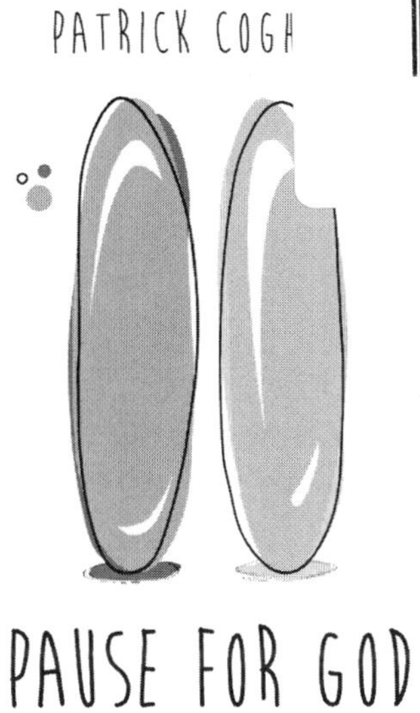

Bible readings taken from the NRSVA

First Published in 2021 by Kevin Mayhew Ltd,

Fengate Farm,

Rattlesden,

Bury St Edmunds,

Suffolk, IP30 0SZ

ISBN (paperback) 9781838581084

ISBN (eBook) 9781838581091

Paperback product code 1501688

eBook product code 1501689

Created with Vellum

CONTENTS

ACKNOWLEDGMENTS

My thanks to my wife, June for her constant support in all my work.

ABOUT THE AUTHOR

Patrick is the Minister at Worstead Baptist Church in Meeting Hill (North Norfolk). He is also the chaplain of Aylsham and district Care Trust (ACT), and the manager of ACT Counselling Services – both of which are based in the ACT Centre, in Aylsham. ACT is a Christian community care charity, and does a lot of work with older people. The ACT Centre is part of the St Michael's Care Complex.

In his work as a minister, chaplain and counsellor, Patrick has had considerable experience of working with people of most age groups, in the context of providing ministry and care.

Patrick is married to June and they have two grown-up children – Rachel and Jonathan – and their first grandchild. For his leisure Patrick enjoys quality family time, gardening, dog walking and going out on his red motorcycle.

Patrick has been an enthusiastic author for many years, having had his first book published in 2001. He has written a variety of Christian resources for different age groups, and some family novels.

INTRODUCTION

Pause for God – 366 daily moments with God is an accessible, user friendly, off the page, easy to follow, but also challenging resource. The reader is encouraged to understand and put into action the teaching of scripture; and, whilst so doing, to practice the art of journaling, to spend time 'in the moment' doing mindfulness type of meditation, to make a prayer response to scripture, and to address any issues linked with the aim of the session that might be difficult to achieve. It looks at both the everyday application of the Bible, and also the eternal. The resource is laid out in such a way that it can be dipped in and out of during the course of a busy day.

Pause for God – 366 daily moments with God is ideal for relatively new Christians and those who are more spiritually mature, who are eager to know how to outwork their faith in daily living. Also for busy people, including parents of young children, who maybe struggle to find uninterrupted quiet time.

Format:

- The header **What the Bible says about**... gives the overall theme for the month or part of the month.
- The title introduces the theme of the individual session.
- The date is given.
- The strap line is a short, but challenging statement which develops the theme, and introduces the Bible verse, or verses.
- The Bible verse, or occasionally two or three verses, directly relate to the theme. Most of the Bible verses are looked at as 'stand-alone' verses. However, where the wider story needs to be read, in order to understand the verse in context, then the full Bible passage is given beforehand: for example, the account of the Christmas story – **In Telling the story.**

The ***'My Journal'*** section (in italics) encourage the reader to practice the art of journaling; and space is allocated for this to happen. Either a question, series of short questions, or a topic is briefly outlined for the reader to consider; and then to **write down their response**, what God is saying to them through the material, points for prayer, and any other significant personal thoughts. There are no right or wrong answers. The journal is entirely for the reader's own benefit; and it can be very helpful to look back on, in the future, as well as at the time of writing it.

The **Meditate** section challenges the reader to spend a few minutes 'in the moment', doing some mindfulness type of meditation, examining the theme further, focusing on a particular aspect outlined by the author.

The prayer of response, which follows includes space for any additional points for prayer to be included.

The prayer can be used as it is, adapted or added to. Once again, as well as being an off the page prayer, it develops further the theme that runs through the session. It is a personal response prayer... It is not a substitute for your own personal prayer requests: bringing your needs and the needs of others to God; remembering to pray for the kingdom; and giving thanks.

'Doers of the word' (aim) (based on James 1:22)**:** is once again what it says on the label, highlighting an active response to the session. It translates the theme of the session into a statement of action.

Underneath the **'Doers of the word'** section the reader is challenged to consider any issues regarding putting the aim of the session into action, with which they might struggle.

NB:

We need to remember that the Bible is God's word (2 Timothy 3:16-17) – God speaking to each one of us... But are we really listening to what he is saying to us (Mark 9:7 and James 1:19)? As you, the reader, use this resource, listen to what God is saying to you, through his word.

God is calling us to listen to what he is saying to us in his word; and to 'do' or put into practice what he tells us:

Then a cloud overshadowed them, and from the cloud there came a voice, 'This is my Son, the Beloved, listen to him!'
(Mark 9:7)

All scripture is inspired by God and is useful for teaching, for reproof, for correction, and for training in righteousness, so that everyone who belongs to God may be proficient, equipped for every good work.
(2 Timothy 3:16-17)

You must understand this, my beloved: let everyone be quick to listen, slow to speak, slow to anger.
(James 1:19)

But be doers of the word, and not merely hearers who deceive themselves.
(James 1:22)

WELCOME

Welcome to **Pause for God: 366 daily moments with God**.

Please let me share with you some thoughts about self-care before you embark on these reflective times with God – for a year.

Life is so busy for so many people in the modern world; maybe you fall into this category, and that is why you have chosen this particular resource – in the hope of being able to dip in and out of it during the busyness of the day. Perhaps you have a particularly demanding job; live a particularly demanding lifestyle; are bringing up very young children, or taxying around teenagers; or maybe you are a carer for someone. In the busyness of life, especially when caring for others, self-care is just so important and should not be neglected.

So what does that mean in practical terms?

- Making the time to be with God.
- In worship, Bible study, prayer and fellowship.
- To receive his healing, encouragement and refreshment.
- And sometimes to just rest and 'be' in his presence.
- Giving yourself permission to have some 'you' time.
- To rest.
- To relax.
- To exercise.
- Maybe to pursue some kind of hobby.
- And to eat (avoid missing out meals).

This resource is part of your self-care, helping to facilitate you to spend some of your quality time with God, on a daily basis. Finding that 'you' time is entirely up to you to organise; but you could begin by crossing out slots of time in your diary or calendar.

May God bless you in the year ahead.

1

NEW YEAR

What the Bible says about **new things (New Year)**

A new day

1st January

Each new day is a wonderful gift from God; full of new opportunities and potential: to be entered into with thankfulness, boldness and faith.

This is the day that the Lord has made;
Let us rejoice and be glad in it.

(Psalm 118:24)

'My Journal':

- *At the start of a new day, a new month, a new year... What are your overwhelming feelings?*

Meditate on the fact that today is a day God has created. He has created it with love and purpose. It is a gift for you. But sometimes those fears, worries and anxieties can appear to steal away the promise of the new day. What would your prayer be at the start of a new day, a new month, or a new year?

Lord God.

It is your day: you have created it and filled it with unimaginable potential!

Thank you for the gift of a new day, a new month and a new year.

Please be with me in the new day, the new month, and the New Year; whatever my feelings might be about it.

Help me not to feel guilty if my feelings are negative ones; but enable me to be confident in you.

Be with me when I feel like celebrating.

Be with me when my mood is low, or I am feeling anxious.

And be with me, when I struggle to think beyond one day at a time, as a result of how I am feeling, or my age.

I pray for your blessing upon the new day, new month and new year that lies ahead: for me, for those who I love and care about, and for those who I meet on a regular basis.

In Jesus' name.

Amen.

'Doers of the word' (aim): To give thanks to God for each new day, each new month, and each New Year.

Is there anything that you think you might find difficult about achieving the aim?

A new song

2nd January

The psalmist uses the analogy of life being like singing a song or playing a tune: living the Christian life is like a 'new song' sung to God; or a beautiful tune including the very best harmonies, played for God.

I will sing a new song to you, O God;
upon a ten-stringed harp I will play to you.

(Psalm 144:9)

'My Journal':

- *What kind of lifestyle does God desire from us?*

Meditate on what kind of song you are singing; or tune you are playing… and who it is for? For example: Are you endeavouring to live a Christ like lifestyle? Is your life oozing with love for others? Are you witnessing in word and deed? And is it all for the Triune God: God the Father, Jesus the Son, and the Holy Spirit?

Lord.

You want me to be singing a metaphorical song and playing a metaphorical tune that is harmonious and based on love – for you - and one that will benefit others!

Thank you that you pour your love into our lives, to share with those around us.

Please help me to live a life that is radiating your love and compassion.

Let the lyrics be pleasing to you.

And let the tune be harmonious.

(Include any additional topics for prayer or thanksgiving, arising from this study)

In Jesus' name.

Amen.

'Doers of the word' (aim): To live the kind of life that is like a new song or a harmonious tune, sung or played in a way to bring joy to God.

Is there anything that you think you might find difficult about achieving the aim?

What the Bible says about **new things (New Year)**

A new name

3rd January

Names are often associated with belonging to a particular club, organisation or vocation. As followers of Jesus, we are known as Christians: part of the 'Church', part of the 'body of Christ', a member of the 'family of God'... Belonging brings with it privileges; but it also comes with responsibilities.

The nations shall see your vindication,
and all the kings your glory;
and you shall be called by a new name
that the mouth of the Lord will give.

(Isaiah 62:2)

'My Journal':

- *What do you consider to be some of the privileges of being a Christian, alongside some of the responsibilities?*

Meditate on what it means to you, as a follower of Jesus, to be called a Christian. Is it a name that you own with pride – or do you look upon it with a degree of embarrassment… or even disown it, at times?

Almighty God.

As followers of Jesus we are known as Christians – we are your people!

Thank you that you want to have a personal relationship with each one of us.

Please help me to be proud to be part of your family; and willing to take on the responsibilities that go with it – and own the name!

Fill me afresh with the Holy Spirit, and enable me to be able to live up to the name; and glorify you.

(Include any additional topics for prayer or thanksgiving, arising from this study)

In Jesus' name.

Amen.

'Doers of the word' (aim): To live up to the new name God has given us as followers of Jesus.

Is there anything that you think you might find difficult about achieving the aim?

What the Bible says about **new things (New Year)**

New every morning
4th January

Every day is filled with an abundance of God's love, mercy and faithfulness. What a great incentive to get up in the mornings!

The steadfast love of the Lord never ceases,
his mercies never come to an end;
they are new every morning;
great is your faithfulness.

(Lamentations 3:22-23)

'My Journal':

- *Which of God's attributes is most precious or significant to you: his love, mercy, faithfulness... or something else?*

Meditate: Spend some time prayerfully resting in, and being immersed in God's love.

Lord.

Your love, mercy and faithfulness never end.

Thank you that each new day we can depend on them.

Please enable me to help lead others to get to know you, so that they might experience your love, mercy and faithfulness, in their own lives.

And fill me with your love to share with others.

(Include any additional topics for prayer or thanksgiving, arising from this study)

In Jesus' name.

Amen.

'Doers of the word' (aim): To remember and act upon the love, mercy and faithfulness of God.

Is there anything that you think you might find difficult about achieving the aim?

What the Bible says about **new things (New Year)**

A new spirit
5th January

Through Jesus and the power of the indwelling Holy Spirit, we are given a new spirit, and one heart. We are empowered, transformed and united by the indwelling Holy Spirit.

I will give them one heart, and put a new spirit within them; I will remove the heart of stone from their flesh and give them a heart of flesh.

(Ezekiel 11:19)

'My Journal':

- *What do you think it means to have a new spirit within us?*

Meditate on the analogy of changing a heart of stone into a heart of flesh: from a hard heart which is resistant to making any positive response to God, to one that not only relates to him, but also shares his love with those around them.

Heavenly Father.

You place a new spirit within us; and you change our hearts.

Thank you that you long for us all to be in relationship with you – and to be more like you.

Thank you that you are renewing me spiritually – through my personal relationship with Jesus.

Please fill me afresh with the Holy Spirit.

Grant me a willingness to change.

Encourage me to allow you to fully soften my heart.

And help me to enter into a really close relationship with you – through Jesus.

(Include any additional topics for prayer or thanksgiving, arising from this study)

In Jesus' name.

Amen.

'Doers of the word' (aim): To have a new spirit within us, and a heart of flesh.

Is there anything that you think you might find difficult about achieving the aim?

What the Bible says about **new things (New Year)**

New wine

6th January

Jesus instigates and enables a new way of doing things to take place; but it must not be compromised by confusing it with how things used to be done.

'Neither is new wine put into old wineskins; otherwise, the skins burst, and the wine is spilled, and the skins are destroyed; but new wine is put into fresh wineskins, and so both are preserved.'

(Matthew 9:17)

'My Journal':

- *Jesus warns that sometimes we have to let go of how things used to be done, and fully adopt the new way of doing things. What do you think about this concept, in respect to Jesus' mission to save humankind from sin and its consequences?*

Meditate on how this concept can also apply in our individual church congregations, when God speaks to us about doing new things.

Lord Jesus.

You introduced a completely new way of doing things.

Thank you that through giving your life on the cross, you were the ultimate sacrifice that need never be repeated – for the forgiveness of sin.

Thank you that you rose from the dead, and you are alive today.

Thank you that when we enter into a personal relationship with you, based on repentance and faith, we experience your salvation.

Please grant me the acceptance of all these things.

Help me to be willing to accept – and respond to - new things in my life and my church congregation, when it is of you.

(Include any additional topics for prayer or thanksgiving, arising from this study)

In your name.

Amen.

'Doers of the word' (aim): To be prepared to do new things, or old things in a new way; when it is God's will.

Is there anything that you think you might find difficult about achieving the aim?

What the Bible says about **new things (New Year)**

The new covenant

7th January

My understanding of a covenant is that it is like a contract; where there is value offered on both sides: on God's part, it is the offer of forgiveness, through entering into a personal relationship with the risen Jesus; on our part, we need to respond positively to the call to follow Jesus – and make a commitment.

And he did the same with the cup after supper, saying, 'This cup that is poured out for you is the new covenant in my blood.'

(Luke 22:20)

'My Journal'

- *The cup of wine represents the shedding of Jesus' blood on the cross making it possible for God to be able to offer forgiveness for sin. What a high price to pay! What a demonstration of love! What are your thoughts?*

Meditate on what the required response involves, when choosing to follow the risen Jesus.

Loving heavenly Father.

You have made it possible for us to enter into a new covenant with you: one which offers us forgiveness for sin, through following Jesus.

Thank you that Jesus has paid the price for sin when he died on the cross, and rose again.

Please help me as I strive to follow Jesus: to repent; to be committed; to give of my time and energy; to focus on him; and to choose God centred priorities.

(Include any additional topics for prayer or thanksgiving, arising from this study)

In Jesus' name.

Amen.

'Doers of the word' (aim): To be part of the new covenant.

Is there anything that you think you might find difficult about achieving the aim?

What the Bible says about **new things (New Year)**

A new birth

8th January

Jesus talks about the importance of dying to our old sinful way of life, and being reborn into a new God centred way of life – in order to enter into the kingdom.

Jesus answered him, 'Very truly, I tell you, no one can see the kingdom of God without being born from above.'

(John 3:3)

'My Journal':

- *What kind of things would you like to leave behind, that are associated with your old way of life – before becoming a Christian?*

Meditate on the things of God (e.g. love, compassion, generosity and honesty), associated with the new way of life that you are striving to live.

Lord Jesus.

Through you, we can be spiritually reborn: dying to our old sinful lifestyle and being reborn into a new God centred life.

Thank you for making that possible.

Please help me to be able to let go of any areas of my old lifestyle that I am still holding onto; and help me to always keep a focus on the kingdom.

Fill me afresh with the Holy Spirit, to empower me.

Help me to always hold onto the hope of spending eternity in your presence.

(Include any additional topics for prayer or thanksgiving, arising from this study)

In Jesus' name.

Amen.

'Doers of the word' (aim): To be spiritually reborn – through Jesus – and enter into God's eternal kingdom.

Is there anything that you think you might find difficult about achieving the aim?

What the Bible says about **new things (New Year)**

A new creation
9th January

The ultimate in having a fresh start is achieved through having a personal relationship with Jesus – becoming a new creation, where the old has been totally replaced with the new.

So if anyone is in Christ, there is a new creation: everything old has passed away; see, everything has become new!

(2 Corinthians 5:17)

'My Journal':

- *What are some of the main characteristics of Christ, to which you would aspire?*

Meditate on the concept of becoming a new creation in Christ – where everything becomes new. Prayerfully strive to attain it. Celebrate it as you progressively move closer towards it.

Lord Jesus.

You really want me to become a new creation!

Thank you that through being 'in' you, I am able to be that new creation – where everything is new.

Please fill me afresh with the Holy Spirit; to renew me completely...

To progressively transform me into your likeness.

Help me to be willing to allow the Holy Spirit complete freedom to work in my life.

(Include any additional topics for prayer or thanksgiving, arising from this study)

In your name.

Amen.

'Doers of the word' (aim): To be a new creation.

Is there anything that you think you might find difficult about achieving the aim?

What the Bible says about **new things (New Year)**

Clothed with a new self

10th January

Paul uses the analogy of changing clothes to describe the practical outworking of being a Christian: talking about removing one piece of clothing which represents the practices of our old way of life, before coming to faith, and replacing it with a new piece of clothing, representing the new way of life.

Do not lie to one another, seeing that you have stripped off the old self with its practices and have clothed yourselves with the new self, which is being renewed in knowledge according to the image of its creator.

(Colossians 3:9-10)

'My Journal':

- *The analogy is describing a choice or decision which has been made quite emphatically; and yet there seems to be confusion about the fact that the two options are mutually exclusive. Jot down anything that God says to you about it.*

Meditate on what things Paul is referring to, in practical terms, when he highlights the need for honesty about how we live our lives, by commanding, 'Do not lie.' Bear in mind the new self he is talking about involves our everyday behaviour being according to God's values.

Lord Jesus.

You want our Christian faith to be outworking into our everyday lives, in the way that we behave!

Thank you that you are our perfect example.

Please help me to study scripture more; so that I can discover more about that example, which you have set for me to follow.

Fill me afresh with your Holy Spirit, to help me to be that person you would have me be – copying your example to me.

Help me to demonstrate practical qualities like honesty, respect, generosity, faithfulness, and conscientiousness.

And enable me to prevent compromise from creeping into my life.

(Include any additional topics for prayer or thanksgiving, arising from this study)

In your name.

Amen.

'Doers of the word' (aim): To learn more about Jesus' example to us, and to demonstrate those same Christ like qualities, in our everyday lives.

Is there anything that you think you might find difficult about achieving the aim?

What the Bible says about **acceptance** - by God

Known by God

11th January

God knows everything there is to be known about each one of us: the good things and the things that we might rather he didn't know. Because of that, we can't pull the wool over God's eyes about anything to do with ourselves.

And even the hairs of your head are all counted.

(Matthew 10:30)

'My Journal':

- *How well does your partner/best friend/colleague at work/mum/dad know you?*

2

ACCEPTANCE

What the Bible says about **acceptance** – by God

Welcomed, warts and all!

12th January

God knows that we have all fallen short of his expectations of us (Romans 3:23); but none of us are too broken to turn to Jesus – to be welcomed – and to receive his forgiveness, restoration and eternal hope.

And the Pharisees and the scribes were grumbling and saying, 'This fellow welcomes sinners and eats with them.'

(Luke 15:2)

'My Journal':

- *Consider the significance of the phrase 'warts and all'... When we turn to Jesus, we come to him with 'everything'! Make some notes about your thoughts.*

Meditate on this: despite our faults and failings, Jesus longs to welcome us all to himself; so that, through him, we can all enter into his Kingdom. How does that make you feel?

Loving Lord Jesus.

Your love for us is unconditional!

Thank you that you love us all, warts and all – and that you welcome us all to come to yourself, with all our faults and failings.

Thank you that you offer us forgiveness, when we enter into a personal relationship with you – based on repentance and in faith – and you welcome us into the kingdom.

Please help me to have an ever closer relationship with you.

(Include any additional topics for prayer or thanksgiving, arising from this study)

In your name.

Amen.

'Doers of the word' (aim): To respond positively to Jesus' welcome - knowing that he accepts us warts and all, as we come to him – and through him, to enter into the kingdom.

Is there anything that you think you might find difficult about achieving the aim?

What the Bible says about **acceptance** – by God

Sought by God

13th January

The mission of Jesus is to seek out and save those who are spiritually lost: to replace hopelessness with eternal hope, and to replace meaningless with fulfilment.

'For the Son of Man came to seek out and to save the lost.'

(Luke 19:10)

'My Journal':

- *Most of us probably have some kind of childhood memory of getting separated from one or other parent, in a large shop or somewhere similar – and the resulting joy of being reunited. Make a note of your feelings at the time.*

- Meditate on the mission of Jesus to find the spiritually lost, by drawing some comparisons with being spiritually lost and found. What is your personal experience?

Lord Jesus.

Your mission was, and still is, to find the spiritually lost!

Thank you that the spiritually lost can be found, through following you.

Please help me to follow you more closely every day; and give me the confidence to tell those who are still spiritually lost that they too can be found - by following you.

Replace any feelings of hopelessness in my life with eternal hope, and any feelings of meaningless with fulfilment.

(Include any additional topics for prayer or thanksgiving, arising from this study)

In your name.

Amen.

'Doers of the word' (aim): To make a positive response to being sought by Jesus; and spreading the word to others who are still spiritually lost.

Is there anything that you think you might find difficult about achieving the aim?

What the Bible says about **acceptance** – by God

Valued by God
14th January

On a more obvious level, this verse speaks about love; but it is also describing how much God values each one of us – enough to allow his Son, Jesus, to give his life on the cross for us all – paying the penalty for sin.

'For God so loved the world that he gave his only Son, so that everyone who believes in him may not perish but may have eternal life.'

(John 3:16)

'My Journal':

- *How does it feel to be valued that much?*

Meditate on how much you value yourself as a result; and how you put that into practice, in terms of things like respecting yourself, expecting respect from others, or applying self-care.

Loving heavenly Father.

You love us unconditionally, and value us all!

Thank you for loving us enough to allow your only Son, Jesus, to die on the cross, paying the penalty for sin.

Thank you that he rose from the dead, and is alive today.

And through him, we can have eternal life, and freedom from guilt and shame.

Thank you that this act of love is also a sign of how much you value each one of us.

Thank you that you value me…

Please help me to value myself and others.

(Include any additional topics for prayer or thanksgiving, arising from this study)

In Jesus' name.

Amen.

'Doers of the word' (aim): To feel loved and valued by God, to value each other, and to value ourselves.

Is there anything that you think you might find difficult about achieving the aim?

What the Bible says about **acceptance** – by God

God's promises

15th January

God has made us so many promises, spelled out in the Bible; and we can be assured that he is able to fulfil each and every one of them – and he will! All available through entering into a personal relationship with Jesus.

Being fully convinced that God was able to do what he had promised,

(Romans 4:21)

'My Journal':

- *Spend a few minutes thinking about promises: promises that have been made to you by other people, and promises that you have made to other people. How many of them have been kept; and how many of them have been broken? How did the different outcomes feel?*

Meditate on the fact that God's promises will never fail – he will never let us down. How does that feel?

Faithful God.

Your promises – with eternal potential and significance – never fail!

Thank you that you are the God of amazing promises, available through our relationship with Jesus - and all of them, ones that you will fulfil.

Thank you that you are dependable.

Please help me to trust in your promises, claim them, and base my life on them.

Heal the hurt that has been caused in my life by being let down by others who have broken promises made to me.

Heal the hurt that I have caused by breaking promises that I have made to others.

Empower me to fulfil the promises I make.

(Include any additional topics for prayer or thanksgiving, arising from this study)

In Jesus' name.

Amen.

'Doers of the word' (aim): To respond to, and trust in God's eternal promises; and to keep the promises that we make to others.

Is there anything that you think you might find difficult about achieving the aim?

What the Bible says about **acceptance** – by God

Loved by God

16th January

In modern society, the love that we experience from other people so often comes with conditions – I will love you if you look or behave in a particular way - but God's love is completely unconditional. Acceptance means that no matter who we are, or what we have done, God still showers his love upon us.

See what love the Father has given us, that we should be called children of God; and that is what we are. The reason the world does not know us is that it did not know him.

(1 John 3:1)

'My Journal':

- *If it is your life experience, jot down some notes about the kind of things over which you have felt unfairly judged.*

Meditate in the knowledge that God accepts you into his love 'just as you are', and without any conditions.

Loving God.

Your love is unconditional!

Thank you for your love that you shower upon us all!

Thank you that we don't have to earn that love, or in any way, be worthy of receiving it.

Thank you for your love for me.

Please help me to recognise that you really do love unconditionally.

Help me to experience that love in all its fullness.

And grant me the enablement to love others with that same kind of love.

(Include any additional topics for prayer or thanksgiving, arising from this study)

In Jesus' name.

Amen.

'Doers of the word' (aim): To acknowledge and receive God's unconditional love; and to love others in the same way.

Is there anything that you think you might find difficult about achieving the aim?

What the Bible says about **acceptance** – of each other in the Church

One body

17th January

Paul uses the metaphor of the Church being the Body of Christ: in other words, Jesus' followers, through the generations, continuing his work here on earth. As he does this, he begins by speaking about the importance of unity.

For just as the body is one and has many members, and all the members of the body, though many, are one body, so it is with Christ.

(1 Corinthians 12:12)

'My Journal':

- *Consider what unity is really about. It is about working together, with a common purpose; but it is also about those qualities that are necessary for a strong team to be established. Jot down what you believe some of those qualities to be, in a Christian context; and why they are so important.*

Meditate on the fact that the most fundamental source of our unity is the personal relationship we share with the Triune God.

Lord Jesus.

It is your will that your Church should be united!

Thank you for the privilege of being called to be part of your body – the Church… continuing your work here on earth.

Please help us to work together with a common purpose, demonstrating those important team building qualities like acceptance, tolerance, communication, respect and honesty.

Help me to walk close to you; fill me afresh with the Holy Spirit; and help me to live in obedience to the Father.

Let me be focused on you constantly.

(Include any additional topics for prayer or thanksgiving, arising from this study)

In your name.

Amen.

'Doers of the word' (aim): To focus on Jesus, and to work together with others, for unity in the Church.

Is there anything that you think you might find difficult about achieving the aim?

What the Bible says about **acceptance** – of each other in the Church

Uniquely different

18th January

Paul indicates the diversity of temperaments, backgrounds, skills and callings of the people that make up the Church: we are all uniquely different, and we should celebrate that diversity.

Indeed, the body does not consist of one member but of many.

(1 Corinthians 12:14)

'My Journal':

- *Spend some time considering and making a list of what makes you uniquely different; your strengths and your weaknesses.*

Meditate on God's love and creative power, as he created you to be unique; and the benefits of diversity. Remember things like the wealth of talents and abilities gathered together in your church congregation.

Creator God.

You created us to be uniquely different; but at the same time, united through following Jesus!

Thank you for diversity in the Church.

Please help me to recognise and celebrate those talents and abilities that make me, and those in my church congregation, uniquely different.

Let the variety of personalities, backgrounds and callings work together in a positive way, resulting in strength rather than division.

(Include any additional topics for prayer or thanksgiving, arising from this study)

In Jesus' name.

Amen.

'Doers of the word' (aim): To celebrate and build on the diversity in the Church.

Is there anything that you think you might find difficult about achieving the aim?

What the Bible says about **acceptance** – of each other in the Church

Of equal importance

19th January

It is so easy to get into squabbles about who is the more important; whether it be in the home, at work, in social activities or even in the Church. Paul calls us to recognise our interdependency in many ways; and also the importance, even of those more menial tasks – those tasks that can so easily be overlooked, until they don't get done for one reason or another.

The eye cannot say to the hand, 'I have no need of you', nor again the head to the feet, 'I have no need of you.'

(1 Corinthians 12:21)

'My Journal':

- *Imagine the scenario Paul sets before us: how ridiculous it would be for the different parts of the human body to try to make out that they could quite easily and successfully manage to function without the other parts of the body. Jot down some notes on how this metaphor might apply to the Church.*

Meditate on the concept that whatever role you might be playing in your church congregation; it is of equal importance in the overall ministry of the church, as everyone else's roles. Consider some of the many roles that are necessary for the ministry of your church congregation to happen.

Lord Jesus.

You never strived for importance!

Thank you for the privilege of having a role to play in the Church.

Please help me to value that role, however important or menial it might seem.

Help me to offer it up to you; to do it to the best of my ability; to further your kingdom through doing it; and to glorify your name.

Thank you for everyone else who plays a role in the Church – enabling it to function and to provide an ongoing witness and ministry.

Please help us all to value each other, and the roles that we play, equally.

(Include any additional topics for prayer or thanksgiving, arising from this study)

In your name.

Amen.

'Doers of the word' (aim): To value each other equally; including the roles that we play in the Church. No-one is more important than another.

Is there anything that you think you might find difficult about achieving the aim?

What the Bible says about **acceptance** – of each other in the Church

Caring for each other
20th January

Paul emphasises the need for care in the Church. It is right that we should care for those in our wider communities; but we also need to remember to care for each other in the church family – and accept that we all have needs.

That there may be no dissension within the body, but the members may have the same care for one another.

(1 Corinthians 12:25)

'My Journal':

- *Some people are more vocal about everything than others. Some people are quicker to ask for help than others. Some people have more up front, public roles in the church congregation; and are more noticed generally. Paul is saying that we should care for each other equally. What does that mean in practice?*

Meditate on the type of care that we should be offering each other, in our church congregations.

Loving heavenly Father.

It is your will that we should care for each other!

Thank you that you care for us.

Please help me to care for others in my church congregation.

Help me to remember to ask those, who are aren't as vocal as others about expressing themselves, how they are.

Help me to reassure those, who are not confident to ask for their needs to be met, that it is okay to do so.

And help me to notice those whose needs so often seem to go unnoticed.

(Include any additional topics for prayer or thanksgiving, arising from this study)

In Jesus' name.

Amen.

'Doers of the word' (aim): To care for each other in the Church.

Is there anything that you think you might find difficult about achieving the aim?

What the Bible says about **acceptance** – of each other in the Church

It is Christ's body!
21st January

It's all on the label, as they say! - The body of Christ! The Church is metaphorically Jesus' body; let's never forget that fact. As such, our focus should always be on him.

Now you are the body of Christ and individually members of it.

(1 Corinthians 12:27)

'My Journal':

- *What does it mean to focus on Jesus? And how can we do that?*

Meditate on the person of Jesus, in one or more of those ways.

Lord Jesus.

The Church is your body: it is to you that we should be looking and focusing on!

Thank you that you are always with me; guiding, helping and encouraging.

Please help me to constantly be focused on you; and let my relationship with you enrich my relationships with others.

Guide me to say and do the things that you would have me say and do.

Help me to follow your example.

Grant me the discernment to recognise your voice, as I listen.

And give me the courage to go through those doors that you open up for me.

Help me to avoid those things that distract me from focusing on you.

(Include any additional topics for prayer or thanksgiving, arising from this study)

In your name.

Amen.

'Doers of the word' (aim): To focus on Jesus.

Is there anything that you think you might find difficult about achieving the aim?

3

CREATED IN THE IMAGE OF GOD

What the Bible says about being **created in the image of God**

Created in the image of God

22nd January

It is so easy to nonchalantly quote that God created humankind in his image: but do we miss the importance of what that means to us?

Then God said, 'Let us make humankind in our image, according to our likeness; and let them have dominion over the fish of the sea, and over the birds of the air, and over the cattle, and over all the wild animals of the earth, and over every creeping thing that creeps upon the earth.'

(Genesis 1:26)

'My Journal':

- *We are all created in God's image. Why is that so significant; and what does that have to say about our standing in God's creation?*

Meditate on what 'having dominion over' means in practical terms: things like having a responsibility to take care of the world in which we live – including all the creatures.

Creator God.

You created us all in your image: to be like you!

Thank you that you have placed us in such a privileged position in your creation.

Please help me to always be aware of the responsibility that comes with being created in your image; and to behave in an appropriate way.

Let my decision making, be in keeping with having dominion over the creatures.

(Include any additional topics for prayer or thanksgiving, arising from this study)

In Jesus' name.

Amen.

'Doers of the word' (aim): To appreciate and respond positively to the fact that we are all created in the image of God.

Is there anything that you think you might find difficult about achieving the aim?

What the Bible says about being **created in the image of God**

Demonstrate a degree of sovereignty

23rd January

Having a degree of sovereignty comes with practical and spiritual responsibilities: certainly, we need to outwork that sovereignty by demonstrating Christ like characteristics in our lives.

God blessed them, and God said to them, 'Be fruitful and multiply, and fill the earth and subdue it; and have dominion over the fish of the sea and over the birds of the air and over every living thing that moves upon the earth.'

(Genesis 1:28)

'My Journal':

- *Make a list of the characteristics of Christ; bearing in mind the fact that we should implement them as we utilise the degree of sovereignty that we have been given within God's world.*

Meditate on how we should implement those Christ like characteristics in practice, as we seek to utilise the degree of sovereignty that we have been given within God's world. Obviously, we have responsibilities regarding how we care for the planet; but we also have responsibilities to strive to run our families, neighbourhoods, workplaces, nations and church congregations in ways that are glorifying to God.

Father God.

You have granted us all a degree of sovereignty!

Thank you that you have placed your trust in us to take on leadership roles in your world.

Please empower humankind to take on those roles in responsible ways: taking care of the planet, but also, striving to conduct leadership roles utilising Christ like characteristics.

Enable me to glorify you in the leadership roles that you have called me to… *(name those roles)*; and help me to do my bit in taking care of the planet.

(Include any additional topics for prayer or thanksgiving, arising from this study)

In Jesus' name.

Amen.

'Doers of the word' (aim): To fulfil that calling to sovereignty in a way that is glorifying to God, and at the same time meeting the responsibilities that come with it.

Is there anything that you think you might find difficult about achieving the aim?

What the Bible says about being **created in the image of God**

To be creative

24th January

Like God, we have creative skills – obviously to a much lesser degree - in varying types and quantities. He has given them to us to use in his service, to further his kingdom, and to glorify his name.

Thus the heavens and the earth were finished, and all their multitude. And on the seventh day God finished the work that he had done, and he rested on the seventh day from all the work that he had done.

(Genesis 2:1-2)

'My Journal':

- *Write a list of your creative skills?*

Meditate over something you have created – in an attitude of praise and thanksgiving to God.

Almighty God.

You are the great creator God; the creator of all things!

Thank you for your amazing creation; and that you have given us all some kind of creative skills, to be used to brighten our lives, and the lives of others.

Please help me to use my creative skills in positive ways; including in ways that will help to build your kingdom.

Help me to always remember that, linked in with your creative skills, we are reminded of the importance of rest, as well as work – and to act upon that principle.

(Include any additional topics for prayer or thanksgiving, arising from this study)

In Jesus' name.

Amen.

'Doers of the word' (aim): To be creative for God.

Is there anything that you think you might find difficult about achieving the aim?

What the Bible says about being **created in the image of God**

To have a work ethic

25th January

God is at work all around us. We see Adam placed into the Garden of Eden to work in it and maintain it. It is God's intention for us to take up a work ethic.

The Lord God took the man and put him in the garden of Eden to till it and keep it.

(Genesis 2:15)

'My Journal':

- *Look outside for a few minutes – at the garden, or up into the sky - and list some of the ways in which you can see God at work. How does that make you feel?*

Meditate on your own work – it might be a paid job, work in the voluntary sector, or something like being a parent or carer – consider how you can include God in that work to a greater extent, and how you can glorify him more, through that work.

Creator God.

You have set us the example of working and resting!

Thank you that you have given us many different contexts in which we are able to follow your example and your ordinance of work.

Please help me to further your kingdom and glorify your name through my work.

Encourage me to take you to work with me, each day.

Help me to be conscientious in performing the tasks I have before me.

Enable me to bring blessing to others as I carry out those tasks.

And let me witness to others in my work.

(Include any additional topics for prayer or thanksgiving, arising from this study)

In Jesus' name.

Amen.

'Doers of the word' (aim): To do our work for God – whatever that work might be.

Is there anything that you think you might find difficult about achieving the aim?

What the Bible says about being **created in the image of God**

Relating to each other
26th January

The Triune God – God the Father, Jesus the Son, and the Holy Spirit – demonstrates the perfect relationship to us, as the three persons in fellowship together. We were never created not to have company.

Then the Lord God said, 'It is not good that the man should be alone; I will make him a helper as his partner.'

(Genesis 2:18)

'My Journal':

- *Jot down some names of people with whom you have a really close relationship. What makes that relationship so important?*

Meditate on the fact that it is not good for us to be alone.

Triune God.

Father, Son and Holy Spirit.

You created us to be in relationship with you and with each other!

Thank you that you have placed people around me to offer support, help and encouragement – particularly if I become isolated as a result of my circumstances.

Thank you that you demonstrate the perfect example of relationship; and you highlight that we have a need to relate with others.

Please help me to allow other people into my life.

And enable me to find a way around those circumstances that make isolation all too easy.

(Include any additional topics for prayer or thanksgiving, arising from this study)

In Jesus' name.

Amen.

'Doers of the word' (aim): To relate with each other.

Is there anything that you think you might find difficult about achieving the aim?

What the Bible says about being **created in the image of God**

Relating with God
27th January

It was always God's intention to be in a relationship with each one of us – humankind. Obviously, this happens in the beginning, until the Fall; because we see God walking in the Garden of Eden with Adam and Eve – in the cool of the evening breeze.

They heard the sound of the Lord God walking in the garden at the time of the evening breeze, and the man and his wife hid themselves from the presence of the Lord God among the trees of the garden.

(Genesis 3:8)

'My Journal':

- *The Great Creator God planned his creation with the intention of being in relationship with the people he was to create. What a privileged position we are in! Make some notes on your thoughts.*

Meditate on the closeness of the relationship between God the Father, Jesus the Son and the Holy Spirit – the Triune God. Three persons in one. Remember that it is in God's image we have been created – to be in a close relationship with him!

Creator God.

You created us all, because you wanted to be in a close relationship with us.

Thank you that you have placed humankind in such a privileged position in your creation – to be able to know you in a personal way.

Please help me to walk closely to Jesus daily, to allow the indwelling Holy Spirit to work fully in my life, and to live in obedience to you.

Help me to make time for you: to study the Bible, to spend time in prayer and listening... and to do your will.

(Include any additional topics for prayer or thanksgiving, arising from this study)

In Jesus' name.

Amen.

'Doers of the word' (aim): To share in a close relationship with the Triune God.

Is there anything that you think you might find difficult about achieving the aim?

What the Bible says about being **created in the image of God**

Be holy
28th January

What is holiness? I guess we could say that it is all about being like God, even when it means being different from society.

For I am the Lord your God; sanctify yourselves therefore, and be holy, for I am holy.

(Leviticus 11:44a)

'My Journal':

- *The writer of Leviticus uses the two concepts of sanctification and holiness in the same verse. It reinforces the idea of sometimes having to walk away from some of the practices, beliefs and values that society portrays – because they are not in keeping with the will of God. Jot down some notes about when and how you think this might apply to your life.*

Meditate on how it might feel to be different from your peers, in order to be 'holy'.

Holy God.

We should aspire to doing your will!

You want us to be like you: sharing in your values and working towards demonstrating more of your characteristics in our lives.

Thank you that you want what is best for us, for the kingdom, and for our relationship with you.

Please help me to be prepared to be different, when it is necessary in order to attain sanctification and holiness.

Give me a desire to be more like you; and to do your will.

(Include any additional topics for prayer or thanksgiving, arising from this study)

In Jesus' name.

Amen.

'Doers of the word' (aim): To strive to acquire holiness.

Is there anything that you think you might find difficult about achieving the aim?

What the Bible says about being **created in the image of God**

Eternal potential

29th January

One of the characteristics of our lives on earth is that our lifespans are limited; and at some point we will face physical death – unless Jesus returns first! Despite that, being created in the image of God means that we have eternal potential – we can spend eternity in God's heavenly kingdom, through being in relationship with Jesus.

And he said to them, 'Truly I tell you, there is no one who has left house or wife or brothers or parents or children, for the sake of the kingdom of God, who will not get back very much more in this age, and in the age to come eternal life.'

(Luke 18:29-30)

'My Journal':

- *Jesus is speaking about focus and commitment in this verse of scripture, when he speaks about making sacrifices for the sake of the kingdom. Following Jesus, can result in us being faced with having to make some very difficult choices. Jot down any difficult choices you are facing at the present time.*

Meditate on Jesus speaking about the rewards of living the Christian life, of love and witness, not just being for eternity, but also during our lives here on earth.

Lord Jesus.

It is through following you that we are assured of eternal life in your heavenly kingdom!

Thank you that we can have the assurance of eternal life, when we are in a personal relationship with you.

Please help me to be confident of my eternal future, through walking with you daily.

Thank you that, as well as there being eternal rewards for living the Christian life of love and witness, there are all kinds of blessings in our lives here on earth.

As I look forward to the promise of your wonderful heavenly kingdom, please help me not to miss the joys of living for you, here and now.

(Include any additional topics for prayer or thanksgiving, arising from this study)

In your name.

Amen.

'Doers of the word' (aim): To be assured of eternal life in God's heavenly kingdom.

Is there anything that you think you might find difficult about achieving the aim?

What the Bible says about being **created in the image of God**

A glorious body
30th January

As followers of Jesus, we are promised that, after we die, we will receive new resurrection bodies: bodies that are no longer susceptible to things like pain, sickness or wearing out.

He will transform the body of our humiliation so that it may be conformed to the body of his glory, by the power that also enables him to make all things subject to himself.

(Philippians 3:21)

'My Journal':

- *What might it be like to no longer have to endure suffering which results from the transient nature of our earthly bodies?*

Meditate on the wonderful hope that this verse contains for those of us who are suffering through the weaknesses of our earthly bodies, at the present time.

Almighty God.

You are able to give us new resurrection bodies that will not fail us or wear out!

Thank you for your promises concerning eternal life, in your heavenly kingdom.

Thank you that all followers of Jesus have the assurance of spending eternity in your presence.

Please help me to be assured, through my faith in Jesus, that I will have a wonderful new body when I die, and I will be resurrected into your eternal kingdom.

Until that time, help me to cope with any suffering linked with my present body and mind.

(Include any additional topics for prayer or thanksgiving, arising from this study)

In Jesus' name.

Amen.

'Doers of the word' (aim): To be filled with hope and reassurance; especially in present day suffering of body or mind.

Is there anything that you think you might find difficult about achieving the aim?

What the Bible says about being **created in the image of God**

Pleasing God

31st January

We can please God by the way that we live our lives; when we do his will. It is a wonderful thought, that despite our faults and weaknesses, we can actually do that. Our aim should be to increasingly please him as we also attain greater spiritual maturity.

Finally, brothers and sisters, we ask and urge you in the Lord Jesus that, as you learned from us how you ought to live and please God (as, in fact, you are doing) you should do so more and more.

(1 Thessalonians 4:1)

'My Journal':

- *As Christians, we give ourselves a hard time, so often: talking about the times when we cause God sadness, because of sin and failure in our lives. In reality, there are times when we please God. Jot down how that makes you feel.*

Meditate on the words 'more and more' in the verse: it implies that pleasing God is an ongoing journey of progressively getting to know his heart better, allowing the Holy Spirit to work increasingly in our lives, and becoming more Christ like.

Loving God.

We want to be like you!

Thank you that we can please you, by being more like you, and from doing your will.

Please fill me afresh with your Holy Spirit, to transform and empower me to be more like you, to know something of your heart, and to do your will.

Help me to say and do those things that are pleasing to you.

And enable me to achieve ever greater spiritual maturity.

(Include any additional topics for prayer or thanksgiving, arising from this study)

In Jesus' name.

Amen.

'Doers of the word' (aim): To please God.

Is there anything that you think you might find difficult about achieving the aim?

4

FOLLOWING JESUS

What the Bible says about **following Jesus**

Nothing of our own to offer

1st February

Let's stop trying to earn our way into God's kingdom: we need to accept that it is something we can't afford – and that is spiritual poverty!

'Blessed are the poor in spirit, for theirs is the kingdom of heaven.'

(Matthew 5:3)

'My Journal':

- *Consider the different areas in which society encourages us to be independent; and then jot down some thoughts about the implications of needing to depend on Jesus, and our relationship with him, to give us entry into the kingdom – although it is a free gift.*

Meditate on what it would mean to have to let go of something that you have become dependent on, that is currently restricting your dependency on Jesus, in some way – and jot down some thoughts.

Risen Lord Jesus.

What an amazing gift!

Thank you that you paid the price for the whole of humankind to be forgiven, set free from sin's consequences, and enabled to enter into your eternal heavenly kingdom, when you gave your life on the cross.

Please help me to recognise my own spiritual poverty, and enable me to depend entirely on you and what you have done to make it possible for me to enter into the kingdom.

Forgive me for those things I have done that have saddened you.

Give me the strength to let go of, or hold lightly, anything that is standing in the way of me achieving that dependency on you.

(Include any additional topics for prayer or thanksgiving, arising from this study)

In your name.

Amen.

'Doers of the word' (aim): To fully depend on Jesus; and what he has achieved for us.

Is there anything that you think you might find difficult about achieving the aim?

Letting go

2nd February

Following Jesus inevitably means letting go of certain beliefs, forms of behaviour, and priorities from our past; things that are not pleasing to God. That might feel like a loss (almost like a bereavement) - but with God in our lives, the rewards are always greater than the losses!

'Blessed are those who mourn, for they will be comforted.'

(Matthew 5:4)

'My Journal':

- *Sketch a picture of a cobweb in your journal. And then think about the concept of any 'cobwebby corners' that are still remaining in your life – areas that are not according to the teaching of Jesus or the values of God. Name them on your drawing.*

Meditate on how you might begin to clean up those 'cobwebby' corners; in the power of the Holy Spirit.

Loving heavenly Father.

The Bible is such an amazing instruction book!

Thank you for the teaching in the Bible, concerning how I should live my life.

Please help me to recognise those areas of my beliefs, behaviour and the priorities I set that are contrary to your will and standards – those cobwebby corners of my life - and through the power of the indwelling Holy Spirit, enable me to clean them up.

Thank you that I will never lose out when I give up anything that is not honouring to you.

Thank you that you offer comfort in times of loss.

(Include any additional topics for prayer or thanksgiving, arising from this study)

In Jesus' name.

Amen.

'Doers of the word' (aim): To do some prayerful spring cleaning in our lives.

Is there anything that you think you might find difficult about achieving the aim?

Meekness is not a weakness

3rd February

The values portrayed in the beatitudes appear to be so opposite to those that society often seems to reflect: submission to God – linked with selflessness - is the key to real success and fulfilment in terms of God's kingdom.

'Blessed are the meek, for they will inherit the earth.'

(Matthew 5:5)

'My Journal'

- *Consider, and make some notes on, what submission to God constitutes and how it can be outworked into our daily living.*

Meditate on how you visualise meekness.

Almighty God.

Thank you that you are the Creator God, who is all knowing, all seeing, and all powerful – you know what is best for us!

Thank you that submission to your will – linked with selflessness - is the key to success and fulfilment in life.

Please help me to see meekness as something to which I should aspire; and not as a weakness.

Help me to understand what your values are; and empower me, through your Holy Spirit, to apply those values in my daily living.

Thank you that the blessings you shower upon us, as a result of living your way, are experienced now and for eternity *(name some of those blessings).*

(Include any additional topics for prayer or thanksgiving, arising from this study)

In Jesus' name.

Amen.

'Doers of the word' (aim): To overcome self-centredness and fully submit to God.

Is there anything that you think you might find difficult about achieving the aim?

What a feast

4th February

We all have a spiritual need, void or emptiness (hunger or thirst) that can only be filled (satisfied) by God: God is longing to fill it – to nourish and satisfy spiritually.

'Blessed are those who hunger and thirst for righteousness, for they will be filled.'

(Matthew 5:6)

'My Journal':

- *Try to recall a time in your life when you were really hungry or thirsty. Write down when it was, and how it made you feel?*

Meditate on a time when you had a celebration meal, and were able to eat and drink as much as you wanted. What did it feel like to have your hunger and thirst more than satisfied on that occasion? Consider a spiritual comparison: that God is our source of spiritual nourishment.

Dear Lord.

Only you can satisfy us spiritually!

Thank you that you provide an abundance of spiritual nourishment, with which we can be filled.

Please help me to be filled as I spend time pursuing things like praise, worship, Bible study and prayer; and in my daily walk with Jesus.

And let me experience spiritual refreshment from you, as well.

Let the church congregation that I belong to be a supportive and encouraging one – for the benefit of all of us.

(Include any additional topics for prayer or thanksgiving, arising from this study)

In Jesus' name.

Amen.

'Doers of the word' (aim): To be spiritually nourished and refreshed.

Is there anything that you think you might find difficult about achieving the aim?

What the Bible says about **following Jesus**

Mercy goes two ways
5th February

Because we sometimes make bad choices in our lives, those which are not pleasing to God (sin), we all need his mercy (forgiveness): and we are called to demonstrate mercy (forgiveness) to others as well.

'Blessed are the merciful, for they will receive mercy.'

(Matthew 5:7)

'My Journal'

- *Mercy involves forgiveness. Consider for a moment, exactly what it means to the person being forgiven – base it on your own personal experience; and jot down some notes.*

Meditate on the concept of mercy involving forgiveness. Consider for a moment exactly what forgiveness means to the person doing the forgiving – base it on your own personal experience.

Gracious God.

It is your desire to forgive!

Thank you that when we enter into a personal relationship with Jesus - based on repentance and faith – you forgive us for our sin!

Please forgive me for those times when I continue to fall short of your expectations of me…

Encourage me to seek forgiveness from those who I have hurt in some way; and help me to forgive those who have done something to harm me or cause me pain.

(Include any additional topics for prayer or thanksgiving, arising from this study)

In Jesus' name.

Amen.

'Doers of the word' (aim): To experience God's forgiveness ourselves; to seek forgiveness from others; and to demonstrate forgiveness to others.

Is there anything that you think you might find difficult about achieving the aim?

Living the lifestyle

6th February

Following Jesus involves learning more about him, and living the lifestyle (according to his teaching and example): and by so doing we will 'see God' – in other words, we will begin to understand more about the true nature of God himself.

'Blessed are the pure in heart, for they will see God.'

(Matthew 5:8)

'My Journal':

- *From your understanding of the Bible, jot down some of the facets of the nature of Jesus.*

Meditate on your list for a few minutes: God the Father has the same nature as that of his Son, Jesus.

Lord Jesus.

You are the perfect example!

Thank you for being an example to us.

Thank you that, not only do you tell us how we should live our lives, but you have also shown us.

Thank you that the more we learn about you, the more we learn about the Father.

Please help me to discover more about you by studying more of the Bible; empower me to put what I learn into practice, in my own life; and help me to understand more about the Father's nature, as a result.

Fill me afresh with the power of the indwelling Holy Spirit.

(Include any additional topics for prayer or thanksgiving, arising from this study)

In your name.

Amen.

'Doers of the word' (aim): To get to know more about Jesus; to live the lifestyle; and to understand more about God the Father.

Is there anything that you think you might find difficult about achieving the aim?

What the Bible says about **following Jesus**

Taking on the family likeness
7th February

The Christian life involves pursuing peace – endeavouring to defuse conflict and division. As children of God, we should be striving to take on the family likeness of God - amongst other things, he is the God of peace.

'Blessed are the peacemakers, for they will be called children of God.'

(Matthew 5:9)

'My Journal':

- *Think about the various characteristics you have inherited from your parents, or grandparents – the family likeness. Jot down your thoughts.*

Meditate on taking on the family likeness of God; and how it makes you feel.

Loving heavenly Father.

We can be called children of God!

Thank you that when we enter into a personal relationship with Jesus, knowing him as our Lord and Saviour, we enter into your heavenly family – becoming your children.

Please help me to progressively take on more of your family likeness.

As others look at me, may they see something of you, in the things that I say and do.

(Include any additional topics for prayer or thanksgiving, arising from this study)

In Jesus' name.

Amen.

'Doers of the word' (aim): To try to take on the family likeness of God.

Is there anything that you think you might find difficult about achieving the aim?

What the Bible says about **following Jesus**

There will be hardships

8th February

Living the Christian life is not without difficulties; many people will oppose the values and teaching of God: but the reward is to be part of God's kingdom.

'Blessed are those who are persecuted for righteousness' sake, for theirs is the kingdom of heaven.'

(Matthew 5:10)

'My Journal':

- *List some of the many different forms of persecution we might experience as Christians in the 21st century western world.*

Meditate on ways in which you have actually experienced persecution, for your faith – maybe even at work. How do you deal with it? Is there a better way?

Almighty God.

Your values, and the way of life which you desire us to pursue, are the best!

Thank you that you have passed on your values to us, to be followed – for our own benefit.

Thank you that you have made it possible for us to enter into the Christian lifestyle, through following Jesus.

Please empower me to live according to your will and teaching – and to endure persecution for the sake of living life your way.

Strengthen me, grant me more faith and fill me afresh with the Holy Spirit.

(Include any additional topics for prayer or thanksgiving, arising from this study)

In Jesus' name.

Amen.

'Doers of the word' (aim): To endure persecution when it is for the sake of helping to build God's kingdom.

Is there anything that you think you might find difficult about achieving the aim?

What the Bible says about **following Jesus**

There will be a reward

9th February

Let's be clear about this, the reward for enduring persecution, for the sake of God's kingdom, is to spend eternity in heaven: there can be no greater reward than that!

'Rejoice and be glad, for your reward is great in heaven, for in the same way they persecuted the prophets who were before you.'

(Matthew 5:12)

'My Journal':

- *Many of the biblical descriptions of heaven describe it as being like a wonderful feast of good food and drink* (e.g. Isaiah 25:6-8)*. What does that say to you about what heaven is like? You might even like to sketch a picture in your journal (it could be symbolic).*

Meditate in the knowledge that there will be an abundance of good things in heaven, for our benefit and for us to enjoy – including a limitless supply of spiritual nourishment.

Father in heaven.

You are awesome!

Thank you that you are a powerful God.

Please empower me to endure any persecution that I am subjected to for your sake.

Thank you that the reward for following Jesus is eternal life in your heavenly kingdom.

It doesn't get any better than that!

Thank you for the eternal blessings that you are preparing for me in heaven *(name some of those blessings).*

(Include any additional topics for prayer or thanksgiving, arising from this study)

In Jesus' name.

Amen.

'Doers of the word' (aim): To rejoice, even in times of persecution, in the knowledge of the reward to come.

Is there anything that you think you might find difficult about achieving the aim?

Be salty
10th February

Jesus emphasises that we should not lose our saltiness, as we endeavour to be salt in the world around us. In other words, we must not become like salt that no longer has those familiar qualities of salt – it is of no use.

'You are the salt of the earth, but if salt has lost its taste, how can its saltiness be restored? It is no longer good for anything, but is thrown out and trampled under foot.'

(Matthew 5:13)

'My Journal':

- *Salt has various qualities: flavour, of course; it is antiseptic (or cleansing); and it can be quite abrasive. Consider the ways in which we can be salt, by unpacking the metaphor. Make some notes.*

Meditate on how you can put that into practice, and be 'salt' in the different areas of your life.

Lord Jesus.

You have commanded us to be salt!

Thank you that you want us to serve you by being like salt in the world – in a spiritual context.

Thank you that you will empower us to do that, through the indwelling Holy Spirit.

Please help me to spread the flavour of the joy of being in relationship with you – through witnessing and words of personal testimony.

Enable me to be a cleansing example to society, by setting a good moral example – in the way that I behave.

And give me the strength of character to be a little bit abrasive when needed, as I stand up for your values.

Help me to be really 'salty' salt!

(Include any additional topics for prayer or thanksgiving, arising from this study)

In your name.

Amen.

'Doers of the word' (aim): To be salt – really 'salty' salt.

Is there anything that you think you might find difficult about achieving the aim?

Let the light shine

11th February

We all have the opportunity to spread the light of God in a world where there is a lot of darkness, linked with sin and evil. So let's be light, and let's not hide that light from our families, friends, colleagues and neighbours.

'You are the light of the world. A city built on a hill cannot be hidden. No-one after lighting a lamp puts it under a bushel basket, but on the lampstand, and it gives light to all in the house. In the same way, let your light shine before others, so that they might see your good works and give glory to your Father in heaven.'

(Matthew 5:14-16)

'My Journal':

- *We are able to spread the 'light' as we live according to the will and purposes of God; touching other people's lives as we share things like love, peace, patience, generosity, compassion and hope. Write a list of ways in which we can end up in hiding that light.*

Meditate for a few moments on the very simple concept of light overcoming the darkness – like a candle burning on a winter's evening – then apply the metaphor to the light of God overcoming the darkness of sin and evil.

God of light.

You are the light that overcomes the darkness of sin and evil in the world!

Thank you that you provide the opportunity for us to be in the light of living in your love and will.

Thank you for all the different expressions of your love; and that walking in your will brings abundant blessings to us.

Please help me to walk daily in your light, and by so doing, to pass on that light to others.

Help me not to be tempted to hide that light; maybe through embarrassment, as a result of the lack of courage, or even because there are times when I allow myself to be tempted to deviate from your will and purposes.

(Include any additional topics for prayer or thanksgiving, arising from this study)

In Jesus' name.

Amen.

'Doers of the word' (aim): To allow the light of God to shine through our lives.

Is there anything that you think you might find difficult about achieving the aim?

What the Bible says about **following Jesus**

Jesus fulfils the law

12th February

Don't be fooled into thinking that the law of God, in the Old Testament, is no longer relevant or applicable to today. Much of Jesus' teaching is to reinforce and explain the importance, relevance and application of the law, to all generations.

'Do not think that I have come to abolish the law or the prophets; I have not come to abolish but to fulfil.'

(Matthew 5:17)

'My Journal':

- *Under the heading 'The purpose of law' write a list of reasons why God's law is so important to us today; and then spend some time focusing on what you have written.*

Meditate on the abundance of God's love expressed in his law; and prayerfully allow yourself to be immersed in that love.

Lord God.

Your law is a demonstration of your love for us; it reflects your nature; and it is a revelation of your will!

Your law is relevant to us today, it is for our benefit, and it is there to help establish your kingdom here on earth – just as it is in heaven!

Thank you for your law.

Thank you that Jesus not only explains the deeper nature of the law; he also lives it out in his life on earth, as our example.

Please empower me, through the indwelling Holy Spirit, to also live out your law on a daily basis, in my life... and, by so doing, become more like you and further your kingdom.

(Include any additional topics for prayer or thanksgiving, arising from this study)

In Jesus' name.

Amen.

'Doers of the word' (aim): To try to understand God's law better; and to apply it to our daily living.

Is there anything that you think you might find difficult about achieving the aim?

There is power in words

13th February

It is not just violent and unkind actions that are wrong, it is the anger from which those type of actions can arise: and the associated harsh critical and contemptuous words, which can be really damaging.

'But I say to you that if you are angry with a brother or sister, you will be liable to judgement; and if you insult a brother or sister, you will be liable to council; and if you say, "you fool", you will be liable to the hell of fire.'

(Matthew 5:22)

'My Journal':

- *Maybe you have been the victim of verbal abuse, in the context of being bullied or controlled; or you might have been at the receiving end of a harsh critical voice that you have grown up with. Perhaps, looking back, you have been that voice, to yourself or to someone else. Jot some notes down about the power of words - to build up or to tear down.*

Meditate on God's love for you; and then prayerfully seek some words of encouragement and affirmation from him: he might lead you to a verse of scripture, he could remind you of some words that a wise Christian friend has recently expressed to you, or he could just utter something into your heart.

Lord God.

Words are so powerful: they can build up, or they can hurt and destroy!

Thank you that your words are the type that encourage and help us to be the people that you would have us be.

Please help me to control destructive anger in my life; and only use those words that are kind and helpful to others.

Forgive me for sometimes allowing destructive anger to take hold, and for those words that I have said in the past that were neither kind nor helpful.

Have your healing touch upon me, for those words that have been said to me which have been damaging – and maybe still have a negative influence on me.

Help me to meditate on the positive and affirming things that you say to me through scripture and in other ways – and be built up by them.

(Include any additional topics for prayer or thanksgiving, arising from this study)

In Jesus' name.

Amen.

'Doers of the word' (aim): To control destructive anger, and to choose the words that we say, thoughtfully and carefully – and to listen to those words that build up and affirm.

Is there anything that you think you might find difficult about achieving the aim?

Taking a ruthless approach to sin

14th February

A really fundamental principle, highlighted in Jesus' teaching, is that we should do all that we can to separate ourselves from sources of temptation - whenever and wherever we possibly can. He is not suggesting that we really mutilate our bodies when he says:

'If your right eye causes you to sin, tear it out and throw it away; it is better for you to lose one of your members than for your whole body to be thrown into hell.'

(Matthew 5:29)

'My Journal':

- *This illustration portrays a very drastic scenario. That highlights the seriousness of the message Jesus is putting across. Temptation is a major issue, with possible eternal consequences. Jot down any areas of temptation in your life that could be eradicated by you.*

Meditate on some of the tools we have to use in the fight against temptation.

Lord Jesus.

We must deal harshly with temptation, because it can so easily lead us into sin.

Thank you for your teaching and example, both of which are so relevant to us in how we should deal with temptation (Matthew 4:1-11).

Thank you that you can empower us through the indwelling Holy Spirit to do just that.

Please fill me afresh with the Holy Spirit; and help me to eradicate or lessen any areas of temptation that I am able – grant me wisdom, discernment, self-control, and strength of character.

Enable me to say 'no' to the pull of remaining temptations.

(Include any additional topics for prayer or thanksgiving, arising from this study)

In your name.

Amen.

'Doers of the word' (aim): To deal harshly with the temptation that is likely to cause us to sin.

Is there anything that you think you might find difficult about achieving the aim?

What the Bible says about **following Jesus**

Forgiveness is better than revenge

15th February

I understand that the idea of 'an eye for an eye and a tooth for a tooth' was originally to limit revenge, to no more than the original offence: but Jesus wants us to forgive and not seek any revenge at all.

'You have heard that it was said, "An eye for an eye and a tooth for a tooth." But I say to you, Do not resist an evildoer.'

(Matthew 5:38-39a)

'My Journal':

- *Are you someone who believes that there should be a 'payback' time?*

Meditate on offering forgiveness instead of revenge. – Even when the person who has hurt you in some way is not necessarily seeking your forgiveness; but you can give it anyway! What are your thoughts about that.

Lord Jesus.

Your way is to forgive!

Thank you that your forgiveness is complete, when we enter into a personal relationship with you – based on repentance and faith.

Please forgive me for those times when I have done something that is not according to your teaching or example.

Help me to forgive others for those times when they have hurt me in some way – even when they show no remorse.

Enable me to let go of any thoughts about seeking revenge.

(Include any additional topics for prayer or thanksgiving, arising from this study)

In your name.

Amen.

'Doers of the word' (aim): To forgive those who have done something to hurt us – as completely as God forgives us.

Is there anything that you think you might find difficult about achieving the aim?

Even my enemies?

16th February

Hatred is probably more usually associated with how people feel about their enemies: but Jesus instructs us to love them – and pray for anyone who persecutes us.

'But I say to you, Love your enemies and pray for those who persecute you.'

(Matthew 5:44)

'My Journal':

- *Hatred is a very strong negative emotion; and one which modern society connects closely with 'enemies'. Ask yourself if there is someone in your life who you would class as an enemy. Consider what your feelings are towards that person (or people); and how the concept of loving them might feel. Jot down your thoughts.*

Meditate on the benefits of praying for, instead of retaliating against those who persecute you.

Loving heavenly Father.

Your nature is love!

Thank you for loving me.

Please help me, not to just love those who are 'lovable' but also to love those whom I might class as enemies.

Empower me to pray for those who persecute me.

(Include any additional topics for prayer or thanksgiving, arising from this study)

In Jesus' name.

Amen.

'Doers of the word' (aim): To learn to love our enemies, and pray for those who persecute us.

Is there anything that you think you might find difficult about achieving the aim?

What the Bible says about **following Jesus**

The things that last

17th February

When we pass away, we can't take anything with us, from the physical world. Wealth and possessions are transient – but the things of God are eternal.

'Do not store up for yourselves treasures on earth, where moth and rust consume and where thieves break in and steal; but store up for yourselves treasures in heaven, where neither moth nor rust consumes and where thieves do not break in and steal. For where your treasure is, there your heart will be also.'

(Matthew 6:19-21)

'My Journal':

- *Think about the significance of the fact that even our physical bodies wear out. Only the things of God are eternal; and that includes us, in a spiritual context - through Jesus. What are your thoughts?*

Meditate upon this. Visualise in your mind's eye, a cartoony wooden treasure chest... It's your treasure chest! What's are you striving to acquire in your life, in order to fill it? Is it material wealth and possessions, or is it the things of God? Where is your heart?

Loving God.

Treasure from you never rusts, and it is not eaten by moths!

Thank you that heavenly treasure is eternal: please help me to set my heart on the things of you.

Please grant me the enablement to hold onto those things that are of this physical world, lightly...

And to only hold those things of you, tightly.

Let the treasure that I earnestly strive to build up, be heavenly treasure – those things that will last.

(Include any additional topics for prayer or thanksgiving, arising from this study)

In Jesus' name.

Amen.

'Doers of the word' (aim): To invest in those things of eternal value: the things of God.

Is there anything that you think you might find difficult about achieving the aim?

What the Bible says about **following Jesus**

Using our senses

18th February

God gave us five senses: sight, hearing, taste, touch, and smell – to enable us to gather knowledge and wisdom.

'The eye is the lamp of the body. So, if your eye is healthy, your whole body will be full of light.'

(Matthew 6:22)

'My Journal':

- *In what way do the kind of things that we feast our senses on either have a very positive effect on us - on our whole beings - or a very negative one?*

Meditate on this thought; and then prayerfully allow God to pour his light into your life.

Almighty God.

Sight, hearing, taste, touch and smell!

Thank you for the senses that you have given me; to enable me to gain and accumulate knowledge and wisdom.

Please help me to use those senses to gather that which is positive and healthy – to be focused on Jesus – and to fill my whole being with your light.

(Include any additional topics for prayer or thanksgiving, arising from this study)

In Jesus' name.

Amen.

'Doers of the word' (aim): To focus our senses on that which is good and healthy – especially, being open to absorbing the light of God into our whole beings, in all its expressions.

Is there anything that you think you might find difficult about achieving the aim?

One or the other!

19th February

Even in the best scenarios, divided loyalties will inevitably lead to compromise. In terms of dividing our loyalties between God and materialism, they are such opposites that it is bound to lead to disaster.

'No-one can serve two masters; for a slave will either hate the one and love the other, or be devoted to the one and despise the other. You cannot serve God and wealth.'

(Matthew 6:24)

'My Journal':

- *Spend a bit of time jotting down some notes about what it means to serve God alone. What does that constitutes in practical terms?*

Meditate on what it means, in practical terms, to let go of, or hold 'lightly' wealth and possessions – and selfish ambitions.

Almighty God.

You desire to be our master!

Thank you that you are worthy of our full commitment.

Please help me to give you my undivided loyalty at all times.

Enable me to hold lightly onto wealth and the material possessions of this world.

Strengthen me to avoid giving in to those distractions that can so easily take my full focus away from you.

Help me to serve only you.

Protect me from spiritual attack.

(Include any additional topics for prayer or thanksgiving, arising from this study)

In Jesus' name.

Amen.

'Doers of the word' (aim): To serve only God.

Is there anything that you think you might find difficult about achieving the aim?

No need to worry
20th February

God provides for the wild animals and birds through the natural order of his creation. How much more will he provide for humankind: God values each one of us, so much!

'Look at the birds of the air; they neither sow nor reap not gather into barns, and yet your heavenly Father feeds them. Are you not of more value than they?'

(Matthew 6:26)

'My Journal':

- *Jesus is not disputing that we have physical needs: for warmth, shelter, clothing, food, drink, etc. And he is not saying that we don't need to work. What he is challenging us with, is the fact that so many of us spend too much time and effort worrying about how those things that we need will be provided. What do you think?*

Meditate on the fact that Jesus gave his life on the cross for you (John 3:16).) That proves how much you are valued by God.

Loving heavenly Father.

You value and care for us all!

Thank you for your provision.

Please help me to trust in you, and your provision, more - and to worry less.

In particular, help me not to worry about those things that I have no control over, anyway.

Help me not to be as dependant, as I am, on the things of this physical world, in which I live.

(Include any additional topics for prayer or thanksgiving, arising from this study)

In Jesus' name.

Amen.

'Doers of the word' (aim): To trust in God's provision, rather than resorting to worrying.

Is there anything that you think you might find difficult about achieving the aim?

What good does worry do?

21st February

There are some outcomes over which we have control; some outcomes that are completely beyond our control; and some outcomes that might never happen anyway. At the risk of stating the obvious, worry can be an awful waste of time and effort.

'And can any of you by worrying add a single hour to your span of life?'

(Matthew 6:27)

'My Journal':

- *How does the scenario that Jesus describes in this verse, highlight our dependency on God for so many things that are completely out of our hands?*

Meditate on the things that we can do, in an effort to lengthen our lives, as compared with worry, that is more likely to do the opposite.

Almighty God.

What good does worry do?

Indeed, we cannot add a single hour to the length of our lives by worry – in fact, we are more likely to shorten our lives as a result of worry and anxiety.

Please help me to recognise the futility – even the destructive quality – of worry.

And empower me to progressively replace worry with trust – trust in you.

Help me to remember to apply self-care.

(Include any additional topics for prayer or thanksgiving, arising from this study)

In Jesus' name.

Amen.

'Doers of the word' (aim): To understand, and make a positive response, to the futility of worry.

Is there anything that you think you might find difficult about achieving the aim?

What the Bible says about **following Jesus**

Worry can spoil today
22nd February

Worrying about tomorrow can demand so much of our energy and focus; that it ends up in spoiling today: and the opportunities that it has within it, to serve God.

'So do not worry about tomorrow, for tomorrow will bring worries of its own. Today's trouble is enough for today.'

(Matthew 6:34)

'My Journal':

- *What kind of God given opportunities do you know that today holds; and how can you prepare to face any additional, unexpected opportunities?*

Meditate, and learn from, what happened yesterday: consider the opportunities that you grasped – and any that you missed, because of worry.

Almighty God.

The future is in your hands!

Thank you that through my relationship with Jesus, my eternal future is safe in your hands.

Please grant me the confidence and assurance to believe that, and act upon it.

Enable me to focus on today's opportunities, and not to waste them by worrying about tomorrow.

Help me to learn some positive lessons from those times when I have wasted opportunities, because of worry.

(Include any additional topics for prayer or thanksgiving, arising from this study)

In Jesus' name.

Amen.

'Doers of the word' (aim): Not to spoil today, for the sake of worrying about tomorrow.

Is there anything that you think you might find difficult about achieving the aim?

Judgement

23rd February

Being judged is not a nice thought, when on the receiving end; and yet we often seem to be so eager to judge others.

'Do not judge, so that you may not be judged.'

(Matthew 7:1)

'My Journal':

- *Jot down some hypothetical ways in which we might be tempted to pass judgements on each other.*

Meditate on the significance of the saying of Jesus, in this verse. – It is quite a warning, isn't it?

Lord.

You love to forgive!

Thank you that, through Jesus, we can be forgiven for all the bad things we have ever done; but help us to be warned that if we judge others, you will judge us.

Please help me not to make judgements on others – probably most would be on very superficial things anyway.

It is not my place to judge them.

(Include any additional topics for prayer or thanksgiving, arising from this study)

In Jesus' name.

Amen.

'Doers of the word' (aim): Not to be tempted to make judgements on other people.

Is there anything that you think you might find difficult about achieving the aim?

What the Bible says about **following Jesus**

The ball's in your court!
24th February

Everything we could ever need – I mean, really need – is available: it is up to us to claim it.

'Ask, and it will be given to you; search, and you will find; knock, and the door will be opened for you.'

(Matthew 7:7)

'My Journal':

- *Consider what Jesus is saying in this verse. Eternal blessings and the empowerment by the indwelling Holy Spirit, are there for the asking. The deeper truths of scripture will be revealed to those who seek. And entry into the kingdom is immediate for those who knock on the door... All linked with our personal relationship with Jesus. Jot down your thoughts on this.*

Meditate on the fact that the essence of this verse is, everything that is being offered is free of charge – by grace – made possible through Jesus' act of love on the cross.

Lord Jesus.

You command us to ask, search and knock!

Thank you that you have promised when we ask; it will be given to us.

Thank you that you have promised when we search; we will find.

And thank you that you have promised when we knock; the door will be opened to us.

Thank you for all these things in terms of salvation, through our relationship with you – by grace!

But in a wider context, please help me to know your will: knowing what to ask for; knowing what to search for; and knowing on what doors to knock.

Enable me to discover and benefit from all those things that you have prepared for me, into eternity.

(Include any additional topics for prayer or thanksgiving, arising from this study)

In your name.

Amen.

'Doers of the word' (aim): To be confident enough to ask, search, and knock.

Is there anything that you think you might find difficult about achieving the aim?

What the Bible says about **following Jesus**

A good bench mark to remember

25th February

The Bible speaks a lot about how we should behave towards each other; but maybe the best summary of this is in the words of Jesus, when he says:

'In everything do to others as you would have them do to you; for this is the law and the prophets.'

(Matthew 7:12)

'My Journal':

- *How do you like to be treated by other people?*

Meditate for a moment on how you treat other people… and how that compares with the way you like to be treated by them.

Lord Jesus.

What amazing advice!

Thank you for instructing us to behave towards others as we would have them behave towards us.

Please help me to value myself, as you value me.

Grant me an awareness and understanding of how I like to be treated; and empower me to threat others in that same way.

(Include any additional topics for prayer or thanksgiving, arising from this study)

In your name.

Amen.

'Doers of the word' (aim): To have a clear awareness of how we like to be treated by others, as a guide as to how we should treat them.

Is there anything that you think you might find difficult about achieving the aim?

The wide gate leads to destruction

26th February

Jesus speaks about the importance of making the right choice in how we live our lives: he compares it to the gate which we chose to go through, and the road that it leads to. The wide gate, leads to the broad road, leading to destruction. That is, the road which represents the type of life where anything goes.

'Enter through the narrow gate; for the gate is wide and the road is easy that leads to destruction, and there are many who take it.'

(Matthew 7:13)

'My Journal':

- *In the case of Christianity; good boundaries are set on the basis of the Bible. What are the consequences of not having good boundaries; as represented by the wide road?*

Meditate on the fact that the wide road also represents a life of not being in relationship with God. And this road, we are told, leads to destruction – in particular, to spiritual destruction. Think about that for a few minutes.

Lord Jesus.

You warn us against a life with no biblically based boundaries – and no relationship with you.

Thank you for that warning, and for providing us with another way – the narrow road.

Please help me to avoid the wide road which leads to destruction; and to speak up in helping others to avoid that road.

Help me to make the right spiritual and lifestyle choices – and set the right boundaries.

(Include any additional topics for prayer or thanksgiving, arising from this study)

In your name.

Amen.

'Doers of the word' (aim): To make the right lifestyle and spiritual choices – those which do not lead to destruction... and set the right boundaries.

Is there anything that you think you might find difficult about achieving the aim?

What the Bible says about **following Jesus**

The narrow gate leads to life
27th February

The road that leads to life – life in all its fullness, and life that is eternal – is a difficult road to travel along. It begins with entering into a personal relationship with Jesus; and setting up some strict scripturally based boundaries.

'For the gate is narrow and the road is hard that leads to life, and there are few who find it.'

(Matthew 7:14)

'My Journal':

- *What might some of those 'hard' things be, that are part of following the metaphorical narrow road?*

Meditate on your relationship with Jesus; and then spend some time prayerfully affirming it, and aspiring to experience eternal life it all its fullness, as a result.

Lord Jesus.

You are the way to real life: life in all it's fullness, and life which is eternal.

Thank you that our relationships with you are the way to receiving that 'life'.

Please help me to walk closely to you each day.

Enable me to live in obedience to the will of the Father.

Equip me to follow your teaching.

Give me the willingness to follow the leading by the Holy Spirit.

And help me to live out the Christian life of love and witness.

Help me to give up those things in my life that are not in keeping with living your way; and give me perseverance when things are particularly difficult.

(Include any additional topics for prayer or thanksgiving, arising from this study)

In your name.

Amen.

'Doers of the word' (aim): To travel down the narrow road by doing things God's way.

Is there anything that you think you might find difficult about achieving the aim?

Words are easy

28th February

Words are easy! It's one thing to profess to be a Christian; it is something else to really commit to Jesus, and live the lifestyle that matches that profession. Jesus highlights the importance of putting into practice those things that we say about our faith – so that they are not just empty words.

'Not everyone who says to me, "Lord, Lord", will enter into the kingdom of heaven, but only one who does the will of my Father in heaven.'

(Matthew 7:21)

'My journal':

- *How does your confession of faith in Jesus compare with your lifestyle – do they match? Are you putting into practice all that you say about it?*

Meditate in the knowledge that, when we are truly committed to following Jesus, he fills us with the power of the indwelling Holy Spirit: to cleanse, transform, empower, and give us the desire to live a lifestyle of doing the will of God... so that our actions might reflect our words.

Lord Jesus.

It is your desire that our faith should not be in words only!

Thank you that through making a commitment to following you, we enter into your eternal kingdom.

Please let my commitment to do that be more than just empty words.

Help me to be truly committed to you.

And let my lifestyle match up with the words that I speak.

(Include any additional topics for prayer or thanksgiving, arising from this study)

In your name.

Amen.

'Doers of the word' (aim): To put into practice those things that we say about our faith.

Is there anything that you think you might find difficult about achieving the aim?

What the Bible says about **following Jesus**

A good foundation

29th February

What is the most secure foundation on which we could ever build our lives? - The key to entering into the kingdom, discovering real fulfilment in life and having the assurance of eternal life. The answer to this question is in the words of Jesus when he says:

'Everyone then who hears these words of mine and acts on them will be like a wise man who built his house on rock.'

(Matthew 7:24)

'My Journal':

- *Hearing and acting on the teaching of Jesus involves prayerfully reading the Bible; understanding what God is saying through those words of scripture; making a positive response; and it includes being in relationship with Jesus. Jot some notes down about the foundation of your life.*

Meditate on the qualities of rock as a foundation; and then apply the analogy to your own life, in a spiritual context.

Lord Jesus.

You are the perfect foundation to life!

Thank you that you provide the only really firm foundation.

Through dying on the cross paying the penalty for sin.

By rising again, defeating death, and being alive today.

And by offering forgiveness for sin, fulfilment to life, and eternal hope – all available, through us entering into a personal relationship with you... based on repentance and faith.

Please help me to commit to being in that relationship with you; and build my life on the firm and unshakable foundation you offer.

(Include any additional topics for prayer or thanksgiving, arising from this study)

In your name.

Amen.

'Doers of the word' (aim): To build our lives on firm foundations.

Is there anything that you think you might find difficult about achieving the aim?

5

LENT

What the Bible says about the **Baptism of Jesus (Lent)**

1st March

Telling the story

Then Jesus came from Galilee to John at the Jordan, to be baptised by him. John would have prevented him, saying, 'I need to be baptised by you, and do you come to me?' But Jesus answered him, 'Let it be so now; for it is proper for us in this way to fulfil all righteousness.' Then he consented. And when Jesus had been baptised, just as he came up from the water, suddenly the heavens were opened to him and he saw the Spirit of God descending like a dove and alighting on him. And a voice from heaven said, 'This is my Son, the Beloved, with who I am well pleased.'

(Matthew 3:13-17)

...To be looked at in detail over the next five days

Lord God.

Thank you for the truth of scripture, and that it is relevant to every generation.

Thank you for this passage of scripture which looks at the baptism of Jesus.

Please help me to understand what I have just read; and to meditate upon it today.

(Include any additional topics for prayer or thanksgiving, arising from this study)

In Jesus' name.

Amen.

What the Bible says about the **Baptism of Jesus (Lent)**

Baptism
2nd March

Jesus doesn't need to be baptised because he is sinless, but he wants to set an example for us to follow – it is God's will for us to be baptised.

Then Jesus came from Galilee to John at the Jordan, to be baptised by him.

(Matthew 3:13)

'My Journal':

- *Jot down some thoughts about the symbolism of baptism: both in terms of cleansing from sin; and in terms of dying to an old way of life, and being reborn into a new way of life following Jesus.*

Meditate on the fact that Jesus is sinless; which makes him our perfect example, in every way.

Loving heavenly Father.

It is your will that we should be baptised!

Thank you that we are able to leave a self-centred lifestyle behind, and move into a God-centred one – through entering into a personal relationship with Jesus.

Please help me to make that commitment.

Fill me afresh with the power of your indwelling Holy Spirit, empowering me to live a God-centred lifestyle.

Help me to follow Jesus' example not just in baptism, but in all things.

(Include any additional topics for prayer or thanksgiving, arising from this study)

In Jesus' name.

Amen.

'Doers of the word' (aim): Jesus ordains the act of baptism, for us to follow.

Is there anything that you think you might find difficult about achieving the aim.

What the Bible says about the **Baptism of Jesus (Lent)**

Misunderstood

3rd March

John the Baptist desperately wants to serve Jesus, and do the right thing: in so doing, he almost fails to carry out God's will for him – this could even be the pinnacle of his calling.

John would have prevented him, saying, 'I need to be baptised by you, and do you come to me?'

(Matthew 3:14)

'My Journal':

- *Sometimes in our eagerness to serve, we can misunderstand what Jesus is calling us to do – and, in so doing, miss important opportunities. Can you think of any specific examples in your own life?*

Meditate on the significance of those occasions when our plans to witness and serve, are not God's plans.

Father God.

My desire is to serve you!

Thank you that you want me to serve you; and that you have a plan of what you want me to do.

Please help me, in my enthusiasm to serve, not to end up not really listening to your guidance – and maybe doing things that you don't want me to be doing… and vice versa.

Enable me to be a good servant of you.

(Include any additional topics for prayer or thanksgiving, arising from this study)

In Jesus' name.

Amen.

'Doers of the word' (aim): To listen to God's leading with regards to those things he wants us to be doing for him.

Is there anything that you think you might find difficult about achieving the aim?

What the Bible says about the **Baptism of Jesus (Lent)**

The right time

4th March

Let us always remember that God's timing is perfect: there is a right time for Jesus to be baptised - Jesus uses the word 'now'.

But Jesus answered him, 'Let it be so now, for it is proper for us in this way to fulfil all righteousness.' Then he consented.

(Matthew 3:15)

'My Journal':

- *Consider the concept and application that God's timing is perfect. Every aspect of God's plan has a 'right time' to happen. What are your thoughts?*

Meditate on the importance of patience as we eagerly seek to serve Jesus, in the world around us.

Almighty God.

You have a right time for everything!

Thank you that you have a plan for my life (Jeremiah 29:11) – and a wider plan for the whole of creation – both are perfect plans.

And every phase of those plans has a time when it should happen.

Please forgive me for my impatience; for those times when I try to hurry you along – not wanting to wait for your timing.

Grant me more patience.

(Include any additional topics for prayer or thanksgiving, arising from this study)

In Jesus' name.

Amen.

'Doers of the word' (aim): To realise and accept that, in God's eyes, there is a right time for everything – and to have patience to wait for that time.

Is there anything that you think you might find difficult about achieving the aim?

What the Bible says about the **Baptism of Jesus (Lent)**

Filled with the Holy Spirit
5th March

We can experience the power of God within us, through being filled with the indwelling Holy Spirit – when we are in a relationship with Jesus.

And when Jesus had been baptised, just as he came up from the water, suddenly the heavens were opened to him and he saw the Spirit of God descending like a dove and alighting on him.

(Matthew 3:16)

'My Journal':

- *Think about the significance of living with the power of God within us: in terms of knowing the fullness of God's love, receiving his guidance, being strengthened and empowered, benefitting from his wisdom, and being progressively transformed into the likeness of Jesus himself. Jot down your thoughts.*

Meditate on the example Jesus sets us, of not even thinking about embarking on living the Christian life of love and witness without relying on the power of the indwelling Holy Spirit.

Lord Jesus.

Even you received the indwelling Holy Spirit, in preparation for beginning your ministry on earth!

Thank you that, through being in relationship with you, we are filled with the Holy Spirit.

Please fill me afresh.

Empower me to be the person you would have me be; and to say and do the things you would have me say and do.

(Include any additional topics for prayer or thanksgiving, arising from this study)

In your name.

Amen.

'Doers of the word' (aim): To be filled with the power of the indwelling Holy Spirit.

Is there anything that you think you might find difficult about achieving the aim?

What the Bible says about the **Baptism of Jesus (Lent)**

God's Son

6th March

We are left in no doubt as to who Jesus is, when Matthew informs us:

And a voice from heaven said, 'This is my Son, the beloved, with whom I am well pleased.'

(Matthew 3:17)

'My Journal':

- *Let there be no confusion: Jesus is the Son of God. Jesus is divine as well as human. Think about it, and jot down your response.*

Meditate on the significance of God coming down to earth, through his Son, Jesus.

Risen Lord Jesus.

You are the Son of God!

You came down to live amongst us in human form – but also divine!

Thank you that you came to communicate God's love to us - unconditional love.

And the greatest demonstration of that love was when you died on the cross, paying the penalty for our sin.

Please help me to realise the significance of that; and make a positive response to you – and to serving you.

(Include any additional topics for prayer or thanksgiving, arising from this study)

In your name.

Amen.

'Doers of the word' (aim): To reciprocate the unconditional love that God showers upon us.

Is there anything that you think you might find difficult about achieving the aim?

What the Bible says about the **temptations of Jesus (Lent)**

7th March

Telling the story

Then Jesus was led up by the Spirit into the wilderness to be tempted by the devil. He fasted for forty days and forty nights, and afterwards he was famished. The tempter came and said to him, 'If you are the Son of God, command these stones to become loaves of bread.' But he answered, 'It is written,

"One does not live by bread alone,
but by every word that comes from the mouth of God."'

Then the devil took him to the holy city and placed him on the pinnacle of the temple, saying to him, 'if you are the Son of God, throw yourself down; for it is written,

"He will command his angels concerning you",
and "On their hands they will bear you up,
so that you will not dash your foot against a stone."'

Jesus said to him, 'Again it is written, "Do not put the Lord your God to the test."'

Again, the devil took him to a very high mountain and showed him all the kingdoms of the world and their splendour; and he said to him, 'All these I will give you, if you will fall down and worship me.' Jesus said to him, 'Away with you, Satan! for it written,

"Worship the Lord your God,
and serve only him."'

Then the devil left him, and suddenly angels came and waited on him.

(Matthew 4:1-11)

… To be looked at over the next eight days

Lord God.

Thank you for the truth of scripture, and that it is relevant to every generation.

Thank you for this passage of scripture that looks at Jesus being tempted in the wilderness.

Please help me to understand what I have just read; and to meditate upon it today.

(Include any additional topics for prayer or thanksgiving, arising from this study)

In Jesus' name.

Amen.

What the Bible says about the **temptations of Jesus (Lent)**

In the wilderness
8th March

The Spirit leads Jesus into the wilderness (to be tempted) for a purpose: it is time out from the busyness and pressures of everyday life, in order to prepare for his forthcoming ministry.

Then Jesus was led up by the Spirit into the wilderness to be tempted by the devil.

(Matthew 4:1)

'My Journal':

- *Lent is a time when we should step aside from the busyness and pressures of life, in order to spend time examining our spiritual lives, including our relationships with Jesus, as we prepare for Easter. Jot down your immediate thoughts on this.*

Meditate on what you could do, in order to improve your spiritual life and your relationship with Jesus?

Risen Lord Jesus.

Lent is a time to consider our relationship with you!

Thank you that, through your death and resurrection, it is possible to be in relationship with you.

Please help me to prayerfully examine my relationship with you; and discover ways of making it a closer and deeper one.

Enable me to be prepared for Easter; and to make a positive response of renewed commitment and service to you.

Empower me not to allow distractions to prevent me from being focused on you and kingdom building.

(Include any additional topics for prayer or thanksgiving, arising from this study)

In your name.

Amen.

'Doers of the word' (aim): To prepare for Easter, by making a positive response of renewed commitment and service to Jesus.

Is there anything that you think you might find difficult about achieving the aim?

What the Bible says about the **temptations of Jesus (Lent)**

Jesus understands

9th March

Jesus knows what it is like to be hungry, to be vulnerable, and to be tempted. This passage highlights his humanity, as well as his deity.

He fasted for forty days and forty nights, and afterwards he was famished.

(Matthew 4:2)

'My Journal':

- *Make some notes as you consider the concept of Jesus' humanity. By the end of his life on earth, he really understands the things that we go through.*

Meditate on the knowledge that Jesus understands, and can empathise with, what it means to be human, and to live in a broken world?

Risen Lord Jesus.

You know what it is like to be hungry!

You know what it is like to suffer!

You know what it is like to face opposition and temptation!

You know what it is like to face physical death!

Thank you that you know what it is like to be human; and because of that, you understand the things we endure as we go through life.

Please grant me the assurance that you understand.

(Include any additional topics for prayer or thanksgiving, arising from this study)

In your name.

Amen.

'Doers of the word' (aim): To be assured that Jesus understands what it is like to be human.

Is there anything that you think you might find difficult about achieving the aim?

What the Bible says about the **temptations of Jesus (Lent)**

Feeding the hungry
10th March

The tempter (the devil) is never far away; especially when we are walking in God's will for us: he loves to try to wreck the plans and purposes of God.

The tempter came and said to him, 'If you are the Son of God, command these stones to become loaves of bread.'

(Matthew 4:3)

'My Journal':

- *Jesus could put an end to starvation in the world, with an enormous miracle; but it wouldn't solve the problem of people turning their backs on God. Make a note of your thoughts in response to that statement.*

Meditate on the concept that Jesus does care about the poor - he goes on to demonstrate that during his ministry - but his priority is our spiritual wellbeing. We should follow Jesus' example. Consider what that means.

Risen Lord Jesus.

Our greatest needs are not always the most obvious ones; but the devil loves to try to persuade us that they are!

Thank you that you understand our physical needs for things like food and drink; and you do provide through your creation – but in a broken world, it does not get shared equally.

Please help me not to become too focused on physical needs; to the extent of losing sight of any other possible needs – especially spiritual ones.

Give me the confidence, and help me to prioritise in such a way as to speak to others about you – as well as sharing your love in caring, compassionate ways.

Empower me to stand up to the devil's attempt to defeat God's plans and purposes for my life.

(Include any additional topics for prayer or thanksgiving, arising from this study)

In your name.

Amen.

'Doers of the word' (aim): To remember that our greatest needs – and the needs of others - are not always the most obvious physical ones.

Is there anything that you think you might find difficult about achieving the aim?

What the Bible says about the **temptations of Jesus (Lent)**

Correct priorities
11th March

Jesus' way of dealing with temptation is by looking at scripture: on that basis he refuses to give in to the devil.

But he answered, 'It is written,
"One does not live by bread alone,
but by every word that comes from the mouth of God."'

(Matthew 4:4)

'My Journal':

- *All the answers concerning dealing with temptation are there, in the Bible. Write down your thoughts.*

Meditate on the fact that Scripture says we need spiritual food, as well as physical food (things like worship, prayer and Bible study). Jesus' response points us towards making our spiritual needs the main priority. What are your priorities, in order of importance?

Risen Lord Jesus.

You know what we really need!

Thank you that you recognise our physical needs for things like food and drink; but, at the same time, you know that our greatest need is spiritual: to be forgiven, cleansed, restored in our relationship with the Triune God, and filled with eternal hope.

Please help me to think about physical, emotional and spiritual needs; but with a focus and emphasis on spiritual needs.

Help me to relate to you, the Father and the Holy Spirit; and prepare me for eternity in your presence.

(Include any additional topics for prayer or thanksgiving, arising from this study)

In your name.

Amen.

'Doers of the word' (aim): To make it a priority to receive spiritual nourishment.

Is there anything that you think you might find difficult about achieving the aim?

What the Bible says about the **temptations of Jesus (Lent)**

Putting God to the test

12th March

The whole point about faith, is that it is all about believing those things of God, even when there is no physical proof of them (Hebrews 11:1). The devil loves to attack our faith by planting doubts and encouraging us to demand that proof.

Then the devil took him to the holy city and placed him on the pinnacle of the temple, saying to him, 'if you are the Son of God, throw yourself down, for it is written,

"He will command his angels concerning you",
and "On their hands they will bear you up,
so that you will not dash your foot against a stone."'

(Matthew 4:5-6)

'My Journal':

- *The devil tries to persuade Jesus to perform a spectacular stunt; putting God the Father to the test at the same time. Real faith is about believing, without physical proof. Write down some thoughts about your experience of faith.*

Meditate on the demanding of signs. Are there times when you are tempted to demand signs from God, instead of asking for more faith, and the discernment to recognise his calling?

Father God.

You are the God of truth, and are always faithful in keeping your promises.

Thank you that we can accept your promises in faith.

Please increase my faith.

Help me not to demand physical signs for those things that I should be believing anyway.

(Include any additional topics for prayer or thanksgiving, arising from this study)

In Jesus' name.

Amen.

'Doers of the word' (aim): To ask God to increase our faith, rather than asking for physical signs, all the time.

Is there anything that you think you might find difficult about achieving the aim?

What the Bible says about the temptations of Jesus **(Lent)**

Unchanging values

13th March

The old saying goes, 'Some things never change': it is usually used in a contemptuous way... But it can be a really positive thing to have that kind of unchanging point of reference.

Jesus said to him, 'Again it is written, "Do not put the Lord your God to the test."'

(Matthew 4:7)

'My Journal':

- *Constantly in Jesus' ministry, he refers back to what it says in the Scriptures. It is like a 'benchmark' which is unchanging, on which he bases his every action and response. Is that how you view the Bible?*

Meditate on looking at the Bible in that way: both as being unchanging in terms of God's nature and values being constant; and in terms of the Bible being that kind of all-inclusive resource.

Loving God.

You never change; and neither do your values.

Thank you that the teaching in the Scriptures doesn't change.

Please help me to understand it's relevance to me today; and apply it to everyday situations that I am faced with.

And help me to base all my choices and decisions on your word.

(Include any additional topics for prayer or thanksgiving, arising from this study)

In Jesus' name.

Amen.

'Doers of the word' (aim): To constantly refer back to scripture as we make choices, decisions, plans and responses.

Is there anything that you think you might find difficult about achieving the aim?

What the Bible says about the **temptations of Jesus (Lent)**

Conformity

14th March

It is so easy to be tempted to conform to the pressure of society: by our peers, by the world of advertising, and by the ever variable set of values that society places before us.

Again, the devil took him to a very high mountain and showed him all the kingdoms of the world and their splendour; and he said to him, 'All these I will give you, if you will fall down and worship me.'

(Matthew 4:8-9)

'My Journal':

- *Sadly, society doesn't always take its lead from God; and so, often, conformity to society can lead to doing things that are more pleasing to the plans and purposes of the devil, rather than those of God. What are your thoughts?*

Meditate on the way that conformity can lead to obtaining all kinds of things that have their own attraction, like acceptance, popularity or even celebrity status - but at what cost?

Loving heavenly Father.

Your ways are always best!

Thank you that you have an eternal plan for our wellbeing.

Please help me not to be tempted to deviate from your plans, with the consequences of entering into the devil's plans.

Help me not to give in to the temptation of compromise or conformity; when it means deviating from your will.

(Include any additional topics for prayer or thanksgiving, arising from this study)

In Jesus' name.

Amen.

'Doers of the word' (aim): To avoid the temptation to fall into the trap of doing things the devil's way.

Is there anything that you think you might find difficult about achieving the aim?

What the Bible says about the **temptations of Jesus (Lent)**

God alone!
15th March

Our focus, commitment, and obedience should be to God alone.

Jesus said to him, 'Away with you, Satan! for it written,
"Worship the Lord your God,
and serve only him."'

(Matthew 4:10)

'My Journal':

- *What does it mean to worship only God?*

Meditate on what other people or things could act as a distraction from worshiping God.

Almighty God.

You are worthy of our worship!

Thank you that you are the great creator God; and it is right that we should worship you.

Please help me to worship only you.

Help me not to worship wealth and materialism.

Help me not to worship self-centred ambitions.

Help not to exalt celebrities to such a level that they are robbing you of some of the worship due to you.

And help me not to steal, for other things, the time that is due to you.

Fill me afresh with the power of the indwelling Holy Spirit, empowering me to live my whole life – all that I am, and all that I say and do – as an act of worship to you.

(Include any additional topics for prayer or thanksgiving, arising from this study)

In Jesus' name.

Amen.

'Doers of the word' (aim): To worship only God.

Is there anything that you think you might find difficult about achieving the aim?

What the Bible says about the **temptations of Jesus (Lent)**

Cared for by the Father

16th March

Jesus is not alone. God the Father has been close by, even during this time of vulnerability and temptation. God cares for us and, through our relationship with Jesus, will never leave us.

Then the devil left him, and suddenly angels came and waited on him.

(Matthew 4:11)

'My Journal':

- *It is often at our most vulnerable times that we experience the greatest closeness to God. Jot down your thoughts.*

Meditate on the reality of God still being with us, at our most vulnerable times; whether it be in times of temptation, or in some other form of vulnerability. When do you feel most vulnerable?

Our loving heavenly Father.

You shower us with your love and care!

Thank you for your amazing unconditional love.

Thank you that, through my relationship with Jesus, you will never leave me.

Please help me to believe that.

Help me to be prepared to ask for help when I need it.

And help me to accept your care; even when I am at my most vulnerable.

Enable me to demonstrate your love and care to others.

(Include any additional topics for prayer or thanksgiving, arising from this study)

In Jesus' name.

Amen.

'Doers of the word' (aim): To receive God's care; particularly during those most vulnerable times.

Is there anything that you think you might find difficult about achieving the aim?

What the Bible says about **being called (Lent)**

17th March

Telling the story

As he walked by the sea of Galilee, he saw two brothers, Simon who is called Peter, and Andrew his brother, casting a net into the lake – for they were fishermen. And he said to them, 'Follow me, and I will make you fish for people.' Immediately they left their nets and followed him. As he went from there, he saw two other brothers, James son of Zebedee and his brother John, in the boat with their father Zebedee, mending their nets, and he called them. Immediately they left the boat and their father, and followed him.

(Matthew 4:18-22)

…To be looked at over the next five days

Lord God.

Thank you for the truth of scripture, and that it is relevant to every generation.

Thank you for this passage of scripture that looks at Jesus calling his first disciples, as he prepares for ministry.

Please help me to understand what I have just read; and to meditate upon it today.

(Include any additional topics for prayer or thanksgiving, arising from this study)

In Jesus' name.

Amen.

What the Bible says about **being called (Lent)**

Jesus is looking for ordinary people to serve him

18th March

We don't have to be in a position of power or authority; we don't have to be highly academic; and we don't have to have celebrity status for Jesus to call us to serve him – sometimes in quite amazing ways!

As he walked by the Sea of Galilee, he saw two brothers, Simon, who is called Peter, and Andrew his brother, casting a net into the lake – for they were fishermen.

(Matthew 4:18)

'My Journal':

- *Use of the word 'ordinary' might sound a bit condescending; but it is not meant to be. It is intended to give the ring of inclusivity. We can all be used to serve Jesus, in some way. Jot down your response.*

Meditate, prayerfully, on the things that Jesus might be calling you to do.

Lord Jesus.

You call us to serve you!

Thank you that you offer us the privilege of serving you.

Thank you that we don't have to be in a position of power or authority; we don't have to be highly academic; and we don't have to have celebrity status for you to call us to serve you.

Please help me to be willing to respond positively to your calling to me.

Fill me afresh with your Holy Spirit, and empower me to use those skills with which you have equipped me, for the kingdom.

And help me to know how you want me to use those skills in your service.

(Include any additional topics for prayer or thanksgiving, arising from this study)

In your name.

Amen.

'Doers of the word' (aim): To be willing to respond positively to the call of Jesus, to serve him.

Is there anything that you think you might find difficult about achieving the aim?

What the Bible says about **being called (Lent)**

A new type of fishing
19th March

You might have experienced river or sea fishing; but have you ever fished for people? – Because that is what Jesus calls us to do, when we follow him!

And he said to them, 'Follow me, and I will make you fish for people.'

(Matthew 4:19)

'My Journal':

- *Consider the following, and make some notes. Who are we fishing for? What is the purpose of fishing for them? And what is the bait that we are using?*

Meditate on serving Jesus in this way. Is fishing for people something you feel you could do, by sharing the love of Jesus with others in practical ways; by chatting about Jesus; and by sharing words of personal testimony? – With God's help, of course!

Lord Jesus.

It is your desire that all of your followers should fish for people – leading them towards the kingdom!

Thank you that the kingdom is available to everyone, through you.

Please help me to be effective in my fishing: through acts of kindness, chatting to others about you, and sharing words of personal testimony – backed up by an appropriate lifestyle of obedience to the Father.

Empower me through the Holy Spirit.

Let the catch of people into the kingdom be a really good one!

(Include any additional topics for prayer or thanksgiving, arising from this study)

In your name.

Amen.

'Doers of the word' (aim): To fish people into the kingdom.

Is there anything that you think you might find difficult about achieving the aim?

Following Jesus

20th March

Following Jesus involves being in a personal relationship with him; living in obedience to his guidance and teaching; and striving to become more like him.

Immediately they left their nets and followed him.

(Matthew 4:20)

'My Journal':

- *Are you following Jesus in every respect?*

Meditate on the significance of Peter and Andrew leaving their nets and following Jesus. Remember that fishing was their job – their source of income – so, trusting Jesus, they walk away from their business. Sometimes we have to make significant sacrifices in order to follow Jesus.

Lord Jesus.

You call us to follow you!

Thank you that you call us in that way.

Please help me to respond positively to that calling.

Help me to be prepared to make any sacrifices that I need to, in order to follow you.

Help me to have a close relationship with you; to live in obedience to you, following your teaching, guidance and example; and to be more like you.

(Include any additional topics for prayer or thanksgiving, arising from this study)

In your name.

Amen.

'Doers of the word' (aim): To follow Jesus – even if it means making significant sacrifices!

Is there anything that you think you might find difficult about achieving the aim?

Called by Jesus
21st March

We are all called to serve Jesus: it is not an easy calling to fulfil, but what a privilege it is! Let's not miss the opportunity.

As he went from there, he saw two other brothers, James son of Zebedee and his brother John, in the boat with their father Zebedee, mending their nets, and he called them.

(Matthew 4:21)

'My Journal':

- *How do you view being called by Jesus, to serve him? Is it just another chore; is it something that you hadn't bargained for; or is it a real privilege?*

Meditate on the nature of your calling to serve Jesus: that is, where Jesus has called you to serve; and in what ways he has called you to serve.

Lord Jesus.

It is such a privilege to be called by you – to serve!

Thank you for your calling: please help me to respond positively.

Help me not to allow busyness to prevent me from fully entering into your calling to me.

Teach me the right priorities I should demonstrate in my life.

And, if my calling is to serve where I am, don't let me get distracted by thoughts of living and working in exotic places.

Grant me contentment and fulfilment in my life.

(Include any additional topics for prayer or thanksgiving, arising from this study)

In your name.

Amen.

'Doers of the word' (aim): To respond to the privilege of being called to serve, by Jesus – and not miss the opportunity.

Is there anything that you think you might find difficult about achieving the aim?

What the Bible says about **being called (Lent)**

An instant response
22nd March

Act now! Don't waste time! James and John make an instant response to Jesus.

Immediately they left the boat and their father, and followed him.

(Matthew 4:22)

'My Journal':

- *Have you made a positive response to Jesus' calling to follow him and to serve him; or are you still hesitating – reluctant to commit? Remember that James and John's response is instant and decisive – 'Immediately'.*

Meditate on what you are already doing; or feel that you could do, to respond to Jesus' calling?

Lord Jesus.

You need an instant response from us!

Thank you for your calling to me, to follow you; to serve you; and for me to perform specific tasks.

Please help me to respond positively to your callings, and instantly.

Help me not to procrastinate; but to be decisive.

And grant me the enablement and empowerment to fulfil your callings to me.

(Include any additional topics for prayer or thanksgiving, arising from this study)

In your name.

Amen.

'Doers of the word' (aim): To always respond instantly to Jesus, every time he calls us to do something.

Is there anything that you think you might find difficult about achieving the aim?

What the Bible says about **Christ like living (Lent)**

This is love

23rd March

John emphasises that there is nothing new about love – it has been the basis of all God's commandments since the beginning of time - and can be seen constantly in the example that Jesus sets before us to emulate, in his life on earth.

And this is love, that we walk according to his commandments; this is the commandment just as you have heard it from the beginning – you must walk in it.

(2 John 6)

'My Journal':

- *The reason that all the commandments are about love in practice, is because they are all reflections of the nature of God - and God's nature is love! Consider that, and then make some notes: maybe it changes your attitude towards obeying God's commandments in some way.*

Meditate on the concept of personally walking according to God's commandments.

God of love.

All the commandments are an expression of your nature!

Thank you that during Jesus' life on earth, we see him living out those commandments – as our example.

Please empower me, through the Holy Spirit, to live in obedience to you; and at the same time to emulate Jesus – loving one another!

Help me to walk according to your commandments – in terms of them becoming intrinsic to my whole lifestyle.

(Include any additional topics for prayer or thanksgiving, arising from this study)

In Jesus' name.

Amen.

'Doers of the word' (aim): To apply God's commandments as an outworking of his love, within us.

Is there anything that you think you might find difficult about achieving the aim?

What the Bible says about **Christ like living (Lent)**

Live in Jesus' teaching
24th March

There is an intrinsic link between striving to live a Christ like life, and relationship with the Triune God (God the Father, Jesus the Son, and the Holy Spirit): the one cannot exist in isolation of the other.

Everyone who does not abide in the teaching of Christ, but goes beyond it, does not have God; whoever abides in the teaching has both the Father and the Son.

(2 John 9)

'My Journal':

- *The phrase 'abide in the teaching of Christ' has the connotation of not straying from that teaching, at all. Wise words! Make some notes as you consider its significance for you.*

Meditate on the phrase: 'Has both the Father and the Son'. It denotes relationship. Think about the connection between behaviour and relationship in this particular context.

Lord Jesus.

Thank you for your teaching.

Life changing teaching!

Please help me to 'abide' in your teaching; not deviating from it at all.

Let it be evidence of my relationship to you, and of my commitment to being in your will.

Fill me afresh with the power of the Holy Spirit, to enable me to live in obedience to you.

(Include any additional topics for prayer or thanksgiving, arising from this study)

In your name.

Amen.

'Doers of the word' (aim): To live according to Jesus' teaching daily.

Is there anything that you think you might find difficult about achieving the aim?

What the Bible says about **Christ like living (Lent)**

Pray for each other
25th March

There is such value in prayer: it is such a blessing to be prayed for by others, and such a privilege to pray for others.

Beloved, I pray that all may go well with you and that you may be in good health, just as it is well with your soul.

(3 John 2)

'My Journal':

- *On what kind of occasions might we offer prayer to others?*

Meditate on praying for others. We don't need to know the whole situation; because God knows every detail – so useful in confidential situations. Maybe that knowledge opens up the opportunity for you to pray for numerous other people.

Heavenly Father.

Prayer is such a wonderful blessing!

Thank you for the privilege of being able to come to you in prayer.

Thank you that prayer is a 'gift' that we can offer to other people.

We can pray with and for other people, in so many different situations.

Please grant me the confidence to be able to do that.

And help me to be organised in my own prayer life.

Be with those I love and care about *(expand, giving names and situations).*

(Include any additional topics for prayer or thanksgiving, arising from this study)

In Jesus' name.

Amen.

'Doers of the word' (aim): To remember to pray for others.

Is there anything that you think you might find difficult about achieving the aim?

Walking in the truth

26th March

Christ like living, involves living according to the truth – the truth of God.

I was overjoyed when some of the friends arrived and testified to your faithfulness to the truth, namely, how you walk in the truth.

(3 John 3)

'My Journal':

- *What is truth?*

Meditate on how and where we can source that truth; on which we can base our lives – through Bible study and teaching.

Lord Jesus.

In the Gospels, you describe yourself as the truth!

Thank you, that as we learn more about you, we also learn more about the nature of God.

Thank you, that as we learn more about your life on earth, we also learn more about the way we should live our lives.

Thank you, that as we learn more about your teaching, we also learn more about the kingdom, salvation and eternity.

Please help me to make it a goal to learn more and more about you; and grant me the enablement, through the power of the Holy Spirit, to live according to the truth that you bring to us.

(Include any additional topics for prayer or thanksgiving, arising from this study)

In your name.

Amen.

'Doers of the word' (aim): To base our lives on the truth of God (sourced from the Bible).

Is there anything that you think you might find difficult about achieving the aim?

What the Bible says about **Christ like living (Lent)**

No greater joy
27th March

John, in his love and compassion, reflects the joy that God feels for us when we are walking in the truth: living lives based on his truth - the truth of scripture.

I have no greater joy than this, to hear that my children are walking in the truth.

(3 John 4)

'My Journal':

- *Bearing in mind that the Bible teaches us the truth about God and our eternal futures in relationship with him, how does that affect the way in which you handle scripture?*

Meditate on your feelings about the Bible's relevance to all generations -still on the subject of the truth of scripture?

Our loving heavenly Father.

We can bring joy to you; by living in your truth!

Thank you for the truth of the Bible; and its relevance to all generations.

Please fill me afresh with the Holy Spirit; and help me to live according to the truth of scripture.

Forgive me for those times when I fail to live up to your standards, and fail to be within your will.

(Include any additional topics for prayer or thanksgiving, arising from this study)

In Jesus' name.

Amen.

'Doers of the word' (aim): To bring joy to God, by living in his truth.

Is there anything that you think you might find difficult about achieving the aim?

What the Bible says about **Christ like living (Lent)**

Hospitality and welcoming strangers
28th March

The Bible promotes the practice of hospitality; even to the extent of welcoming strangers.

Beloved, you do faithfully whatever you do for the friends, even though they are strangers to you.

(3 John 5)

'My Journal':

- *Is the church congregation, to which you belong, a welcoming one? If so, what makes it so?*

Meditate on the ways in which the church congregation, to which you belong, offers practical hospitality in any way.

Heavenly Father.

It is your will that we should offer hospitality to others; especially to those who come into the Church!

Thank you that you give us a love to share, even with those people we don't know; which leads us to demonstrate compassion and acts of generosity and kindness.

Please let the church congregation to which I belong be welcoming to those whom you send to us: giving a warm welcome and demonstrating hospitality.

(Include any additional topics for prayer or thanksgiving, arising from this study)

In Jesus' name.

Amen.

'Doers of the word' (aim): To promote hospitality taking place in and through our church congregations, to which we belong.

Is there anything that you think you might find difficult about achieving the aim?

What the Bible says about **Christ like living (Lent)**

Loving behaviour that is worthy of God

29th March

It is God's will that we, his followers, are noticed; but for the right reasons. In this context, it is about sharing his love with others.

They have testified to your love before the church. You will do well to send them on in a manner worthy of God.

(3 John 6)

'My Journal':

- *What are people saying about your behaviour, and that of the church congregation to which you belong – is the love that you are demonstrating worthy of God?*

Meditate on how love in action, often in very practical ways, is a huge witness to other people – the God whom we follow is a God of love!

Loving God.

You love us all so much!

Thank you for your amazing, unconditional love for us all.

Thank you for your amazing, unconditional love for me.

Please fill me so full of that love, that it just pours out into my whole lifestyle; day by day.

Let me be noticed for the right reasons.

And forgive me for those times when I am noticed for the wrong reasons.

Help me to be a good witness of you.

(Include any additional topics for prayer or thanksgiving, arising from this study)

In Jesus' name.

Amen.

'Doers of the word' (aim): To be noticed by others, because of our love.

Is there anything that you think you might find difficult about achieving the aim?

What the Bible says about **Christ like living (Lent)**

Imitating the right things
30th March

We must choose good role models in order to follow their example – or imitate how they behave. The best role model is Jesus himself.

Beloved, do not imitate what is evil but imitate what is good.

(3 John 11a)

'My Journal':

- *Think about the various role models who you have looked up to, over the years. What qualities made those role models good?*

Meditate for a few minutes on looking to Jesus as your example, to follow in your life. Note is compassion, his obedience to the Father, and his demonstration of unconditional love in action.

Lord Jesus.

You are just the best example we could ever have!

Thank you that you are the perfect role model to follow.

Thank you for all those other people that you have placed in my life, who have been important to me – who I have learned from, and benefitted from imitating *(give names).*

Please help me to only imitate that which is good.

And help me to follow your example in all things.

Enable me to be a good example to others.

(Include any additional topics for prayer or thanksgiving, arising from this study)

In your name.

Amen.

'Doers of the word' (aim): To imitate what is good – in particular, to follow Jesus' example.

Is there anything that you think you might find difficult about achieving the aim?

What the Bible says about **Christ like living (Lent)**

Our behaviour says it all

31st March

Our behaviour is the evidence of whether or not we are in relationship with the Triune God (God the Father, Jesus the Son, and the Holy Spirit).

Whoever does good is from God; whoever does evil has not seen God.

(3 John 11b)

'My Journal':

- *Consider the concept described in the verse: good behaviour is the evidence of a close relationship and daily walk with God; and bad behaviour is the evidence of the absence of God in a person's life. Jot down your thoughts.*

Meditate on how this concept relates to your life?

Almighty God.

All good things are from you!

Thank you that a personal relationship with you enables us to do good.

Please help me to have that close relationship with you, through Jesus; and grant me the enablement to evidence that commitment by demonstrating goodness in my choices, decisions, words and actions.

(Include any additional topics for prayer or thanksgiving, arising from this study)

In Jesus' name.

Amen.

'Doers of the word' (aim): To do good on a daily basis.

Is there anything that you think you might find difficult about achieving the aim?

6

EASTER

What the Bible says about **Jesus' triumphal entry into Jerusalem (Easter)**

1st April

Telling the story

After he had said this, he went on ahead, going up to Jerusalem.

When he had come near Bethphage and Bethany, at the place called the Mount of Olives, he sent two of the disciples, saying, 'Go into the village ahead of you, and as you enter it you will find tied there a colt that has never been ridden. Untie it and bring it here. If anyone asks you, "Why are you untying it?" Just say this: "The Lord needs it." So those who were sent departed and found it as he had told them. As they were untying the colt, its owners asked them, 'Why are you untying the colt?' They said, 'The Lord needs it.' Then they brought it to Jesus; and after throwing their cloaks on the colt, they set Jesus on it. As he rode along, people kept spreading their cloaks on the road. As he was now approaching the path down from the Mount of Olives, the whole multitude of the disciples began to praise God joyfully with a loud voice for all the deeds of power that they had seen, saying,

'Blessed is the king who comes in the name of the Lord!'

'Peace in heaven, and glory in the highest heaven!'

Some of the Pharisees in the crowd said to him, 'Teacher, order your disciples to stop.' He answered, 'I tell you, if these were silent, the stones would shout out.'

(Luke 19:28-40)

... to be looked at over the next four days.

Lord God.

Thank you for the truth of scripture, and that it is relevant to every generation.

Thank you for this passage of scripture that looks at Jesus' triumphal entry into Jerusalem.

Please help me to understand what I have just read; and to meditate upon it today.

(Include any additional topics for prayer or thanksgiving, arising from this study)

In Jesus' name.

Amen.

What the Bible says about **Jesus' triumphal entry into Jerusalem (Easter)**

Never been ridden
2nd April

The plan is for Jesus to ride into Jerusalem: but why would he chose a donkey that has never been ridden before? – It certainly has the potential for a miracle to be worked here.

Saying, 'Go into the village ahead of you, and as you enter it you will find tied there a colt that has never been ridden. Untie it and bring it here.

(Luke 19:30)

'My Journal':

- *The whole incident is out of the ordinary; beginning with the way in which the colt is selected, and continuing with Jesus mounting the young donkey that has never been broken in – to ride it into Jerusalem. And then there is the response from Jesus' supporters. This is an incident that is meant to be noticed and remembered. It is a demonstration of God's power, a reflection of the huge support for Jesus, and it is another confirmation that the build up to Jesus' crucifixion is all part of God's plan. Consider these things, and write down your thoughts.*

Meditate on the God of miracles: this is yet another demonstration of God's power. God is still in control.

Lord God.

You have a wonderful eternal plan for your creation; and you are in control, working out that plan!

Thank you that your plan is a good plan; and that as a follower of Jesus, you want me to be part of it – indeed, I am already part of it.

Please help me to be willing to fully enter into that plan – which has eternal significance.

(Include any additional topics for prayer or thanksgiving, arising from this study)

In Jesus' name.

Amen.

'Doers of the word' (aim): To recognise that the happenings we remember at Easter time are all part of God's plan – he is still in control!

Is there anything that you think you might find difficult about achieving the aim?

What the Bible says about **Jesus' triumphal entry into Jerusalem (Easter)**

God's hand in events

3rd April

Some might say that this was prearranged with the owners of the colt. I like to believe that God's hand was behind this – intervening – speaking into the hearts and minds of the people concerned!

So those who were sent departed and found it as he had told them.

(Luke 19:32)

'My Journal':

- *I always say that there is no such thing as luck or coincidence – but it is God's hand at work in our lives. What do you believe? Does that add to your confidence?*

Meditate on the importance of listening to the guidance of God; being quick to respond to his leading; and to trust that what he says will happen – it will come to fruition.

Our loving heavenly Father.

You speak into the hearts and minds of people; and amazing things happen!

Thank you that you are involved in the world today; and in our lives, if we let you.

Please help me to be a good listener to you, as you seek to speak words of guidance into my heart and mind.

Help me to be willing and responsive to go to the places you instruct me to go to; to do the things you would have me to do; and to say the things you would have me say.

Fill me with trust in you; and help me to be confident that the future is safe in your hands.

(Include any additional topics for prayer or thanksgiving, arising from this study)

In Jesus' name.

Amen.

'Doers of the word' (aim): To trust in, and respond to God speaking into our hearts and minds.

Is there anything that you think you might find difficult about achieving the aim?

What the Bible says about **Jesus' triumphal entry into Jerusalem (Easter)**

The triumphal entry
4th April

This time, riding a donkey colt; but we are told in Revelation that when Jesus returns (his second coming) he will be mounted on a white horse, as the ultimate victor (Revelation 19:11-16).

As he rode along, people kept spreading their cloaks on the road. As he was now approaching the path down from the Mount of Olives, the whole multitude of the disciples began to praise God joyfully with a loud voice for all the deeds of power that they had seen,

(Luke 19:36-37)

'My Journal':

- *In what ways have you experienced the power of God at work, in your own life?*

Meditate on the significance of Jesus' entry into Jerusalem, on this occasion, being a triumphal one. Even though Jesus is heading towards his inevitable death (and resurrection), by so doing, he is going to pay the price that none of us can afford to pay ourselves. He is going to pay the penalty for sin, and thus, he is going to pay the cost of salvation. This triumphal entry is a forerunner of Jesus' second coming, when he will win the final victory over sin and evil. We can share in the victory, through following Jesus. Jot down your thoughts.

Lord Jesus.

You have won the victory!

Thank you that you have paid the penalty for sin, and by so doing, paid the cost of salvation.

Thank you that when you return, you will win the final victory over sin and evil.

Please help me to believe that you will be coming again.

Help me to respond to your victory by being in a close relationship with you, serving you, and sharing the message of salvation with others.

(Include any additional topics for prayer or thanksgiving, arising from this study)

In your name.

Amen.

'Doers of the word' (aim): To celebrate and share in the victory of the risen Jesus, over sin and evil; and talk to others about it.

Is there anything that you think you might find difficult about achieving the aim?

What the Bible says about **Jesus' triumphal entry into Jerusalem (Easter)**

The natural expression

5th April

A close relationship with Jesus will find its natural expression in witnessing and sharing personal testimony: telling others about our daily walk with him.

Some of the Pharisees in the crowd said to him, 'Teacher, order your disciples to stop.' He answered, 'I tell you, if these were silent, the stones would shout out.'

(Luke 19:39-40)

'My Journal':

- *Recall a time when you heard some great news: remember that feeling of needing to tell someone before you burst. Describe the incident?*

Meditate on how you feel about sharing words of testimony with others. Consider if your feelings, about sharing your personal experiences of Jesus, are similar to the occasion you have just recalled. It could be that the 'great news' was actually to do with your coming to faith!

Lord Jesus.

We have great news to share!

Thank you that our relationship with you is something amazing.

Please help me to be so excited and full of joy about it, that I just cannot keep quiet.

Help me to recognise the opportunities you place before me to share testimony.

Give me confidence.

Help me to know the right words to say.

And let others respond positively to my witness.

(Include any additional topics for prayer or thanksgiving, arising from this study)

In your name.

Amen.

'Doers of the word' (aim): To excitedly chat to people about Jesus.

Is there anything that you think you might find difficult about achieving the aim?

What the Bible says about **Jesus cleansing the temple (Easter)**

6th April

Telling the story

Then he entered the temple and began to drive out those who were selling things there; and he said, 'It is written,

"My house shall be a house of prayer"; but you have made it a den of robbers.'

Every day he was teaching in the temple. The chief priests, the scribes, and the leaders of the people kept looking for a way to kill him; but they did not find anything they could do, for all the people were spellbound by what they heard.

(Luke 19:45-48)

... to be looked at over the next four days.

Lord God.

Thank you for the truth of scripture, and that it is relevant to every generation.

Thank you for this passage of scripture concerning Jesus' cleansing of the temple.

Please help me to understand what I have just read; and to meditate upon it today.

(Include any additional topics for prayer or thanksgiving, arising from this study)

In Jesus' name.

Amen.

What the Bible says about **Jesus cleansing the temple (Easter)**

Stand up and be counted
7th April

Jesus demonstrates to us the importance of making a stand against those things that are not in agreement with God's purposes or values: we need to be prepared to be unpopular sometimes.

Then he entered the temple and began to drive out those who were selling things there.

(Luke 19:45)

'My Journal':

- *Have you ever had to make a stand against something? What was it, and how did it feel? Did it feel okay to demonstrate controlled anger?*

Meditate on some of the qualities necessary to make that stand: things like, having an adequate knowledge and understanding of scripture; and, of course, having the confidence and courage to do it.

Lord Jesus.

You are our perfect example in all things!

Thank you that, in your life on earth, you demonstrated to us what it means to stand up for what is right.

Please help me to do the same.

Show me those issues that are not according to God's will and values.

Grant me the strength and boldness to confront them – even when it means standing alone, amongst my peers.

Thank you that I am not actually alone, because you are with me, just as much at those times as any other.

(Include any additional topics for prayer or thanksgiving, arising from this study)

In your name.

Amen.

'Doers of the word' (aim): To stand up for God's values and biblical teaching.

Is there anything that you think you might find difficult about achieving the aim?

What the Bible says about **Jesus cleansing the temple (Easter)**

According to purpose
8th April

We should be vigilant about our church buildings being well used: but they should always be used in ways that are in keeping with our faith, our calling as part of the Church, and the values of God.

And he said, 'It is written,

"My house shall be a house of prayer"; but you have made it a den of robbers.'

(Luke 19:46)

'My Journal':

- *What does Jesus mean by 'A house of prayer' – in practical terms?*

Meditate for a moment on what the modern equivalent of the scenario, highlighted in this verse, might be: that is, ways in which the church building could be misused for financial gain today.

Lord God.

Your house is a house of prayer!

Thank you that you have given us a vision for the use of our church buildings.

To be places where people can meet with you: in worship, praise, prayer and Bible teaching – and somewhere that they can experience unconditional love in action.

Please help me to do my part in making sure that the building, of the congregation to which I belong, is always used in a way that is glorifying to you and furthering of the kingdom.

(Include any additional topics for prayer or thanksgiving, arising from this study)

In Jesus' name.

Amen.

'Doers of the word' (aim): To make good use of our church buildings, but in a way that complies with the Christian ethos and calling to witness – and to love and care.

Is there anything that you think you might find difficult about achieving the aim?

What the Bible says about **Jesus cleansing the temple (Easter)**

Hostility and persecution

9th April

It takes a lot of boldness and courage to stand up against a well-established organisation or system, when things go wrong. People will get upset at being challenged, and hostility and persecution may arise.

Every day he was teaching in the temple. The chief priests, the scribes, and the leaders of the people kept looking for a way to kill him.

(Luke 19:47)

'My Journal':

- *Has there been an occasion when you were challenged to confront an organisation or system in this way? Jot down some notes about what you did, and the repercussions of it.*

Meditate on what God is saying to you now. Is he calling you to confront an organisation or system in this way? What is the organisation or system? What is the issue that you feel led to confront? How does God want you to make that challenge?

Lord Jesus.

You have set us the example of confronting things like injustice, loss of vision and direction, and corruption in the Church and other organisations and systems!

Thank you that when we do that; we are not alone, but you empower us through the Holy Spirit.

Please grant me the courage and boldness to be prepared to endure confrontation, and face possible opposition and persecution.

Help me to know what things need changing.

Show me the way to do it: in order to be effective; but in a way that is within the law and glorifying to you.

And pour out your transforming power to bring about positive change.

(Include any additional topics for prayer or thanksgiving, arising from this study)

In your name.

Amen.

'Doers of the word' (aim): To aspire to have the courage to confront injustices and corruption in society, and maybe in the Church – and face the opposition!

Is there anything that you think you might find difficult about achieving the aim?

What the Bible says about **Jesus cleansing the temple (Easter)**

Faultless and preaching with authority

10th April

There is nothing new about trying to dig up some scandal about someone in the public eye, in order to bring about their downfall from power, popularity or influence. But there is no scandal to dig up, concerning Jesus: he is faultless, everything he teaches is truthful, and he has real authority.

But they did not find anything they could do, for all the people were spell-bound by what they heard.

(Luke 19:48)

'My Journal':

- *What is the significance of following someone who has no 'skeletons in the cupboard', and who speaks with truth and authority?*

Meditate on how people in your own life have matched up to that description. How do you match up to it? We have all fallen short, except Jesus!

Lord Jesus.

You are dependable, honest and trustworthy: and you speak with authority!

Thank you that you are the perfect example of how we should live our lives – because you have done nothing wrong and have no dark secrets!

Please help me to always make a positive response to you and your teaching; and strive to emulate your perfect example to me.

(Include any additional topics for prayer or thanksgiving, arising from this study)

In your name.

Amen.

'Doers of the word' (aim): To always remember, and make a positive response to the dependability, authority and trustworthiness of Jesus.

Is there anything that you think you might find difficult about achieving the aim?

What the Bible says about **the plot to kill Jesus (Easter)**

11th April
Telling the story

Now the festival of unleavened bread, which is called the Passover, was near. The chief priests and the scribes were looking for a way to put Jesus to death, for they were afraid of the people.

Then Satan entered into Judas called Iscariot, who was one of the twelve; he went away and conferred with the chief priests and officers of the temple police about how he might betray him to them. They were greatly pleased and agreed to give him money. So he consented and began to look for an opportunity to betray him to them when no crowd was present.

(Luke 22:1-6)

… to be looked at in the next session.

Lord God.

Thank you for the truth of scripture, and that it is as relevant to every generation.

Thank you for this passage of scripture that looks at the plot to kill Jesus.

Please help me to understand what I have just read; and to meditate upon it today.

(Include any additional topics for prayer or thanksgiving, arising from this study)

In Jesus' name.

Amen.

What the Bible says about **the plot to kill Jesus (Easter)**

Satan doesn't take time off

12th April

Let's not believe that God is real, but Satan is not: Satan is at work 24/7, constantly trying to defeat the plans and purposes of God.

Then Satan entered into Judas called Iscariot, who was one of the twelve.

(Luke 22:3)

'My Journal':

- *What does it mean for Satan to enter into someone?*

Meditate on the fact that the only way we can be safe is by walking close to Jesus daily, fully focused on him, obedient to the will of the Father, and filled with the power of the indwelling Holy Spirit. We need to always be aware that we are in a spiritual battle and need God's protection.

Almighty God.

We are in a spiritual battle!

Thank you that you are a powerful God, and you will protect us from the work of Satan when we walk close to you – through Jesus.

Please help me not to doubt the power of Satan; and as a result become complacent.

Let your will be done; and let your plans and purposes be fulfilled.

(Include any additional topics for prayer or thanksgiving, arising from this study)

In Jesus' name.

Amen.

'Doers of the word' (aim): To acknowledge that Satan is real; and he is hard at work.

Is there anything that you think you might find difficult about achieving the aim?

What the Bible says about **the institution of the Lord's Supper (Easter)**

13th April
Telling the story

When the hour came, he took his place at the table, and the apostles with him. He said to them, 'I have eagerly desired to eat this Passover with you before I suffer; for I tell you, I will not eat it until it is fulfilled in the kingdom of God.' Then he took a cup, and after giving thanks he said, 'Take this and divide it among yourselves; for I tell you that from now on I will not drink of the fruit of the vine until the kingdom of God comes.' Then he took a loaf of bread, and when he had given thanks, he broke it and gave it to them, saying, 'This is my body which is given for you. Do this in remembrance of me.' And he did the same with the cup after supper, saying, 'This cup that is poured out for you is the new covenant in my blood. But see, the one who betrays me is with me, and his hand is on the table. For the Son of Man is going as it has been determined, but woe to the one by whom he is betrayed!' Then they began to ask one another which one of them it could be who would do this.

(Luke 22:14-23)

… to be looked at over the next two days.

Lord God.

Thank you for the truth of scripture, and that it is relevant to every generation.

Thank you for this passage of scripture about the institution of the Lord's Supper.

Please help me to understand what I have just read; and to meditate upon it today.

(Include any additional topics for prayer or thanksgiving, arising from this study)

In Jesus' name.

Amen.

What the Bible says about **the institution of the Lord's Supper (Easter)**

Given in love
14th April

Jesus once again predicts his death: he compares the loaf of bread with his body, which will be selflessly given for humankind – a demonstration of his love.

Then he took a loaf of bread, and when he had given thanks, he broke it and gave it to them, saying, 'This is my body which is given for you. Do this in remembrance of me.'

(Luke 22:19)

'My Journal':

- *Consider the selfless love of Jesus that enables him to willingly give his life: suffering and dying for the benefit of humankind. Make a note of anything God says to you.*

Meditate on Jesus' statement, 'Do this in remembrance of me'. Consider the importance of not allowing Jesus' death to be forgotten: in order to highlight his amazing selfless, unconditional love for each one of us; and as an emphasis that we all need to make a positive response to the risen Jesus' sacrificial act.

Risen Lord Jesus.

You willingly suffered and died for humankind!

Thank you for your amazing love for us – demonstrated by your death on the cross.

Undeserved love.

Unending love.

A love that is expressed in so many ways.

And a love that is freely given, without any conditions.

Please help me to always remember what you have done for me; and to make a positive response to it.

Help me to fully commit to following you.

And help me to tell others about your love for them: demonstrated by performing acts of loving kindness.

Equip me, by filling me with your love to share with others.

In your name.

Amen.

'Doers of the word' (aim): To remember: and make a positive response to Jesus' love and sacrifice – demonstrated by his death.

Is there anything that you think you might find difficult about achieving the aim?

What the Bible says about **the institution of the Lord's Supper (Easter)**

Poured out for you
15th April

Jesus shares that his death on the cross – unlike the Old Testament sacrificial system – will be the sacrifice that need never be repeated.

And he did the same with the cup after supper, saying, 'This cup that is poured out for you is the new covenant in my blood.'

(Luke 22:20)

'My Journal':

- *Consider the significance of Jesus' blood being shed for the forgiveness of sin... 'Poured out for you.' Jesus is saying that when his blood is shed on the cross, he will be paying the penalty for all sin, for all people! Make some notes on your thoughts.*

Meditate on the knowledge that Jesus wants us to understand his bloodshed marks a binding agreement between us and God: that through entering into a personal relationship with Jesus – based on repentance and with faith – we are forgiven, set free from the consequences of sin, and enter into God's eternal heavenly kingdom. Consider this alongside the fact that God is faithful and dependable... He will never go back on anything he has promised.

Lord God.

Jesus has paid the penalty for sin, once and for all!

Thank you that we can be assured of receiving your forgiveness, being set free from sin's consequences, and entry into your eternal, heavenly kingdom – through a personal relationship with Jesus.

Thank you that Jesus' blood was poured out for me.

Please help me to commit to following him.

Grant me the assurance that the 'new covenant' contains promise that will be fulfilled – because you are faithful and worthy of our complete trust.

(Include any additional topics for prayer or thanksgiving, arising from this study)

In Jesus' name.

Amen.

'Doers of the word' (aim): To recognise that Jesus' blood was poured out for each one of us; and to make sure that we have entered into that new covenant with God - and know the assurance that it offers.

Is there anything that you think you might find difficult about achieving the aim?

What the Bible says about **the arrest of Jesus (Easter)**

16th April

Telling the story

While he was still speaking, suddenly a crowd came, and the one called Judas, one of the twelve, was leading them. He approached Jesus to kiss him; but Jesus said to him, 'Judas, is it with a kiss that you are betraying the Son of Man?' When those who were around him saw what was coming, they asked, 'Lord, should we strike with the sword?' Then one of them struck the slave of the high priests and cut off his right ear. But Jesus said, 'No more of this!' And he touched his ear and healed him. Then Jesus said to the chief priests, the officers of the temple police, and the elders who had come for him. 'Have you come out with swords and clubs as if I were a bandit? When I was with you day after day in the temple, you did not lay hands on me. But this is your hour, and the power of darkness.'

(Luke 22:47-53)

... to be looked at tomorrow.

Lord God.

Thank you for the truth of scripture, and that it is relevant to every generation.

Thank you for this passage of scripture about the arrest of Jesus.

Please help me to understand what I have just read; and to meditate up it today.

In Jesus' name.

Amen.

What the Bible says about **the arrest of Jesus (Easter)**

God is still in control

17th April

We need to remember that, through the whole of the Easter story, God is in control – it is all part of his plan.

When I was with you day after day in the temple, you did not lay hands on me. But this is your hour, and the power of darkness!'

(Luke 22:53)

'My Journal':

- *Consider the implications of what Jesus is saying in this verse: he is attacking things like hypocrisy, cowardice, rejection, and the power of evil at work in society daily. And yet God is still in control. Jot down your thoughts.*

Meditate on the principle that there are times when God allows bad things to happen to us for a greater purpose; but he doesn't instigate suffering. What is your experience of this, in your own life?

Risen Lord Jesus.

You suffered willingly, paying the penalty for sin – because of your amazing, unconditional love for us all!

Thank you that you love us so much.

Please help me to love you in return.

Help me not to be hypocritical.

Help me not to reject you in any way.

Protect me against the spiritual warfare that I face daily.

And help me to always remember that God doesn't instigate suffering; but sometimes he allows it for his greater purposes – and that, when that happens, he is still in control.

Help me to accept those times of suffering, in faith.

(Include any additional topics for prayer or thanksgiving, arising from this study)

In your name.

Amen.

'Doers of the word' (aim): To learn the lessons from this verse: not to be a hypocrite or coward, not to reject Jesus, and to always remember that we are in a spiritual battle daily – but God is still in control.

Is there anything that you think you might find difficult about achieving the aim?

What the Bible says about **the crucifixion and death of Jesus (Easter)**

18th April
Telling the story

As they led him away, they seized a man, Simon of Cyrene, who was coming from the country, and they laid the cross on him, and made him carry it behind Jesus. A great number of people followed him, and among them were women who were beating their breasts and wailing for him. But Jesus turned to them and said, 'Daughters of Jerusalem, do not weep for me, but weep for yourselves and for your children. For the days are surely coming when they will say, "Blessed are the barren, and the wombs that never bore, and the breasts that never nursed." Then they will begin to say to the mountains, "Fall on us"; and to the hills, "Cover us." For if they do this when the wood is green, what will happen when it is dry?'

Two others also, who were criminals, were led away to be put to death with him. When they came to the place that is called The Skull, they crucified Jesus there with the criminals, one on his right and one on his left. Then Jesus said, 'Father forgive them; for they do not know what they are doing.' And they cast lots to divide his clothing. And the people stood by, watching; but the leaders scoffed at him, saying, 'He saved others; let him save himself if he is the Messiah of God, his chosen one!' The soldiers also mocked him, coming up and offering him sour wine, and saying, 'If you are the King of the Jews, save yourself!' There was also an inscription over him, 'This is the King of the Jews.'

One of the criminals who were hanging there kept deriding him and saying, 'Are you not the Messiah? Save yourself and us.' But the other rebuked him, saying, 'Do you fear God, since you are under the same sentence of condemnation?' And we indeed have been condemned justly, for we are getting what we deserve for our deeds, but this man has done nothing wrong.' Then he said, 'Jesus, remember me when you come into your kingdom.' He replied, 'Truly I tell you, today you will be with me in paradise.'

It was not about noon, and darkness came over the whole land until three in the afternoon, while the sun's light failed; and the curtain of the temple was torn in two. Then Jesus, crying with a loud voice, said, 'Father, into your hands I commend my spirit.' Having said this, he breathed his last. When the centurion saw what had taken place, he praised God and said, 'Certainly this man was innocent.' And when all the crowds who had gathered there for this spectacle saw what had taken place, they returned home, beating their breasts. But all his acquaintances, including the women who had followed him from Galilee, stood at a distance, watching these things.

(Luke 23:26-49)

... to be looked at over the next six days.

Lord God.

Thank you for the truth of scripture, and that it is relevant to every generation.

Thank you for this passage of scripture about the crucifixion and arrest of Jesus.

Please help me to understand what I have just read; and to meditate on it today.

In Jesus' name.

Amen.

What the Bible says about **the crucifixion and death of Jesus (Easter)**

Self-sacrifice
19th April

At the crucifixion, the voice of the soldiers who mock Jesus, reflect what is a deep seated human desire to save ourselves: but Jesus' mission is about giving his life to save others – that is divine! That is the ultimate in real love!

The soldiers also mocked him, coming up and offering him sour wine, and saying, 'If you are the King of the Jews, save yourself!'

(Luke 23:36-37)

'My Journal':

- *Consider for a moment the power of love: that it can overrule the extremely strong natural instinct for self-preservation – for the benefit of others. Love is from God. Jot down your thoughts.*

Meditate on your own life experience, of people who sacrificed their wellbeing, in some way, for the wellbeing of others.

Risen Lord Jesus.

Your love is so strong, that you chose to put the need of humankind before your own wellbeing!

Thank you for loving us so much, that you gave your life on the cross for us – paying the penalty for our sin.

Thank you that you love us, even though we are not worthy of that love.

Please help me to recognise that sacrifice, and understand its significance to me – and the whole of humankind.

Help me to demonstrate selfless love in my own life; by giving of myself, for the benefit of others.

(Include any additional topics for prayer or thanksgiving, arising from this study)

In your name.

Amen.

'Doers of the word' (aim): To recognise the sacrifice that Jesus made for all humankind – when he gave his life on the cross.

Is there anything that you think you might find difficult about achieving the aim?

What the Bible says about **the crucifixion and death of Jesus (Easter)**

Consequences
20th April

It is fundamental to our salvation, that we should first of all recognise that we have all sinned (done things that are not pleasing to God); and that sin brings with it eternal consequences.

But the other rebuked him, saying, 'Do you fear God, since you are under the same sentence of condemnation? And we indeed have been condemned justly, for we are getting what we deserve for our deeds, but this man has done nothing wrong.' Then he said, 'Jesus, remember me when you come into your kingdom.'

(Luke 23:40-42)

'My Journal':

- *Consider the nature of sin for a moment: falling short of God's standards – by whatever degree. In practical terms, in what kind of ways is this demonstrated in everyday life?*

Meditate on the words of the 'other' criminal, and its significance: 'Jesus, remember me when you come into your kingdom.' This might be your own prayer at this time.

Lord Jesus.

You are offering salvation to humankind!

Thank you that you have the power to forgive us and to save us from the consequences of sin.

Thank you that you offer us the opportunity to spend eternity in your kingdom.

Please help me to recognise my own sinfulness, to be repentant of it, and to reach out to you in faith.

(Include any additional topics for prayer or thanksgiving, arising from this study)

In your name.

Amen.

'Doers of the word' (aim): To be repentant: recognising our own sin and its consequences, expressing genuine remorse, and reaching out to Jesus in faith.

Is there anything that you think you might find difficult about achieving the aim?

What the Bible says about **the crucifixion and death of Jesus (Easter)**

The promise of salvation
21st April

One of the most amazing verses of scripture – and one which is so inspiring of eternal confidence – is Jesus' reply to the criminal, who reaches out to him at the cross.

He replied, 'Truly I tell you, today you will be with me in paradise.'

(Luke 23:43)

'My Journal':

- *Pause for a moment and meditate on that reply – Jesus still replies with words of eternal promise to each one of us who reach out to him with repentance and in faith – the promise of salvation! Write down how that feels.*

Meditate on the fact that Jesus' promises never fail. In that light, consider what this verse of scripture has to say about being able to have the assurance of our salvation.

Lord Jesus.

What amazing words of assurance and hope, are held in this verse – the same assurance and hope that we can all know, through you!

Thank you that in a world where there is so much insecurity, we can enter into your kingdom for eternity.

Please grant me the courage and conviction to follow you, in repentance and with faith – trusting you to remember me, in your kingdom.

(Include any additional topics for prayer or thanksgiving, arising from this study)

In your name.

Amen.

'Doers of the word' (aim): To reach out to – and walk with Jesus - in repentance and with faith.

Is there anything that you think you might find difficult about achieving the aim?

What the Bible says about **the crucifixion and death of Jesus (Easter)**

Access to God

22nd April

The system changes with Jesus' death: through his selfless act on the cross, we can all have access into God's presence, through him. The curtain of the temple is torn in two, symbolising this.

It was not about noon, and darkness came over the whole land until three in the afternoon, while the sun's light failed; and the curtain of the temple was torn in two.

(Luke 23:44-45)

'My Journal':

- *Through Jesus we can have direct access into God's presence – through prayer. How amazing is that?*

Meditate on this. Not everyone is open to change, and this verse highlights a very different way of doing things. Are there any changes taking place in your church congregation, at the present time that you are resisting? What are they? Do you believe that they are from God? If so, why are you resisting them?

Heavenly Father.

Because of what Jesus has done for us, we have direct access into your presence through prayer!

Thank you that it was your plan to make that possible.

Please help me to make use of that wonderful opportunity; and spend regular time in your presence, in this way.

And help me to accept change when it is of you.

(Include any additional topics for prayer or thanksgiving, arising from this study)

In Jesus' name.

Amen.

'Doers of the word' (aim): To regularly make use of that opportunity to enter into God's presence through prayer; and to accept changes, when they are of God.

Is there anything that you think you might find difficult about achieving the aim?

What the Bible says about **the crucifixion and death of Jesus (Easter)**

The price has been paid
23rd April

As Jesus 'breathes his last'... we can almost sense it as being with a sigh of relief: this ordeal of incredible abuse, suffering and pain is over – the price has been paid for sin.

Then Jesus, crying with a loud voice, said, 'Father, into your hands I commend my spirit.' Having said this, he breathed his last.

(Luke 23:46)

'My Journal':

- *Ponder on this verse for a few minutes: a verse which highlights what Jesus has done for us – in order that we might be set free from sin and its consequences... in part now, but in full in the future. How does that make you feel?*

Meditate on the suffering of Jesus: he did that for me, and he did that for you. What is your response?

Risen Lord Jesus.

You covered such a huge cost, to make it possible for me to be set free from sin!

Thank you for paying the penalty for sin – my sin!

Please help me never to forget, or to try to belittle, the suffering you endured for me.

Help me to realise the significance of your suffering, to me and to the whole of humankind.

Let my response to you be a positive one.

(Include any additional topics for prayer or thanksgiving, arising from this study)

In your name.

Amen.

'Doers of the word' (aim): To recognise the cost of being given the opportunity to be set free from sin and its consequences.

Is there anything that you think you might find difficult about achieving the aim?

What the Bible says about **the crucifixion and death of Jesus (Easter)**

The point of realisation

24th April

The centurion who is present at the death of Jesus comes to a life changing realisation: recognising Jesus' innocence and who Jesus is – and appears to make a positive response, because we are told that he praises God.

When the centurion saw what had taken place, he praised God and said, 'Certainly this man was innocent.'

(Luke 23:47)

'My Journal':

- *What is the significance of what is being described in this verse: the centurion has been present at this horrendously brutal occasion, where Jesus has been crucified on a wooden cross; he realises that Jesus is innocent of his accusations; and yet he praises God for what has happened?*

Meditate on spiritual enlightenment: you might even have had such a time yourself - that is, a time when God suddenly and dramatically increases our spiritual awareness.

Almighty God.

You are worthy of our praise!

Thank you for all that Jesus achieved, through his life death and resurrection – that we can be set free from the consequences of sin.

Thank you for those times of spiritual enlightenment.

Please help me to recognise and respond positively to them.

Help me to praise you for your power and greatness.

(Include any additional topics for prayer or thanksgiving, arising from this study)

In Jesus' name.

Amen.

'Doers of the word' (aim): To join the centurion, in praising God for what Jesus has achieved in his death and resurrection – salvation for humankind.

Is there anything that you think you might find difficult about achieving the aim?

What the Bible says about **the resurrection of Jesus (Easter)**

25th April

Telling the story

But on the first day of the week, at early dawn, they came to the tomb, taking the spices that they had prepared. They found the stone rolled away from the tomb, but when they went in, they did not find the body. While they were perplexed about this, suddenly two men in dazzling clothes stood beside them. The women were terrified and bowed their faces to the ground, but the men said to them, 'Why do you look for the living among the dead? He is not here, but has risen. Remember how he told you, while he was still in Galilee, that the Son of Man must be handed over to sinners, and be crucified, and on the third day rise again.' Then they remembered his words, and returning from the tomb, they told all this to the eleven and to all the rest. Now it was Mary Magdalene, Joanna, Mary the mother of James, and the other women with them who told this to the apostles. But these words seemed to them an idle tale, and they did not believe them. But Peter got up and ran to the tomb; stooping and looking in, he saw the linen clothes by themselves; then he went home, amazed at what had happened.

(Luke 24:1-12)

… to be looked at over the next three days.

Lord God.

Thank you for the truth of scripture, and that it is relevant to every generation.

Thank you for this passage of scripture about the resurrection of Jesus.

Please help me to understand what I have just read; and to meditate up it today.

(Include any additional topics for prayer or thanksgiving, arising from this study)

In Jesus' name.

Amen.

What the Bible says about **the resurrection of Jesus (Easter)**

Looking in the wrong place
26th April

The women fail to find Jesus in the tomb, because they are looking in the wrong place. There is a profound message contained within that thought.

They found the stone rolled away from the tomb, but when they went in, they did not find the body.

(Luke 24:2-3)

'My Journal':

- *Consider that it is so easy to search for meaning and purpose in life; and yet to look in the wrong places. Write down something of your own experiences of searching.*

Meditate on the fact that we can search for Jesus in a cognitive way - gaining a huge knowledge about him – but never enter into a personal relationship with him... The Bible tells us that without the relationship, we have not found Jesus.

Lord Jesus.

Finding you – and thus discovering meaning and purpose to life – is about being in relationship with you!

Thank you that you want to be in a relationship with me.

Please help me to truly find you: to build up that relationship with you, day by day.

Grant me a walk with you that is an ever closer one.

Help those who are still searching to look in the right place.

(Include any additional topics for prayer or thanksgiving, arising from this study)

In your name.

Amen.

'Doers of the word' (aim): To truly find Jesus; and to develop an ever closer relationship with him.

Is there anything that you think you might find difficult about achieving the aim?

What the Bible says about **the resurrection of Jesus (Easter)**

Fearful of the unknown

27th April

Jesus' body has gone; and two angels are suddenly standing in the tomb, saying that Jesus has risen – is it surprising that the women are terrified? We can easily be fearful of the unexpected, unexplained or impossible.

The women were terrified and bowed their faces to the ground, but the men said to them, 'Why do you look for the living among the dead? He is not here, but has risen.'

(Luke 24:5)

'My Journal':

- *Be comforted in the knowledge that what is impossible for us to do, is possible for God – he does the impossible! Consider that, and then jot down the thoughts that it stimulates.*

Meditate on the significance of Jesus rising from the dead: that he has conquered death, and is a risen Lord and Saviour.

Lord Jesus.

You are alive!

Thank you that you rose from the dead, and you are alive today – a risen Lord and Saviour!

Thank you that we can all have a personal, and life changing relationship with you – which involves receiving eternal life.

Please help me to truly believe that you have risen – and that you have conquered death.

Let my walk with you become closer each day – and let me become more committed to following and serving you.

(Include any additional topics for prayer or thanksgiving, arising from this study)

In your name.

Amen.

'Doers of the word' (aim): To believe that God can do the 'impossible' - Jesus rose from the dead, and is alive today!

Is there anything that you think you might find difficult about achieving the aim?

What the Bible says about **the resurrection of Jesus (Easter)**

A gentle reminder

28th April

Jesus has already told his close followers what would happen in respect to his death and resurrection; and yet the women still don't understand what is happening. It is so important to listen to, understand, remember, believe and respond to the teaching of Jesus.

Remember how he told you, while he was still in Galilee, that the Son of Man must be handed over to sinners, and be crucified, and on the third day rise again.

(Luke 24:6-7)

'My Journal':

- *How do you think Bible study should be approached: that is, how and in what ways? - Things like prayer, listening, understanding and outworking should play a part. Jot down some notes.*

Meditate on how fundamentally important belief is, to the Christian faith. Maybe, more crucially this is a verse of scripture urging us to believe the word of God – the Bible.

Almighty God.

Your word is true!

Thank you for the Bible.

Please help me to prayerfully study scripture, to listen, to understand what I read, to remember, to believe, and to put into practice all that I learn.

(Include any additional topics for prayer or thanksgiving, arising from this study)

In Jesus' name.

Amen.

'Doers of the word' (aim): To prayerfully read, listen, understand, remember, believe and put into practice the word of God – the Bible.

Is there anything that you think you might find difficult about achieving the aim?

What the Bible says about **the ascension of Jesus (Easter)**

29th April

Telling the story

Then he led them out as far as Bethany, and, lifting up his hands, he blessed them. While he was blessing them, he withdrew from them and was carried up into heaven. And they worshipped him, and returned to Jerusalem with great joy, and they were continually in the temple blessing God.

(Luke 24:50-53)

... to be looked at tomorrow.

Lord God.

Thank you for the truth of scripture, and that it is relevant to every generation.

Thank you for this passage of scripture about the ascension of Jesus.

Please help me to understand what I have just read; and to meditate up it today.

(Include any additional topics for prayer or thanksgiving, arising from this study)

In Jesus' name.

Amen.

What the Bible says about **the ascension of Jesus (Easter)**

Jesus ascends into heaven

30th April

After Jesus' death and resurrection – including his various resurrection appearances – he ascends into heaven.

Then he led them out as far as Bethany, and, lifting up his hands, he blessed them. While he was blessing them, he withdrew from them and was carried up into heaven.

(Luke 24:50-51)

'My Journal':

- *Make some notes as you think about the significance of Jesus ascending into heaven. Remember things like, he goes to prepare a place for each of his followers (John 14:1-2); he goes to reign from heaven; he goes to be our advocate; and he goes knowing that he will return one day.*

7

JESUS, WHEN HE SAYS, ‘I AM’

Jesus said, 'I am the bread of life.'

1st May

We all need to be spiritually nourished: to have our spiritual hunger satisfied, and to have our spiritual thirst quenched.

Jesus said to them, 'I am the bread of life. Whoever comes to me will never be hungry, and whoever believes in me will never be thirsty.'

(John 6:35)

'My Journal':

- *In the 21st century western world, for the majority, bread is probably not really the staple food that it used to be. Consider the image portrayed in this verse of scripture, but bearing that in mind. Make some notes on your thoughts.*

Meditate on how long it is, after you have eaten a meal, before you are feeling peckish again. Compare it with the fact that when we are spiritually nourished by Jesus, we will never be hungry or thirsty again – because that source of nourishment is never ending.

Lord Jesus.

You are the 'bread of life'!

You long to nourish and refresh us all spiritually.

Thank you that the spiritual food that you offer not only satisfies completely, but it is also eternal.

Please help me to eat healthily and regularly…

and to remember to self-care - physically and spiritually.

(Include any additional topics for prayer or thanksgiving, arising from this study)

In your name.

Amen.

'Doers of the word' (aim): To have our spiritual hunger and thirst satisfied through a close relationship with Jesus.

Is there anything that you think you might find difficult about achieving the aim?

What the Bible says about **Jesus, when he says, 'I am'**

Jesus said, 'I am the light of the world.'
2nd May

We are very dependent on light. It is common knowledge that light is necessary for life to exist; and life experience tells us that light is necessary to see in the darkness. We are very dependent on the spiritual light that Jesus offers to us.

Again Jesus spoke to them, saying, 'I am the light of the world. Whoever follows me will never walk in darkness but will have the light of life.'

(John 8:12)

'My Journal':

- *What are the qualities that we associate with light?*

Meditate on the spiritual contexts of those qualities that you associate with light – the light that Jesus promises to his followers.

Lord Jesus.

You are the 'light of the world'!

Thank you that you want to pour the light of God into our lives.

Thank you that the spiritual light you offer sustains spiritual life; it is able to overcome the darkness of sin and evil; it shows the way; and it reveals those dark shadowy secrets that we might be concealing in our lives.

Please fill my life with your spiritual light; and let me be light to others.

(Include any additional topics for prayer or thanksgiving, arising from this study)

In your name.

Amen.

'Doers of the word' (aim): To experience the light of Jesus shining in our lives; and share it with others.

Is there anything that you think you might find difficult about achieving the aim?

What the Bible says about **Jesus, when he says, 'I am'**

Jesus said, 'I am from above.'
3rd May

It is good to recognise that there is a difference between the physical world in which we live, and God's eternal heavenly kingdom. He highlights this in the following verse.

He said to them, 'You are from below, I am from above; you are of this world, I am not of this world.'

(John 8:23)

'My Journal':

- *Write down characteristics that you associate with the physical world in which we live: things like, brokenness caused by sin and evil; the transience of possessions; and the reality of physical death.*

Meditate on those characteristics that you associate with God's eternal heavenly kingdom: for example, it is eternal; there will be an end to sin and evil; and we will experience God's amazing love and blessings in all their fullness.

Our loving heavenly Father.

Your kingdom come!

Thank you for the promise of your heavenly kingdom – with all its blessings.

Thank you for the opportunities to serve you, in the world in which we live now.

Please help me to distinguish between the two.

Help me as I look forward to being part of your heavenly kingdom for eternity, not to disregard the importance of my current situation.

(Include any additional topics for prayer or thanksgiving, arising from this study)

In Jesus' name.

Amen.

'Doers of the word' (aim): To recognise the differences between the physical world and God's heavenly kingdom.

Is there anything that you think you might find difficult about achieving the aim?

What the Bible says about **Jesus, when he says, 'I am'**

Jesus said, 'I am.'
4th May

When Jesus claims that he existed before Abraham, and refers to himself as 'I am', he is claiming that he is God – as indeed he is!

Jesus said to them, 'Very truly, I tell you, before Abraham was, I am.'

(John 8:58)

'My Journal':

- *Think about the analogy in this verse, Jesus is claiming his existence before he was born as a baby on earth. Indeed, scripture confirms Jesus' existence, as one person of the Trinity, in creation (John 1:3). Spend some time meditating on this; and jot down some notes.*

Meditate on the fact that when Jesus refers to himself as 'I am' in this context, he is referring to himself with one of the names that God uses for himself. The name 'I Am' (Exodus 3:14) highlights the unchanging nature of God.

Risen Lord Jesus.

You are divine!

Thank you that your nature is unchanging: you have always been, and you will always be.

Please help me to recognise you as being one person of the Trinity; and to appreciate the significance of that to my eternal relationship with you.

(Include any additional topics for prayer or thanksgiving, arising from this study)

In your name.

Amen.

'Doers of the word' (aim): To recognise Jesus as being one person of the Trinity: God the Father, Jesus the Son, and the Holy Spirit.

Is there anything that you think you might find difficult about achieving the aim?

What the Bible says about **Jesus, when he says, 'I am'**

Jesus said, 'I am the gate for the sheep.'

5th May

Surely the whole point of having a gate is so that people (or stock) might enter in through it. When Jesus refers to himself as being a gate for the sheep, his intention is that we (his sheep) should confidently enter in through him (the gate), into the kingdom.

So again Jesus said to them, 'Very truly, I tell you, I am the gate for the sheep... I am the gate. Whoever enters by me will be saved, and will come in and go out and find pasture.'

(John 10:7 and 9)

'My Journal':

- *Jesus says, 'I am the gate.' In other words, the entrance into the kingdom is through Jesus – no other possible route is indicated. Meditate on that thought, and make some notes on your response.*

Meditate on this. Remember a significant gate in your life. Where did it lead to and why was it significant in your life? How significant is Jesus – the gate - in your life, now?

Lord Jesus.

You are the gate!

Thank you that you are the gateway into the kingdom; and there is the promise of salvation and blessing inside the kingdom.

Please let that gate be a significant one in my life.

Help me to not only enter through that gate myself, but also to encourage others to go through it, as well.

(Include any additional topics for prayer or thanksgiving, arising from this study)

In your name.

Amen.

'Doers of the word' (aim): To enter into the kingdom, through Jesus; and encourage others to do so, as well.

Is there anything that you think you might find difficult about achieving the aim?

What the Bible says about **Jesus, when he says, 'I am'**

Jesus said, 'I am the good shepherd.'
6th May

In Jesus' 'I am' statements, he metaphorically describes himself in different ways – on this occasion, it is as the 'good shepherd'... a shepherd who demonstrates commitment to his sheep on a sacrificial level.

'I am the good shepherd. The good shepherd lays down his life for the sheep.'

(John 10:11)

'My Journal':

- *What qualities does the reference to the good shepherd (Jesus), laying down his life for the sheep, speak to us of today?*

Meditate on the implications of those qualities that makes the shepherd (Jesus) a 'good shepherd'.

Lord Jesus.

You are the good shepherd!

Thank you for your selflessness, love and sacrifice.

Thank you that you are truthful and faithful.

Thank you that you have made it possible for the whole of humankind to be saved.

Please help me to experience your salvation in all its fullness.

(Include any additional topics for prayer or thanksgiving, arising from this study)

In your name.

Amen.

'Doers of the word' (aim): To experience the good shepherd's salvation in all its fullness.

Is there anything that you think you might find difficult about achieving the aim?

What the Bible says about **Jesus, when he says, 'I am'**

Jesus said, 'I am the good shepherd.'
7th May

Still in connection with Jesus' statement of 'I am the good shepherd', he goes on to speak about relationship: his relationship with and knowledge of us, and our relationship with and knowledge of him.

'I am the good shepherd. I know my own and my own know me.'

(John 10:14)

'My Journal':

- *What does Jesus know about you? Absolutely everything! How does that make you feel? What difference does knowing that, make to how you live your life?*

Meditate on what you know about Jesus? Are you trying to get to know more about him, and be more like him, in the way that you live your life: for example, to be more loving; to demonstrate more forgiveness; or to base your life more on the truth of Jesus?

Lord Jesus.

You know us all!

You know everything there is to know about me.

Please forgive me for anything in my life that is not glorifying to God, and help me to make appropriate changes.

Help me to get to know you better, and to be more like you.

Fill me afresh with the Holy Spirit.

Help me to allow him complete freedom to work in my life.

(Include any additional topics for prayer or thanksgiving, arising from this study)

In your name.

Amen.

'Doers of the word' (aim): To know Jesus better; and to strive to be more like him.

Is there anything that you think you might find difficult about achieving the aim?

Jesus said, 'I am the resurrection and the life.'

8th May

For those of us who believe in Jesus: even though we die, we will live – that's what Jesus promises in scripture. Physical death is just the beginning of the next chapter to our eternal journey.

Jesus said to her, 'I am the resurrection and the life. Those who believe in me, even though they die, will live.'

(John 11:25)

'My Journal':

- *Meditate on the words of hope contained within this verse: 'Those who believe in me, even though they die, will live.' Isn't that something to which we would all aspire? Make a note of your thoughts.*

Meditate on the words Jesus says, 'I am the resurrection and the life.' He is promising that, through him, we can be resurrected and blessed with eternal life. We know that he has the power to fulfil his promise, because of his own death and resurrection.

Lord Jesus.

You died on the cross, but were resurrected back to life!

Thank you that when we believe in you, even though we will die, we will be raised to eternal life.

Thank you for those amazing words of hope and promise.

Please help me to fully believe in you; and to trust in your promise of being raised to eternal life.

(Include any additional topics for prayer or thanksgiving, arising from this study)

In your name.

Amen.

'Doers of the word' (aim): To live! – Even though we die.

Is there anything that you think you might find difficult about achieving the aim?

What the Bible says about **Jesus, when he says, 'I am'**

Jesus said, 'I am the way, and the truth, and the life.'

9th May

Perhaps you, like me, have a very poor sense of direction: and so, when it comes to our eternal journey, it is so good to have it spelled out to us, when Jesus says:

Jesus said to him, 'I am the way, and the truth, and the life. No-one comes to the Father except through me.

(John 14:6)

'My Journal':

- *This verse has to be one of the most important declarations of who Jesus is, and the purpose of his ministry. Consider the significance of Jesus' words and write down their impact on you.*
- *Through his sacrificial act on the cross, paying the penalty for sin, Jesus provides the 'way' for us to be forgiven, and to be saved from sin's consequences.*
- *Through his resurrection, Jesus is the 'way' to discover eternal life: through entering into a personal relationship with him.*
- *Jesus' life and teaching demonstrates to us the 'truth' of God; in a world where truth is very tainted with lies and deceit.*
- *Through Jesus we enter into eternal 'life', and 'life' in all its fullness.*
- *Through Jesus, we are restored in our relationship with 'God the Father' – only through Jesus.*

Meditate on what you have written down.

Lord Jesus.

You are the way, the truth, and the life!

Thank you that in our search for God, for truth, for meaning to life, and for eternal hope… you are the answer.

Thank you that you spell it out to us, in easy to understand language… and you provide all that we need.

Please help me to respond in a positive way to these words, and this invitation to be in a close daily walk with you.

Help me to know you as my Lord and Saviour.

(Include any additional topics for prayer or thanksgiving, arising from this study)

In your name.

Amen.

'Doers of the word': To respond positively to what Jesus offers to us when he tells us that he is the way, the truth and the life.

Is there anything that you think you might find difficult about achieving the aim?

Jesus said, 'I am the true vine.'
10th May

Spiritual fruitfulness and connection with Jesus are inseparable.

I am the vine, you are the branches. Those who abide in me and I in them bear much fruit, because apart from me you can do nothing.'

(John 15:5)

'My Journal':

- *Consider what connection with Jesus means, in real terms: things like spending time with him, in prayer and Bible study; listening to what he is saying to us; striving to be more like him; being filled with his love to share with others; and receiving the Holy Spirit to cleanse, transform and empower our lives. Jot down your thoughts about how connected you are with Jesus.*

Meditate on the stark reality of what Jesus means when he says: 'Apart from me you can do nothing.' We really do need to remember that; and apply it to our everyday lives. Make some notes of your thoughts.

Lord Jesus.

You are the vine, and we are the branches – that simple analogy says it all!

Thank you that when we connect spiritually with you, you nourish us and enable us to be fruitful – through the power of the indwelling Holy Spirit.

Please help me to do all that I need to do, in order to fully connect with you; and to live a fruitful life.

(Include any additional topics for prayer or thanksgiving, arising from this study)

In your name.

Amen.

'Doers of the word' (aim): To connect with Jesus and be spiritually fruitful.

Is there anything that you think you might find difficult about achieving the aim?

8

LOVE

What the Bible says about **love**

Holistic love for God

11th May

Jesus describes the kind of love we should have for God as flowing from our whole being - expressed emotionally, spiritually and cognitively:

He said to him, "'You shall love the Lord your God with all your heart, and with all your soul, and with all your mind.'"

(Matthew 22:37)

'My Journal':

- *What do you believe is meant by expressing love emotionally, cognitively and spiritually?*

Meditate on whether you really love God with all your heart, with all your soul, and with all your mind.

Almighty God.

You love me so much!

Thank you for your amazing love for me.

Please help me to return that love; feeling it emotionally, understanding the nature of love and its application cognitively, and being able to have an eternal spiritual connexion with you.

Grant me the enablement to remain close to you, even when life is hard *(give details of anything you are struggling with at the moment).*

(Include any additional topics for prayer or thanksgiving, arising from this study)

In Jesus' name.

Amen.

'Doers of the word' (aim): To love God with our whole being.

Is there anything that you think you might find difficult about achieving the aim?

Love is for sharing
12th May

Jesus commands us to love each other; but in the same sentence is the implication that we should love ourselves. Some people find loving themselves a very difficult thing to do.

'And a second is like it: "You shall love your neighbour as yourself."'

(Matthew 22:39)

'My Journal':

- *In what ways can you share the love of God with others; and in what ways can you love yourself, by demonstrating self-care?*

Meditate on ways in which you can demonstrate more love to your neighbours – and consider some names of those who might fall into that category.

Loving heavenly Father.

Thank you that you love us all; and fill us with love to outpour onto those around us!

Please help me to share your love with others.

Without me becoming conceited or proud, help me to love myself - to see myself as you see me.

To recognise those positive qualities that you have given to me; and build on them.

To value myself for those things you are doing through me for the kingdom.

(Name and give thanks for the talents and abilities that you use for God).

(Include any additional topics for prayer or thanksgiving, arising from this study)

In Jesus' name.

Amen.

'Doers of the word' (aim): To love others with Christ like love; and to love ourselves.

Is there anything that you think you might find difficult about achieving the aim?

What the Bible says about **love**

God loves you that much!
13th May

Listen to how much God loves you and I, when you read John 3:16 - it is such a significant verse.

'For God so loved the world that he gave his only Son, so that everyone who believes in him may not perish but may have eternal life.'

(John 3:16)

'My Journal':

- *Consider how this verse makes you feel: to be loved that much; and the significance of entering into a relationship with Jesus, in faith, resulting in receiving eternal life. Think about it. Write some notes.*

Meditate on the word 'perish', in the context of the fact that being in relationship with Jesus, ensures that we will not perish in the eternal picture.

Loving heavenly Father.

You love us so much!

Thank you that you love us all; and that, in your love, you have made it possible for us to have eternal life, through entering into a personal relationship with Jesus – in faith.

I can never thank you enough for that enormous love that you have for me.

Please help me to walk closer to Jesus daily; and to live in your love.

(Include any additional topics for prayer or thanksgiving, arising from this study)

In Jesus' name.

Amen.

'Doers of the word' (aim): To be in relationship with Jesus; and as a result, to live in God's love.

Is there anything that you think you might find difficult about achieving the aim?

What the Bible says about **love**

Love is sacrificial
14th May

Jesus giving his life on the cross is the ultimate demonstration of sacrificial love – Note: 'No-one has greater love'.

'No-one has greater love than this, to lay down one's life for one's friends.'

(John 15:13)

'My Journal':

- *Sacrificial love is all about putting others first. Jesus puts us and our needs before himself and his, when he gives his life on the cross. How does that make you feel?*

Meditate on the fact that sacrificial love can also be demonstrated in ways other than giving our lives physically for the benefit of others. Consider some other ways in which we can lay down our lives for others, things like, sacrificially giving of our time or other resources for the benefit of others.

Risen Lord Jesus.

Your love is sacrificial!

Thank you that you gave your life on the cross, paying the penalty for sin.

Thank you that through my relationship with you, I am forgiven.

Please help me to demonstrate the same kind of sacrificial love towards others: putting their needs before my own – giving of my time and other resources *(name some of those resources).*

(Include any additional topics for prayer or thanksgiving, arising from this study)

In your name.

Amen.

'Doers of the word' (aim): To love others sacrificially – putting their needs before our own.

Is there anything that you think you might find difficult about achieving the aim?

God loved us first

15th May

The ultimate in unconditional love is that God loved us, and allowed his Son Jesus to die on the cross for us, while we were still sinners.

But God proves his love for us in that while we still were sinners Christ died for us.

(Romans 5:8)

'My Journal':

- *In life, love is often conditional; maybe you have experienced that yourself. How did it make you feel at the time – and how do you feel about it now?*

Meditate on the nature of unconditional love – in contrast – to be loved irrespective of behaviour, and not having to win favour in any way. In fact, being loved just as you are. How does that feel?

Almighty God.

Thank you that your love is unconditional.

You love us all, just as we are.

You love us even when we are still guilty of sin; and faced with the consequences of sin – including separation from you.

You love us enough to have allowed your Son Jesus to die on the cross for us – paying the penalty for that sin.

Your love is complete and undeserved.

You loved us first.

Please help me to make an ongoing positive response to your love for me – including to love you in return.

(Include any additional topics for prayer or thanksgiving, arising from this study)

In Jesus' name.

Amen.

'Doers of the word' (aim): To make a positive response to God reaching out to us in unconditional love.

Is there anything that you think you might find difficult about achieving the aim?

What the Bible says about **love**

A key ingredient of love is patience
16th May

The description of Christ like love (God's love) begins with patience – difficult in a society that seems to expect everything to be instant.

Love is patient

(1 Corinthians 13:4a)

'My Journal':

- *What does patience mean in practical terms? Think of some hypothetical examples where it might come into play. Jot down your thoughts.*

Meditate on how good you are at demonstrating patience; and in what areas of your life more patience is needed.

Lord Jesus.

Your love is so amazing!

Thank you for your deep love for us all.

Please help me to be more like you; and to demonstrate that same kind of love in my life.

Grant me patience… because I really lack patience sometimes.

(Include any additional topics for prayer or thanksgiving, arising from this study)

In your name.

Amen.

'Doers of the word' (aim): To exercise more patience, even when under pressure.

Is there anything that you think you might find difficult about achieving the aim?

What the Bible says about **love**

You can't have love without kindness
17th May

Christ like love demonstrates kindness – and that can be so powerful in a society where we hear so much about aggression and abuse.

Love is kind

(1 Corinthians 13:4b)

'My Journal':

- *Think back to a simple act of kindness, that you have been in receipt of recently. Jot down some notes about how it made you feel.*

Meditate for a few minutes on those feelings that you experienced at the time. And then consider ways in which you could demonstrate similar acts of kindness to others?

Lord Jesus.

Your love is kind!

Thank you for your kindness towards us; but also those simple acts of kindness demonstrated by others that bring blessing to us.

Please help me to demonstrate the type of love that expresses itself by performing acts of kindness towards others, in my life.

(Include any additional topics for prayer or thanksgiving, arising from this study)

In your name.

Amen.

'Doers of the word' (aim): To regularly perform acts of kindness towards others.

Is there anything that you think you might find difficult about achieving the aim?

What the Bible says about **love**

Love and envy are incompatible
18th May

Christ like love does not envy – in other words it doesn't allow us to be eaten up with the desire to have something that someone else has got… or to want to claim the things that someone has achieved.

Love is not envious

(1 Corinthians 13:4c)

'My Journal':

- *What kind of the things do we see in society that act as the focus of people's envy of another?*

Meditate on the positive effects of living without envy.

Lord Jesus.

Your love doesn't envy!

Thank you that you set us an example of living a humble lifestyle; and not striving for material possessions or for success in worldly terms.

Please help me not to envy the things that others have: desperate to acquire them for myself.

And help me not to constantly look at the achievements of others: comparing myself with them, envying what they have done.

Let me strive to be the person you would have me be – and discover contentment in doing that.

(Include any additional topics for prayer or thanksgiving, arising from this study)

In your name.

Amen.

'Doers of the word' (aim): To let go of envy, and replace it with contentment.

Is there anything that you think you might find difficult about achieving the aim?

What the Bible says about **love**

Love is not boastful
19th May

Christ like love does not boast – it will not allow us to try to boost our own ego, at the expense of others – especially God.

Love is not... boastful

(1 Corinthians 13:4d)

'My Journal':

- *What different types of things might we be tempted to boast about?*

Meditate on this thought. Christ like love recognises God as being the creator, provider and the one who sustains all things; and that we have nothing to boast about concerning ourselves.

Lord Jesus.

Your love is not boastful!

Thank you that the love you shower upon us is unconditional; and we don't have to compete for it.

Please help me to give the credit to you for those things that I achieve; and not to take that credit for myself.

(Include any additional topics for prayer or thanksgiving, arising from this study)

In your name.

Amen.

'Doers of the word' (aim): To give the credit to God.

Is there anything that you think you might find difficult about achieving aim?

Love is not arrogant

20th May

Christ like love does not go down the road of arrogance – thinking that we are better or more important than everyone else.

Love is not... arrogant

(1 Corinthians 13:4e)

'My Journal':

- *The example of servanthood that Jesus sets us, highlights living with the attitude of humility and putting others before ourselves. In what ways can we demonstrate those same qualities of servanthood today?*

Meditate on some of the occasions and ways in which Jesus puts others before himself, during his life on earth, and in his death.

Lord Jesus.

Your love is not arrogant!

Thank you for your example of humility and putting others first.

Please help me to follow that example.

Help me to be humble; and not to think that I am better than others.

And help me to put the needs of others before my own – but not neglecting self-care.

(Include any additional topics for prayer or thanksgiving, arising from this study)

In your name.

Amen.

'Doers of the word' (aim): To take on a servant role.

Is there anything that you think you might find difficult about achieving aim?

Love is not rude

21st May

Christ like love does not express itself in rudeness – it is polite and respectful at all times, and values others.

Love is not... rude

(1 Corinthians 13:5a)

'My Journal':

- *What kind of behaviour do you associate with respect? Jot down some hypothetical examples.*

Meditate on what society be like if there was more respect for each other.

Lord Jesus.

Your love is not rude!

Thank you that the teaching of the Bible is for our own good; and to make the world a better place.

Please let there be more respect in the world today.

Help me not to be disrespectful to others, in any way, or at any time.

In fact, help me to do all that I possibly can to openly demonstrate respect for other people – in as many different ways that are possible.

(Include any additional topics for prayer or thanksgiving, arising from this study)

In your name.

Amen.

'Doer's of the word' (aim): To treat others and ourselves with respect and courtesy at all times.

Is there anything that you think you might find difficult about achieving the aim?

Love is not irritable

22nd May

Christ like love does not display irritability – things like being over sensitive or quick to anger… or anything else like that.

It (love) does not insist on its own way *(see 30th May for selfless love)**; it is not irritable.*

(1 Corinthians 13:5b)

'My Journal':

- *What kind of things are you over sensitive about?*

Meditate on anger: when it might be justified, and when it is irrational... and what kind of things make you 'fly off the handle'.

Lord.

I don't want to be an irritable person: oversensitive and quick tempered.

Self-control comes to mind.

Avoiding irrational anger and not being over sensitive.

Thank you for your amazing, unconditional love.

Please fill me full of that love: to experience it in all its fullness, and to allow it to overflow onto those around me.

Let it overcome any irritability.

(Include any additional topics for prayer or thanksgiving, arising from this study)

In Jesus' name.

Amen.

'Doers of the word' (aim): To control those momentary feelings of irrational anger, or those negative responses driven by oversensitivity – and not be irritable.

Is there anything that you think you might find difficult about achieving the aim?

What the Bible says about **love**

Love is not resentful
23rd May

Christ like love has no place for resentfulness – it does not begrudge doing an act of kindness or generosity, or think badly of someone else doing the same.

It (love) is not... resentful.

(1 Corinthians 13:5c)

'My Journal':

- *You are probably a person who regularly performs good deeds, and acts of generosity. Is your motivation behind them always out of genuine love and feelings of compassion towards others, or is it sometimes a case of 'I ought to!' – Possibly accompanied by some resentment?*

Meditate for a few moments upon the love and compassion of Jesus: feel it, and allow yourself to be immersed in it. Think about being motivated by Christ like love, when performing those good deeds.

Lord Jesus.

All that you do is motivated by your wonderful love.

Thank you for showering us all with that love: expressed in so many amazing ways.

I am sorry, but I don't always manage to do things with the right motives.

Sometimes I do the 'right thing' for the 'wrong reason'...

Sometimes I do good deeds because I feel 'I ought to' – and then I feel resentment.

Please forgive me for those times; and help me to always have love as my motivation in the future.

Help me not to resent others for anything.

(Include any additional topics for prayer or thanksgiving, arising from this study)

In your name.

Amen.

'Doers of the word' (aim): To avoid harbouring resentment towards others, for whatever reasons.

Is there anything that you think you might find difficult about achieving the aim?

Love rejoices in the truth

24th May

Christ like love focuses on the values of God: endeavouring to live them out in our own lives, and encouraging others to do the same.

It (love) does not rejoice in wrongdoing, but rejoices in the truth.

(1 Corinthians 13:6)

'My Journal':

- *The law of God is an expression of his love and truth. Pause for a moment, and consider the significance of that... How then could love rejoice in anything else, but striving to live in a way that is glorifying to God, based on his truth?*

Meditate on a favourite verse of scripture; in the knowledge that it is God's truth.

Almighty God.

You are the God of truth!

Thank you that everything about you is truth.

Please help me to live according to the truth – to intertwine it into everything that I say and do.

Grant me obedience to your will.

And help me to rejoice in your truth.

(Include any additional topics for prayer or thanksgiving, arising from this study)

In Jesus' name.

Amen.

'Doers of the word' (aim): To rejoice in God's truth, and the lifestyle that is associated with it.

Is there anything that you think you might find difficult about achieving the aim?

Love bears all things

25th May

Christ like love is so powerful – and from it arises forgiveness.

It (love) bears all things

(1 Corinthians 13:7a)

'My Journal':

- *We can all experience acceptance and forgiveness, through being in relationship with Jesus – and receiving his love. Consider what it means to you, to accept and forgive others who may have hurt you in some way. Make some notes.*

Meditate on the part that tolerance plays in what this verse of scripture is instructing us to do. Consider some hypothetical situations (or actual situations in your own life) where more tolerance needs to take place.

Lord.

You offer us all acceptance and forgiveness!

Thank you for your love, which is the basis of both of those things.

Please help me to accept others; without judging them.

Help me to forgive them when they do something to upset me, or cause me pain.

And enable me to demonstrate tolerance in all my relationships.

(Include any additional topics for prayer or thanksgiving, arising from this study)

In Jesus' name.

Amen.

'Doers of the word' (aim): To accept the forgiveness offered to by God (through Jesus), and to forgive others, for things they have done to hurt us in some way – and to demonstrate tolerance in all situations.

Is there anything that you think you might find difficult about achieving the aim?

Love believes all things
26th May

Christ like love is so intrinsically from God that it does not doubt or contradict his word – the Bible.

It (love)... believes all things

(1 Corinthians 13:7b)

'My Journal':

- *Belief is so fundamental to the Christian faith. As well as rejoicing in God's truth, we are called to believe God's truth. Doubt is very detrimental to faith. Jot down some notes on your thoughts.*

Meditate on the fact that doubt is one of the tools contained within Satan's tool box. We should beware! Consider what that means in terms of your daily living.

God of truth.

Everything that is of you is true!

Thank you for the truth and dependability of your word – the Bible.

Please help me to resist any doubts entering into my mind.

Protect me against the work of Satan.

(Include any additional topics for prayer or thanksgiving, arising from this study)

In Jesus' name.

Amen.

'Doers of the word' (aim): To believe God's word - the Bible.

Is there anything that you think you might find difficult about achieving the aim?

Love hopes all things

27th May

Christ like love, due to its whole nature and focus, brings us to that point of being filled with hope.

It (love)... hopes all things

(1 Corinthians 13:7c)

'My Journal':

- *We all need hope. It encourages, motivates and provides purpose. God is our source of eternal hope, through our personal relationship with Jesus. Think about this promise from God, and then jot down your thoughts.*

Meditate on what life would be like without hope.

Loving heavenly Father.

You are our source of hope – in a world that would otherwise be hopeless!

Thank you for that hope, which you have made available to us through Jesus.

Thank you that your love within us is a source of hope.

Please help me to grasp onto that hope; and let it override any feelings of hopelessness that might arise as a result of living in a world that is broken and damaged through sin and evil.

(Include any additional topics for prayer or thanksgiving, arising from this study)

In Jesus' name.

Amen.

'Doers of the word' (aim): To discover our hope in God, and his love.

Is there anything that you think you might find difficult about achieving the aim?

Love endures all things

28th May

Christ like love is very resilient – and it exhibits perseverance.

It (love)... endures all things

(1 Corinthians 13:7d)

'My Journal':

- *Living in a world that has been damaged and broken by sin and evil, we do need to be equipped to be resilient and persevere – in order to cope with whatever we face in life. Being filled with the love of God does that; together with the power of the indwelling Holy Spirit. Spend some time being reassured by that fact, and make some notes on your feelings.*

Meditate on this. Let me bring us back to the knowledge that being filled with the love of God is about being in relationship with God – through Jesus - and all that it entails. That's why love is so powerful! What are your thoughts on that concept?

Lord Jesus.

You demonstrated that love has a resilience about it!

Thank you that your love is an enduring love.

Please enable me – through the love that you pour into my life, and my relationship with you – to endure all the difficulties and trials that life sets before me...

Fill me afresh with the Holy Spirit.

Help me to keep on persevering.

(Include any additional topics for prayer or thanksgiving, arising from this study)

In your name.

Amen.

'Doers of the word' (aim): To allow God to fill us with his love and Holy Spirit, to equip us to endure all that lies ahead of us.

Is there anything that you think you might find difficult about achieving the aim?

What the Bible says about **love**

Love never ends
29th May

Christ like love goes on forever.
Love never ends

(1 Corinthians 13:8a)

'My Journal':

- *One of the most significant reasons why we can depend on God's love, is because it never ends – It is eternal! What are your thoughts on that?*

Meditate for a few moments, prayerfully seeking that God will fill you to overflowing with his love. Absorb his love into your life, to motivate your own responses, and also to share with others.

Eternal God.

Your love never ends!

Praise you for that...

Thank you for that...

Thank you for the knowledge that I can spend eternity in your loving presence – through Jesus.

Please help me to make that commitment.

(Include any additional topics for prayer or thanksgiving, arising from this study)

In Jesus' name.

Amen.

'Doers of the word' (aim): To be filled with God's love, and experience it to all its fullness – eternally.

Is there anything that you think you might find difficult about achieving the aim?

Love is selfless

30th May

We are called to lay down our lives for others by selflessly serving them…

We know love by this, that he laid down his life for us – and we ought to lay down our lives for one another.

(1 John 3:16)

'My Journal':

- *Consider what it meant to Jesus, and what it signifies, when he 'laid down his life for us.' Include the suffering leading up to his death, as well as his actual death. Make some notes on what God says to you.*

Meditate on what John is implying, in practical terms, when he says that 'we ought to lay down our lives for one another'? Things like selflessly giving of our commitment, talents, abilities, time and other resources in order to serve Jesus, by serving others.

Risen Lord Jesus.

You laid down your life for the whole of human kind!

You laid down your life for me!

Thank you for your selfless act of love upon the cross – paying the penalty for sin.

Thank you that you rose again; and are alive today – and that we can, each one of us, enter into an eternal relationship with you… involving hope!

Please help me to serve you as I offer up my commitment and resources in selflessly helping, and witnessing to others.

(Include any additional topics for prayer or thanksgiving, arising from this study)

In your name.

Amen.

'Doers of the word' (aim): To offer all that we have and are up to Jesus, to be used in his service, as we selflessly help, and witness to, others.

Is there anything that you think you might find difficult about achieving the aim?

Love in action...
31st May

John spells out for us, that the kind of love he is talking about, isn't the kind of love that is in word only... it is an active and a truthful love.

Little children, let us love, not in word or speech, but in truth and action.

(1 John 3:18)

'My Journal':

- *What do you think an action based love is all about?*

Meditate on the kind of love that goes much, much further than just empty words: it is a love which literally affects every single thing that we do and say – demonstrated in the life, death and resurrection of Jesus… Divine love!

Loving God.

Your love for us is an active and a truthful love!

Thank you for your unconditional love, which you shower upon us in so many different and amazing ways.

Please fill me so full of that love that it overflows onto those around me: always completely genuine, communicated by using truthful words, and expressed in loving actions.

(Include any additional topics for prayer or thanksgiving, arising from this study)

In Jesus' name.

Amen.

'Doers of the word' (aim): To love in truth and action.

Is there anything that you think you might find difficult about achieving the aim?

9

PENTECOST

Experiencing the power

1st June

Jesus will never challenge us to do anything that he will not equip us to carry out.

But you will receive power when the Holy Spirit has come upon you; and you will be my witnesses in Jerusalem, in all Judea and Samaria, and to the ends of the earth.

(Acts 1:8)

'My Journal':

- *Meditate on this great commission that Jesus sets before us: to be his witnesses in the world around us. How and where we do that is down to our individual calling. Where has Jesus placed you to be his witness; and what has he challenged you to do?*

Meditate on the knowledge that Jesus promises the power of the indwelling Holy Spirit – to equip us to fulfil the task – before he even places the challenge before us. God is good!

Lord Jesus.

You never challenge us to do anything, without equipping us to achieve it!

Thank you for the power of the indwelling Holy Spirit.

Please help me to rise to the challenge of your calling to me; to be your witness in the place where you have put me.

Help me to believe that you will equip me.

And help me to go forward in the knowledge that the Holy Spirit will always dwell within me.

(Include any additional topics for prayer or thanksgiving, arising from this study)

In your name.

Amen.

'Doers of the word' (aim): To experience the power of God.

Is there anything that you think you might find difficult about achieving the aim?

What the Bible says about **the Holy Spirit**

2nd June
Telling the story

When the day of Pentecost had come, they were all together in one place. And suddenly from heaven there came a sound like the rush of a violent wind, and it filled the entire house where they were sitting. Divided tongues, as of fire, appeared among them, and a tongue rested on each of them. All of them were filled with the Holy Spirit and began to speak in other languages, as the Spirit gave them ability.

Now there were devout Jews from every nation under heaven living in Jerusalem. And at this sound the crowd gathered and was bewildered, because each one heard them speaking in the native language of each. Amazed and astonished, they asked, 'Are not all of these who are speaking Galileans? And how is it that we hear, each of us, in our own native language? Parthians, Medes, Elamites, and residents of Mesopotamia, Judea and Cappadocia, Pontus and Asia, Phrygia and Pamphylia, Egypt and the parts of Lybia belonging to Cyrene, and visitors from Rome, both Jews and proselytes, Cretans and Arabs – in our own languages we hear them speaking about God's deeds of power. All were amazed and perplexed, saying to one another, 'What does this mean?' But others sneered and said, 'They are filled with new wine.'

(Acts 2:1-13)

… to be looked at over the next seven days.

Lord God.

Thank you for the truth of scripture, and that it is relevant to every generation.

Thank you for this passage of scripture about the coming of the Holy Spirit.

Please help me to understand what I have just read; and to meditate upon it today.

(Include any additional topics for prayer or thanksgiving, arising from this study)

In Jesus' name.

Amen.

What the Bible says about **the Holy Spirit**

Nothing is by chance

3rd June

There is a right time and a right place for the coming of the Holy Spirit to the disciples.

When the day of Pentecost had come, they were all together in one place.

(Acts 2:1)

'My Journal':

- *God's timing is perfect. The disciples have been waiting for the gift of the Holy Spirit; and today's the day! Is there something that you have been praying about, for which you are awaiting God's answer?*

Meditate on the fact that with God, nothing is by chance. In the case of the coming of the Holy Spirit in Acts chapter 2, God has chosen an occasion when all the disciples are together in one place.

Almighty God.

Your timing is perfect! You know what is best! You don't make mistakes!

And with you nothing is by chance or coincidence!

You planned the coming of the Holy Spirit at Pentecost to the very last detail.

Thank you that you know what is best: the best time, the best place, the best outcome...

Please help me to trust in your perfect timing; in the knowledge that you know when is best.

And grant me the patience to wait when you want me to wait; and grant me the spontaneity to act when the time is right... and the discernment to recognise which is which.

(Include any additional topics for prayer or thanksgiving, arising from this study)

In Jesus' name.

Amen.

'Doers of the word' (aim): To trust in the timing of God, to be patient and to believe that God knows best.

Is there anything that you think you might find difficult about achieving the aim?

Audible

4th June

At Pentecost, the Holy Spirit's arrival is audible.

And suddenly from heaven there came a sound like the rush of a violent wind, and it filled the entire house where they were sitting.

(Acts 2:2)

'My Journal':

- *The sound 'like the rush of violent wind' is perceived as coming down from heaven. Indeed, the Holy Spirit is the gift – from heaven - that has been promised by Jesus, before his ascension. How do you think the disciples feel when they hear it? How would you be feeling?*

Meditate on how the sound of a gale force wind carries: it roars, it shakes the windows and doors, and it whistles as it finds any opening to squeeze through. The sound of the wind at Pentecost cannot be ignored either by those in the house, or outside. Remember that with God, none of this is by chance or coincidence – everything has a purpose.

Risen Lord Jesus.

You promise the gift of the Holy Spirit to all believers!

Thank you for the power of the indwelling Holy Spirit: to transform us more into your likeness; to guide us on our Christian journey; to strengthen us to serve you; and to equip us to fulfil your calling to us.

Please fill me afresh with the power of the Holy Spirit.

Help me to allow the Holy Spirit to work fully in my life.

And help me to recognise and to follow his leading.

(Include any additional topics for prayer or thanksgiving, arising from this study)

In your name.

Amen.

'Doers of the word' (aim): To recognise that the Holy Spirit is the gift that Jesus promises to all believers – from heaven.

Is there anything that you think you might find difficult about achieving the aim?

What the Bible says about **the Holy Spirit**

Visible

5th June

At Pentecost, the Holy Spirit's arrival is visible.

Divided tongues, as of fire, appeared among them, and a tongue rested on each of them.

(Acts 2:3)

'My Journal':

- *What do you suppose is the significance of God sending the Holy Spirit in a visible form?*

Meditate on the significance of the 'Divided tongues'. It implies that the Holy Spirit comes as one, and then divides in order to enter into all those present. There is only one Spirit.

Lord Jesus.

You sent the Holy Spirit to dwell within all your believers!

Thank you for the power of the indwelling Holy Spirit.

Please help my unbelief; and help me to allow the Holy Spirit to work fully in my life.

(Include any additional topics for prayer or thanksgiving, arising from this study)

In your name.

Amen.

'Doers of the word' (aim): To believe in the reality of the one Spirit; and allow him to work fully in our lives.

Is there anything that you think you might find difficult about achieving the aim?

He gave them ability

6th June

Those who have received the Holy Spirit begin to speak in other languages: we are led to believe that they are not language scholars – the Holy Spirit gives them 'ability'.

All of them were filled with the Holy Spirit and began to speak in other languages, as the Spirit gave them ability.

(Acts 2:4)

'My Journal':

- *In what ways do you feel you need the Holy Spirit to equip you in your present situation – in order to fulfil your calling? Make some notes for prayer.*

Meditate on the fact that the Holy Spirit gives us abilities. He gives spiritual gifts – special abilities that will enable us to fulfil a specific calling, maybe for a limited time. He anoints the natural abilities and talents with which we were born. And he equips us for the moment – with the wisdom, strength, etc. that we need. Jot down occasions when the Holy Spirit has done these things in your life.

Almighty God.

Your Holy Spirit gives us 'ability'!

Thank you that when we allow the Holy Spirit to work fully in our lives, he enables us to fulfil our callings.

Please Grant me those spiritual gifts that I need at this time.

Anoint my natural talents and abilities as I offer them up in service.

And please equip me for the moment; on those occasions when I need something of a miracle to happen, enabling me to deal with that situation in a way that is glorifying to you.

Thank you for those times when you have given me 'ability' in the past.

In Jesus' name.

Amen.

'Doers of the word' (aim): To recognise those occasions when the Holy Spirit has given us 'ability'; and not to be afraid to ask for 'ability' for particular situations, in the future.

Is there anything that you think you might find difficult about achieving the aim?

The impossible happens

7th June

When God is at work the impossible can happen – and often does! Demonstrated in the following verse!

And at this sound the crowd gathered and was bewildered, because each one heard them speaking in the native language of each.

(Acts 2:6)

'My Journal':

- *Think about God doing the impossible – the miraculous. Jot down some notes about how that makes you feel.*

Meditate on the effect of God doing the impossible has on society – or do you think some prefer to put it down to coincidence, a bit of luck, or just an unexplained mystery.

Almighty God.

You are the God of miracles!

You are continuously doing things which, in human terms, are totally impossible – but that's what makes you God!

Thank you that you are a powerful God; and that you are at work in our lives, and all around us.

Please help me to always be aware of your hand at work: to notice the impossible happening and attribute it to you; but also to recognise that the small helpful things are from you as well – things like finding that set of lost keys.

(Include any additional topics for prayer or thanksgiving, arising from this study)

In Jesus' name.

Amen.

'Doers of the word' (aim): To recognise the miraculous as being from God.

Is there anything that you think you might find difficult about achieving the aim?

What the Bible says about **the Holy Spirit**

What does this mean?

8th June

There are things that we don't understand about the plans and purposes of God; but let's not allow that to lead to doubts or losing our faith... After all, faith is about believing those things of God that we maybe don't fully understand, or of which we have no tangible evidence.

All were amazed and perplexed, saying to one another, 'What does this mean?'

(Acts 2:12)

'My Journal':

- *What a mixture of feelings: 'amazed' and 'perplexed'. The amazement is good: it is right that we should be amazed at the things God does. But we should prayerfully try to avoid allowing the things we don't understand to cause us to feel perplexed. How do you deal with things connected with your daily walk with Jesus that you don't understand?*

Meditate on the way that faith can overcome lack of understanding, or those things that have no tangible evidence (Hebrews 11:1).

Lord Jesus.

You do amazing things!

Thank you that we don't need to be perplexed by those things that we don't understand concerning the kingdom.

Please help me to leave to faith, everything that I can't understand about the kingdom and kingdom living.

Strengthen my faith.

(Include any additional topics for prayer or thanksgiving, arising from this study)

In your name.

Amen.

'Doers of the word' (aim): To avoid becoming 'perplexed' as a result of the things of God that we don't understand – by relying on faith.

Is there anything that you think you might find difficult about achieving the aim?

Scornful

9th June

It seems so unbelievable that, when we are doing the will of God, we can so often meet with scorn.

But others sneered and said, 'They are filled with new wine.'

(Acts 2:13)

'My Journal':

- *Jot some thoughts down about your own experiences of being scorned or unjustly accused, when you have been serving God in some way?*

Meditate on how it makes you feel to be scorned in this way; and on your response.

Lord Jesus.

People will scorn and mock us because of our faith in you!

Thank you that you understand how that feels, because you had to deal with it in your life on earth.

Please help me not to become discouraged in my Christian life, by those cruel or sarcastic things people may say to me; instead, help me respond by being challenged and empowered as I serve.

(Include any additional topics for prayer or thanksgiving, arising from this study)

In your name.

Amen.

'Doers of the word' (aim): To be prepared to be scorned for the kingdom's sake.

Is there anything that you think you might find difficult about achieving the aim?

What the Bible says about **the Holy Spirit**

Seizing the opportunity
10th June

After receiving the Holy Spirit, Peter demonstrates the boldness and readiness necessary to seize the opportunity.

But Peter, standing with the eleven, raised his voice and addressed them: 'Men of Judea and all who live in Jerusalem, let this be known to you, and listen to what I say.'

(Acts 2:14)

'My Journal':

- *In what ways do you think the Holy Spirit has equipped Peter; enabling him to take the lead on this occasion; and speak with great authority?*

Meditate in the knowledge that your calling may or may not be to preach and teach; but the Holy Spirit will still equip you to fulfil that calling – whatever it might be! Consider possible opportunities to share something about the Christian faith, and your personal experience of Jesus, with others maybe in a less formal way – in the power of the Holy Spirit.

Lord Jesus.

You want us to be ready to speak for you!

Thank you that, through the power of the indwelling Holy Spirit, you equip us to fulfil our callings; including to be ready to seize every opportunity to tell others about you.

Please fill me afresh with the Holy Spirit, and help me to be bold and ready at all times.

(Include any additional topics for prayer or thanksgiving, arising from this study)

In your name.

Amen.

'Doers of the word' (aim): To be ready to seize the God given opportunities to speak up for Jesus.

Is there anything that you think you might find difficult about achieving the aim?

What the Bible says about **the Holy Spirit**

Indecision
11th June

So many people in society today seem to be at that point of indecision, that is: 'To follow Jesus or not to follow Jesus. What shall I do? Shall I or shan't I?'

Now when they heard this, they were cut to the heart and said to Peter and the other apostles, 'Brothers, what should we do?'

(Acts 2:37)

'My Journal':

- *Are you that person? Do you profess to be a Christian, but in reality, you know that you are still sitting on the fence? Consider what a real commitment to Jesus would look like for you, in terms of things like, relationship, focus and time. Make some notes.*

Meditate on the importance of receiving good, scripturally based teaching, delivered with authority – illustrated by the first half of this verse.

Lord Jesus.

You want us to be decisive!

Thank you that you want us all to be in a relationship with you; and to follow you in our daily lives.

Please help me, both to be committed in my relationship with you, but also to be decisive in living out my Christian life.

(Include any additional topics for prayer or thanksgiving, arising from this study)

In your name.

Amen.

'Doers of the word' (aim): To be decisive in committing to, and following Jesus.

Is there anything that you think you might find difficult about achieving the aim?

What the Bible says about **the Holy Spirit**

Gift of the Holy Spirit

12th June

Being filled with the indwelling Holy Spirit isn't something that needs to be earned. The Bible tells us that he is a free gift that we receive through our commitment to Jesus.

Peter said to them, 'Repent, and be baptised every one of you in the name of Jesus Christ so that your sins may be forgiven; and you will receive the gift of the Holy Spirit.

(Acts 2:38)

'My Journal':

- *So often 'special offers' come with conditions. Maybe the offer is of a free gift; but then when we read the small print (t & c's), we discover that it is not quite as straight forward as we might expect. The offer of the free gift of the Holy Spirit, really is what it says it is in this verse. Make some notes on your response.*

Meditate on what that gift means to you in your daily life: for example, ways in which you experience the power of the Holy Spirit in your life; or alternatively, ways in which you would like to experience the power of the Holy Spirit in your life – or a bit of both.

Risen Lord Jesus.

You give the gift of the Holy Spirit to all who follow you in repentance and with faith!

Thank you for that wonderful free gift.

Please help me to accept him, and allow him to work in my life; experiencing his power as I seek to live the Christian life of love and witness.

(Include any additional topics for prayer or thanksgiving, arising from this study)

In your name.

Amen.

'Doers of the word' (aim): To fully experience the power of the indwelling Holy Spirit in our lives.

Is there anything that you think you might find difficult about achieving the aim?

What the Bible says about **the Holy Spirit**

Witnessing in God's power
13th June

To see positive results when we witness, we need to include God; allowing the Holy Spirit to work in and through us.

So those who welcomed his message were baptised, and that day about three thousand persons were added.

(Acts 2:41)

'My Journal':

- *Let's not be discouraged in our witness, by the results that Peter experiences on this occasion – 'about three thousand persons were added'. We are not all called to be international evangelists: for most of us, our experience is a much humbler one. But when we include God, there will be results – so spend some time being encouraged by that! Jot some notes down on your thoughts.*

Meditate on who God is calling you to witness to; and in what ways he wants you to do it.

Lord God.

You want to be involved as we witness to other people, through the Holy Spirit!

Thank you that we are not on our own: you want to be included.

Please be in my witnessing.

Let the Holy Spirit work in and through me.

Let him prepare the lives of those to whom you point me towards.

And let me fulfil my calling; whatever numbers that might involve: millions, thousands, hundred or just a handful.

(Include any additional topics for prayer or thanksgiving, arising from this study)

In Jesus' name.

Amen.

'Doers of the word' (aim): To be effective in our witness, by including God.

Is there anything that you think you might find difficult about achieving the aim?

What the Bible says about **the Holy Spirit**

Proclaiming the message with boldness

14th June

As Christians, don't we all want to proclaim the word of God with boldness? The thing we probably feel we are lacking in, is the 'boldness'.

When they had prayed... they were all filled with the Holy Spirit and spoke the word of God with boldness.

(Acts 4:31)

'My Journal':

- *In context, this verse of scripture describes a physical demonstration of the power of prayer, when it speaks about 'the place in which they were gathered together was shaken'. Think for a moment about the power of prayer. What are your conclusions?*

Meditate on what you need at this time. Consider your own needs; the needs of those close to you; and other needs which God has laid upon your heart which he wants you to be praying about. Maybe that includes the desire for boldness. Remember that there is power in prayer!

Lord Jesus.

You can endow me with that boldness for which I have longed! Please grant it to me.

Thank you that prayer is powerful.

Please help me to believe in the power of prayer; and act upon it.

(Include any additional topics for prayer or thanksgiving, arising from this study)

In your name.

Amen.

'Doers of the word' (aim): To proclaim the message with boldness.

Is there anything that you think you might find difficult about achieving the aim?

What the Bible says about **the Holy Spirit**

Full of faith

15th June

When speaking about the selecting of Stephen for ministry, the writer of Acts refers to his faith and, linked with it, that he is filled with the Holy Spirit. There is a significance to this.

What they said pleased the whole community, and they chose Stephen, a man full of faith and the Holy Spirit, together with Philip, Prochorus, Nicanor, Timon, Parmenas, and Nicolaus, a proselyte of Antioch.

(Acts 6:5)

'My Journal':

- *What is the significance of the link between being full of faith and being filled with the Holy Spirit?*

Meditate on ways in which people might recognise you as being a person who is full of faith and the Holy Spirit. Consider things like, demonstrating belief, trust, hope, truth and love in action – and, of course your relationship with Jesus.

Our loving heavenly Father.

Faith and being filled with the Holy Spirit are intrinsically linked!

Thank you that Jesus has done so much for us; and he is preparing all kinds of eternal blessings for his followers (John 14:1-3).

Please increase my faith, fill me afresh with the Holy Spirit, and help me to walk closely to Jesus daily.

Enable me to be seen by others as a person of faith and filled with the Holy Spirit.

And help me to demonstrate those attributes in my life that reflect this.

(Include any additional topics for prayer or thanksgiving, arising from this study)

In Jesus' name.

Amen.

'Doers of the word' (aim): To be full of faith and the Holy Spirit.

Is there anything that you think you might find difficult about achieving the aim?

Full of grace and power

16th June

Stephen's ministry demonstrates the power of God at work, thanks to his faith and being filled with the Holy Spirit; and he demonstrates grace – something that we associate with the character of God.

Stephen, full of grace and power, did great wonders and signs among the people.

(Acts 6:8)

'My Journal':

- *Bearing in mind that, as followers of Jesus, we are filled with the Holy Spirit, consider why it is that we so often doubt our ability to live out the Christian life of grace, love and witness. Make a note of your thoughts and conclusions.*

Meditate on what exactly having the Holy Spirit dwelling within us really means. Fundamentally, it is God dwelling within us, filling us with his grace, love and power.

Almighty God.

When we enter into a personal relationship with Jesus, you enter into us, through the Holy Spirit!

Thank you that through the Holy Spirit, we are filled with your guidance, your grace, your love, and power from you.

And through him, you begin to restore your image within us.

Please grant me confidence in the knowledge that your power is within me.

(Include any additional topics for prayer or thanksgiving, arising from this study)

In Jesus' name.

Amen.

'Doers of the word' (aim): To be full of grace and power, through the indwelling Holy Spirit.

Is there anything that you think you might find difficult about achieving the aim?

Godly wisdom

17th June

Where is your source of wisdom?

But they could not withstand the wisdom and the Spirit with which he spoke.

(Acts 6:10)

'My Journal':

- *Think about possible sources of wisdom, by which we can be influenced, and their strengths and weaknesses: things like science, philosophy, astrology, life experience, and the wisdom of God - experienced through the indwelling Holy Spirit. Jot down your thoughts.*

Meditate on the fact that this verse of scripture points us towards the wisdom of God, as a result of the Holy Spirit dwelling within us. In context it implies that such wisdom is powerful and effective, and thus is something to be sought in our lives – indeed it should be a priority and point of focus.

Almighty God.

Your wisdom cannot be faulted!

Thank you that we can experience and live according to your wisdom, through the power of the indwelling Holy Spirit.

Please help me to focus on, and base my life on, your wisdom; and help me to recognise those sources of wisdom that are not helpful to follow.

(Include any additional topics for prayer or thanksgiving, arising from this study)

In Jesus' name.

Amen

'Doers of the word' (aim): To live according to the wisdom of God.

Is there anything that you think you might find difficult about achieving the aim?

The face of an angel

18th June

What a wonderful way in which to be described: as having a face 'like the face of an angel'.

And all who sat in the council looked intently at him, and they saw that his face was like the face of an angel.

(Acts 6:15)

'My Journal':

- *What do you think it might mean to have a face 'like the face of an angel'?*

Meditate on this verse of scripture in context: it is all about Stephen being full of the Holy Spirit. It is only through being filled with the indwelling Holy Spirit – and allowing him to work fully in our lives – that we can hope to achieve such things.

Gracious God.

You are loving, kind, warm, full of joy, and, I am sure, have a sense of humour.

Thank you for the cleansing, strengthening, and transforming power of the indwelling Holy Spirit.

I would love to have the face of an angel – in the same way as Stephen did – to reflect your face in some way, in my own face and life.

Please help me, through the power of the Holy Spirit, to be able to achieve that.

(Include any additional topics for prayer or thanksgiving, arising from this study)

In Jesus' name.

Amen.

'Doers of the word' (aim): To strive to have a face like an angel, through allowing the Holy Spirit to work fully in our lives.

Is there anything that you think you might find difficult about achieving the aim?

What the Bible says about **the Holy Spirit**

Led by the Spirit
19th June

The Holy Spirit leads us: it may be to go somewhere or to do something; or it could be not to go somewhere or not to do something.

They went through the region of Phrygia and Galatia, having been forbidden by the Holy Spirit to speak the word in Asia.

(Acts 16:6)

'My Journal':

- *We are possibly more sensitive to listening to God leading us, through the Holy Spirit, to go somewhere or to do something, than we are to him forbidding us – especially when we are filled with enthusiasm. Jot down your thoughts, and maybe personal experiences of this.*

Meditate on some of the ways in which the Holy Spirit might forbid us from going somewhere or from doing something: for example, through relevant words of scripture, when metaphorical doors close, if wise Christian friends are advising us against it, or when we just have an unease about the action.

Lord God.

You guide us through the Holy Spirit!

Thank you that you have a plan for our lives – a good plan – and you show us the way to go (Jeremiah 29:11).

Please fill me afresh with the Holy Spirit.

Help me to listen to his leading, carefully; grant me discernment; and enable me to respond in obedience to you.

(Include any additional topics for prayer or thanksgiving, arising from this study)

In Jesus' name.

Amen.

'Doers of the word' (aim): To be sensitive and obedient to the leading of the Holy Spirit – even when he says a decisive 'no'.

Is there anything that you think you might find difficult about achieving the aim?

Progressively transformed

20th June

Becoming a Christian is the beginning of a lifelong process of transformation: progressively, more and more, into the likeness of Jesus – through the work and power of the indwelling Holy Spirit.

And all of us, with unveiled faces, seeing the glory of the Lord as though reflected in a mirror, are being transformed into the same image from one degree of glory to another; for this comes from the Lord, the Spirit.

(2 Corinthians 3:18)

'My Journal':

- *Are you willing to allow the Holy Spirit to work fully in your life, transforming you? What do you think that constitutes?*

Meditate on some of the aspects of that process of transformation. Things like, being forgiven, spiritually cleansed and made righteous; being filled with Christ like love to share with others; being enabled to know the heart of God more and to live in an ever greater degree of obedience to him; and to be filled with eternal hope.

Lord Jesus.

I want to be more like you!

Thank you that through your death and resurrection, I can be in a life changing relationship with you: leading to forgiveness, cleansing, empowerment and eternal hope.

Please help me to be willing to allow the Holy Spirit to work fully in my life, progressively transforming me more into your likeness.

Thank you that, though I only see you like a reflection now, one day I will see you face to face.

Help me to be ready for that time.

(Include any additional topics for prayer or thanksgiving, arising from this study)

In your name.

Amen.

'Doers of the word' (aim): To be willing to allow the Holy Spirit to work fully in our lives, to bring about that transformation, increasingly into the likeness of Christ.

Is there anything that you think you might find difficult about achieving the aim?

Fruitfulness

21st June

The fruit of the Spirit is in the singular: it is one complete package that we should strive to demonstrate in our daily lives… and it starts with love.

By contrast, the fruit of the Spirit is love... There is no law against such things.

(Galatians 5:22-23)

'My Journal':

- *We're not talking about choosing a few favourite qualities that we would like to demonstrate in our lives; the fruit of the Spirit is one package. Through the power of the indwelling Holy Spirit at work in our lives, we are called to produce all of the fruit of the Spirit, to an ever increasing degree. Consider that for a few minutes; and jot down anything that you feel God is saying to you.*

Meditate on how all the fruit of the Spirit overlap into each other; and cannot be lived in isolation of the others anyway.

Lord Jesus.

You long for us, as your followers, to live spiritually fruitful lives!

Thank you that, the more we allow the Holy Spirit to work in our lives, the more evident the fruit of the Spirit will be.

Please help me to progressively demonstrate more of the fruit of the Spirit each day of my life – always remembering that it is a complete package, and not an opportunity for us to pick and choose which we would like to pursue and which we wouldn't.

Fill me with your love to share with others: let it outpour onto those around me.

(Include any additional topics for prayer or thanksgiving, arising from this study)

In your name.

Amen.

'Doers of the word' (aim): To be spiritually fruitful – including being loving.

Is there anything that you think you might find difficult about achieving the aim?

The fruit of the Spirit – joy

22nd June

True joy is what we experience through being in a personal relationship with Jesus: filled with the indwelling Holy Spirit and reunited with God the Father.

By contrast, the fruit of the Spirit is... joy... There is no law against such things.

(Galatians 5:22-23)

'My Journal':

- *From your own personal experience, how would you describe the joy of being a Christian?*

Meditate on how allowing that kind of joy to shine through our lives is an effective witness to those around us – shining joy into their lives. Consider how you would respond to the question: Why are you so joyful?

Lord Jesus.

You long for us, as your followers, to live spiritually fruitful lives!

Thank you that, the more we allow the Holy Spirit to work in our lives, the more evident the fruit of the Spirit will be.

Please help me to progressively demonstrate more joy in my life: to be more joyful myself and to bring joy to others.

(Include any additional topics for prayer or thanksgiving, arising from this study)

In your name.

Amen.

'Doers of the word' (aim): To demonstrate joy in our lives.

Is there anything that you think you might find difficult about achieving the aim?

The fruit of the Spirit – peace

23rd June

Knowing peace within our lives is so important: to know peace and to help to spread peace in a broken world.

By contrast, the fruit of the Spirit is... peace... There is no law against such things.

(Galatians 5:22-23)

'My Journal':

- *Consider the nature of a peacemaker. Maybe you could jot some notes down from your own personal experience of pacifying situations.*

Meditate on knowing the peace of God within your life – deep down!

Lord Jesus.

You long for us, as your followers, to live spiritually fruitful lives!

Thank you that, the more we allow the Holy Spirit to work in our lives, the more evident the fruit of the Spirit will be.

Please help me to progressively demonstrate more peace in my life – to know more of God's peace and to be more of a peacemaker.

(Include any additional topics for prayer or thanksgiving, arising from this study)

In your name.

Amen.

'Doers of the word' (aim): To demonstrate peace in our lives.

Is there anything that you think you might find difficult about achieving the aim?

What the Bible says about **the Holy Spirit**

The fruit of the Spirit – patience

24th June

The fruit of the Spirit is not an easy option; and that includes patience. In a world where so much seems to be instant, it is easy to struggle with waiting for God's perfect timing.

By contrast, the fruit of the Spirit is... patience... There is no law against such things.

(Galatians 5:22-23)

'My Journal':

- *There are all kinds of reasons for our impatience with regards to God's timing: but consider the implications of those reasons that are fundamentally good qualities. Things like being enthusiastic to serve Jesus, or viewing a need with compassion and a sense of urgency. Make a note of your thoughts.*

Meditate on God's perfect timing, and the need to wait until that time has arrived.

Lord Jesus.

You long for us, as your followers, to live spiritually fruitful lives!

Thank you that, the more we allow the Holy Spirit to work in our lives, the more evident the fruit of the Spirit will be.

Please help me to progressively demonstrate more patience in my life: to wait patiently for your perfect timing, and to demonstrate patience in all my dealings with other people.

(Include any additional topics for prayer or thanksgiving, arising from this study)

In your name.

Amen.

'Doers of the word' (aim): To demonstrate patience in our lives.

Is there anything that you think you might find difficult about achieving the aim?

What the Bible says about **the Holy Spirit**

The fruit of the Spirit – kindness
25th June

Performing acts of kindness isn't just about feeling compassion for others, or seeing the need; it is also about making the effort, and giving the time.

By contrast, the fruit of the Spirit is... kindness... There is no law against such things.

(Galatians 5:22-23)

'My Journal':

- *Performing simple acts of kindness is not necessarily about doing things that will make the newspapers, will be life-changing, or will win over the recipient's lifelong gratitude. Maybe our good deeds will almost go unacknowledged; but not un-noticed. Jot down how you feel about that.*

Meditate on the love and compassion of Jesus – expressed in acts of kindness – described in the Gospels.

Lord Jesus.

You long for us, as your followers, to live spiritually fruitful lives!

Thank you that, the more we allow the Holy Spirit to work in our lives, the more evident the fruit of the Spirit will be.

Please help me to progressively demonstrate more kindness in my life: fill me with your love and compassion for others.

(Include any additional topics for prayer or thanksgiving, arising from this study)

In your name.

Amen.

'Doers of the word' (aim): To demonstrate kindness in our lives.

Is there anything that you think you might find difficult about achieving the aim?

What the Bible says about **the Holy Spirit**

The fruit of the Spirit – generosity
26th June

Generosity isn't just giving gifts at Christmas and birthdays, it is about being generous with our love for others, and how we use our resources – including our time. Generosity is all encompassing.

By contrast, the fruit of the Spirit is... generosity... There is no law against such things.

(Galatians 5:22-23)

'My Journal':

- *Think about the generosity of God – and its expression. Make a list.*

Meditate on your own generosity: how freely do you share Christ like love with others; how generous are you with regards to using your resources for kingdom building; and how freely do you give of your time?

Lord Jesus.

You long for us, as your followers, to live spiritually fruitful lives!

Thank you that, the more we allow the Holy Spirit to work in our lives, the more evident the fruit of the Spirit will be.

Please help me to progressively demonstrate more generosity in my life: to be generous with my love, my time and all the other resources that you have entrusted to me.

(Include any additional topics for prayer or thanksgiving, arising from this study)

In your name.

Amen.

'Doers of the word' (aim): To demonstrate generosity in our lives.

Is there anything that you think you might find difficult about achieving the aim?

The fruit of the Spirit – faithfulness

27th June

Faithfulness is so important to the success of any relationship.

By contrast, the fruit of the Spirit is... faithfulness... There is no law against such things.

(Galatians 5:22-23)

'My Journal':

- *Think about God's faithfulness to us; and the ways in which we might experience it on a daily basis. Make a list.*

Meditate on how we can demonstrate faithfulness in all our relationships; including in our relationships with God.

Lord Jesus.

You long for us, as your followers, to live spiritually fruitful lives!

Thank you that, the more we allow the Holy Spirit to work in our lives, the more evident the fruit of the Spirit will be.

Please help me to progressively demonstrate more faithfulness in my life: help me to faithfully serve you, and to be faithful in all my relationships – including my relationship with you.

(Include any additional topics for prayer or thanksgiving, arising from this study)

In your name.

Amen.

'Doers of the word' (aim): To demonstrate faithfulness in our lives.

Is there anything that you think you might find difficult about achieving the aim?

The fruit of the Spirit – gentleness

28th June

The quality of gentleness is not really one that modern society particularly values or appreciates; and yet, it is held with high esteem in the Bible.

By contrast, the fruit of the Spirit is... gentleness... There is no law against such things.

(Galatians 5:22-23)

'My Journal':

- *How do you think modern society views the characteristic of gentleness?*

Meditate on how do you think the Bible views the characteristic of gentleness?

Lord Jesus.

You long for us, as your followers, to live spiritually fruitful lives!

Thank you that, the more we allow the Holy Spirit to work in our lives, the more evident the fruit of the Spirit will be.

Please help me to progressively demonstrate more gentleness in my life: and demonstrate to society that it is actually a strength – and not a weakness, as it seems to be portrayed so often.

(Include any additional topics for prayer or thanksgiving, arising from this study)

In your name.

Amen.

'Doers of the word' (aim): To demonstrate more gentleness in our lives.

Is there anything that you think you might find difficult about achieving the aim?

The fruit of the Spirit – self-control

29th June

Life is a like a tug of war: battling between the craving to satisfy the desires linked with human nature, and striving to live according to the will of God.

By contrast, the fruit of the Spirit is... self-control. There is no law against such things.

(Galatians 5:22-23)

'My Journal':

- *What does self-control constitute in the 21st century world – especially in our nation? In what areas of our lives do we need to exercise self-control?*

Meditate on us exerting control over our self-centredness, in order to allow the Holy Spirit to be in control of the things we say and do.

Lord Jesus.

You long for us, as your followers, to live spiritually fruitful lives!

Thank you that, the more we allow the Holy Spirit to work in our lives, the more evident the fruit of the Spirit will be.

Please help me to progressively demonstrate more self-control in my life.

Grant me the strength to control my human desires.

Help me to allow the Holy Spirit to take control of those things that I say and do.

(Include any additional topics for prayer or thanksgiving, arising from this study)

In your name.

Amen.

'Doers of the word' (aim): To demonstrate self- control in our lives.

Is there anything that you think you might find difficult about achieving the aim?

What the Bible says about **the Holy Spirit**

Are you listening?

30th June

Listening is so fundamental to the Christian faith – in fact, to any relationship, including our relationship with God.

Let anyone who has an ear listen to what the Spirit is saying to the churches.

(Revelation 2:7a)

'My Journal':

- *Listening involves things like stillness, quiet, focus, not interrupting and not day dreaming. Consider the instruction to 'listen to what the Spirit is saying...' Jot down some thoughts.*

Meditate as you spend some time listening to what the Holy Spirit is saying to you now.

Almighty God.

You want to speak to us through the Holy Spirit.

Thank you that as part of our relationship with you, it is your desire to communicate with us.

Please help me to be a good listener to what you are saying to me.

Help me to be still, quiet and focused – and not interrupt what you are saying to me.

(Include any additional topics for prayer or thanksgiving, arising from this study)

In Jesus' name.

Amen.

'Doers of the word' (aim): To spend time listening to God speaking to us, through the Holy Spirit.

Is there anything that you think you might find difficult about achieving the aim?

10

PRAYER

God answers prayer

1st July

What a comfort it is, to know that God answers prayer.

I cry aloud to the Lord, and he answers me...

(Psalm 3:4a)

'My Journal':

- *God knows best, and his timing is perfect: sometimes his answer is 'yes', but sometimes it is 'no' or 'wait'... but that doesn't mean that we haven't been heard or that God hasn't answered our prayer. Jot down your thoughts.*

Meditate as you spend time in a different kind of prayer. Sometimes we don't need to say anything; we can just spend time in an attitude of prayer, resting in God's presence. Try it for a few minutes; before saying the prayer below.

Lord God.

Thank you that, in a world where so many people don't listen, you are a God who loves to hear our prayers: you listen to every word, and you answer our requests.

Thank you that you know the best way to answer our prayers: sometimes it is with a 'yes', sometimes it is with a 'no', and other times it is with 'wait'.

Please help me to discern your answer to prayer when it is a 'yes' – even if it is in a way that I hadn't expected.

Grant me the humility to accept your answer to prayer when it is a 'no'.

And enable me to demonstrate patience when your answer to prayer is 'wait'.

(Include any additional topics for prayer or thanksgiving, arising from this study)

In Jesus' name.

Amen.

'Doers of the word' (aim): To recognise and accept God's answers to prayer; and, if necessary to learn patience.

Is there anything that you think you might find difficult about achieving the aim?

Heard by God
2nd July

In a society where life is so busy and pressured, and we often feel unheard, unimportant and depersonalised, isn't it amazing to know that God will always hear us, when we speak to him in prayer?

Then when you call upon me and come and pray to me, I will hear you.

(Jeremiah 29:12)

'My Journal':

- *Tell yourself: 'God hears every single word that I say to him, in prayer.' – Make a note of your thoughts.*

Meditate on times in your life when you have felt unheard – So: How does it feel to know that God listens to your prayers?

Almighty God.

You hear us when we pray to you!

Thank you that you hear every single word we say to you in prayer; and that, even when we feel unheard by so much of the world in which we live, you always listen.

Thank you for making me feel loved and important to you.

Please help me to feel free to say what I want to say, when I pray; and not to feel that I have to pray in a particular way, or that I can only pray about certain things.

(Include any additional topics for prayer or thanksgiving, arising from this study)

In Jesus' name.

Amen.

'Doers of the word' (aim): To feel heard by God – Maybe you have never really felt heard by anyone else in your life.

Is there anything that you think you might find difficult about achieving the aim?

Say what's in your heart

3rd July

Prayers don't have to be long or eloquent; and we don't need to use formal language or a formal setting in order to speak to God. We can just chat to God, from anywhere; sharing what is in our hearts.

'When you are praying, do not heap up empty phrases as the Gentiles do; for they think that they will be heard because of their many words.'

(Matthew 6:7)

'My Journal':

- *You might find it helpful to kneel for this – but you don't have to. Spend a few moments praying to God; but using as few words as possible – and then make some notes about how that feels.*

Meditate on the fact that God loves to hear our prayers; so we don't need to catch his attention by using highfaluting words or by babbling. Having said that; there is no time limit on how long we can spend chatting with God – he's always happy to listen! But we should be real with him.

Lord Jesus.

It's not about saying long, eloquent prayers; it's about saying what is in our hearts!

Thank you that the effectiveness of prayer is not about how good we are at praying; but it is about praying with faith and expectation...

It's about being real when we pray.

It's about being honest when we pray.

And it's about sticking to the point when we pray.

Please release my tongue when I pray; grant me a real freedom in my prayer life.

(Include any additional topics for prayer or thanksgiving, arising from this study)

In your name.

Amen.

'Doers of the word' (aim): To speak from the heart when we pray.

Is there anything that you think you might find difficult about achieving the aim?

What the Bible says about **prayer**

Relating to God
4th July

God is the great Creator, who created all things, but he is also a loving parent: we should relate to him in both contexts. This is addressed right at the beginning of what we call 'The Lord's Prayer' – the prayer that Jesus taught us.

'Pray then in this way:
Our Father in heaven,
hallowed be your name.

(Matthew 6:9)

'My Journal':

- *What is your experience of parenting: of being parented or of being a parent? Think about what it means to know God as a parent – the perfect parent. Make a note of your conclusions.*

Meditate on God's amazing creation for a moment. The same God – who is our perfect heavenly parent - created all this. Jot down your response.

Creator God.

You created everything; including humankind!

Thank you that, in your love and desire to relate to us all, you have placed us in the midst of your amazing creation – and you want to be in a relationship with me.

You are the perfect parent.

Thank you that whatever my experience of parenting is; it cannot match with your parenting of me.

Please help me to be able to relate to you, both as the all-powerful, all-knowing and all-seeing Creator God; and also as my loving heavenly Father.

(Include any additional topics for prayer or thanksgiving, arising from this study)

In Jesus' name.

Amen.

'Doers of the word' (aim): To be able to worship and praise God, holding him in awe and wonder; at the same time as having a close personal relationship with him.

Is there anything that you think you might find difficult about achieving the aim?

God's heart's desires should be ours

5th July

Just as God longs to see his kingdom spread across the whole world – for his perfect will to be done – we too should be yearning for that to happen.

Your kingdom come.
Your will be done,
on earth as it is in heaven.

(Matthew 6:10)

'My Journal':

- *You can help to build God's kingdom in the places where you live, work and socialise, by living your life in obedience to the will of God? Write down your thoughts.*

Meditate on any areas of your life in which you might struggle to live according to God's will. Areas like, the plans you make; the way in which you conduct your business; or how you might behave behind closed doors.

Almighty God.

Your will is perfect!

Thank you that you know what is best for us; and our eternal futures – and on that fact, your will is based.

Please help me to know what is on your heart; and to have the same desires as you.

Empower me to live according to your will and purposes in every area of my life.

Let your kingdom be established.

(Include any additional topics for prayer or thanksgiving, arising from this study)

In Jesus' name.

Amen.

'Doers of the word' (aim): To live according to God's will and purposes.

Is there anything that you think you might find difficult about achieving the aim?

God's provision

6th July

Our concept of what we need and when we need it can be very different to what God knows we really need, and the timescale: God provides.

Give us this day our daily bread.

(Matthew 6:11)

'My Journal':

- *Starting off with the beauty and wonder of creation and the supplying of our needs; moving on to things like family, friends and salvation; consider the generosity and provision of God. Make a note of your thoughts.*

Meditate on the role that sharing plays in God' provision to us; and the significance of asking for what we need on a daily basis.

Creator God.

You created all things!

Thank you for the beauty and wonder of your creation.

Thank you that it is a demonstration of your unconditional love, faithfulness and provision to us.

Thank you for seedtime and harvest.

And thank you for all the other resources in your creation.

Thank you for families: biological and church.

Please help me to recognise what I really need; and not waste energy pining for those things that are not necessary.

And provide those things that I need, for me.

Help me to share the abundance with which I am blessed.

(Include any additional topics for prayer or thanksgiving, arising from this study)

In Jesus' name.

Amen.

'Doers of the word' (aim): To understand what we really need; to share God's gifts with others; and trust in God's provision.

Is there anything that you think you might find difficult about achieving the aim?

Live a forgiven lifestyle

7th July

To fully benefit from forgiveness, we need to seek God's forgiveness, forgive others for those times they have hurt us in some way, seek forgiveness from those we have upset… and we need to forgive ourselves.

'And forgive us our debts,
as we also have forgiven our debtors.'

(Matthew 6:12)

'My Journal':

- *Have you asked God for his forgiveness? Is there someone who you need to forgive, or seek forgiveness from? Are you guilty of un-forgiveness of yourself?*

Meditate on the fact that God forgives those, who enter into a personal relationship with Jesus – based on repentance and faith.

Our loving heavenly Father.

The forgiveness you offer is complete!

Thank you that, through entering into a personal relationship with Jesus, we are forgiven for all the bad things we have done.

Please help me to say 'sorry' to you, when I fail in some way.

Help me to forgive others when they hurt me; and to seek forgiveness from others when I hurt them in some way.

And enable me to forgive myself, when you have already forgiven me.

Help me to live a 'forgiven lifestyle'; and not to continually be burdened with guilt through not accepting forgiveness when it is offered, or to hold onto the bitterness of not really forgiving others.

(Include any additional topics for prayer or thanksgiving, arising from this study)

In Jesus' name.

Amen.

'Doers of the word' (aim): To make forgiveness central to our whole lives and our eternal future.

Is there anything that you think you might find difficult about achieving the aim?

The devil is at work

8th July

Temptation is a daily reality: we are surrounded by the lies and deceit of the devil – doing everything that he can to defeat the plans and purposes of God. We need to pray for protection in this spiritual battle.

'And do not bring us to the time of trial,
but rescue us from the evil one.'

(Matthew 6:13)

'My Journal':

- *Jot down a list of some of the ways in which the devil deceives, as he tries to persuade that what we are doing is okay – when it is not.*

Meditate on the knowledge that God can protect us from the work of the devil; and strengthen us when we are faced with temptation.

Almighty God.

You are in control; and you are stronger than all the powers of evil!

Thank you that we can turn to you, as we face the spiritual battle, and you will strengthen and protect us.

Please be with me today as I will face a variety of different temptations, and have to battle against opposition – and the devil will desperately be trying to prevent me from living according to your will and purposes.

Grant me the strength and knowledge of scripture to equip me not to give in to temptation.

Give me a real spirit of perseverance and resilience as I face opposition.

And help me to never turn away from striving to live according to your will and purposes.

(Include any additional topics for prayer or thanksgiving, arising from this study)

In Jesus' name.

Amen.

'Doers of the word' (aim): To look to God for his protection in the spiritual battle.

Is there anything that you think you might find difficult about achieving the aim?

God wants to bless

9th July

Sometimes we seem to think that God is reluctant to answer prayer: but the reality is that God wants to give us good gifts - it is his desire to bless us.

'How much more will your Father in heaven give good things to those who ask him!'

(Matthew 7:11b)

'My Journal':

- *Blessing does not necessarily come in materialistic ways: consider other ways in which God has blessed you, and make some notes.*

Meditate for a moment on God's desire to give us good things. You might like to draw a comparison with your desire to give good gifts to your own children, partner, friends, etc.

Generous heavenly Father.

Thank you that you love to bless us, by showering us with good gifts!

Please help me to recognise that blessings often don't mean those things that can have a monetary value placed upon them.

Instead, it is often those things that cannot be defined in monetary terms that are the greatest blessings.

Thank you for all that you have blessed me with *(give thanks for specific blessings).*

(Include any additional topics for prayer or thanksgiving, arising from this study)

In Jesus' name.

Amen.

'Doers of the word' (aim): To have the confidence to ask God to bless us and those whom we love and care about.

Is there anything that you think you might find difficult about achieving the aim?

Space for God
10th July

Jesus sets us the example of regularly making time to be still and quiet – and prayerful - in God's presence. People use the excuse, 'I am too busy.' The truth is, that the busier we are, almost, the more important it is to make that space.

And after he had dismissed the crowds, he went up into the mountain by himself to pray. When evening came, he was there alone.

(Matthew 14:23)

'My Journal':

- *Obviously, because you are reading this, you have taken some time out to spend with God. But have you been able to make a real space - to be still and quiet with God... alone? If not, can you do that now (in a responsible way) - find a quiet corner, breathe, relax and enjoy the space? How does that feel? Could this be a regular thing?*

Meditate on the fact that as well as needing time to pray, we also need time to listen to God's replies.

Heavenly Father.

You want to spend time with us.

Thank you that it is your desire to do that.

Thank you that it is your desire to spend time with me.

Please help me to be disciplined in making that space for you.

Help me to set aside time from the busyness.

Enable me to avoid the interruptions.

Show me that quiet place where I can go.

And make me listen to your replies as well as making requests in my prayer time.

(Include any additional topics for prayer or thanksgiving, arising from this study)

In Jesus' name.

Amen.

'Doers of the word' (aim): To make space for God amongst the busyness of life.

Is there anything that you think you might find difficult about achieving the aim?

The flesh is weak

11th July

Maybe you hadn't realised that the old saying, 'The spirit is willing, but the flesh is weak' are actually the words of Jesus – it is quite a profound statement, which we would do well to acknowledge and act upon.

'Stay awake and pray that you may not come into the time of trial; the spirit indeed is willing, but the flesh is weak.'

(Matthew 26:41)

'My Journal':

- *Unpick the saying, 'The spirit is willing, but the flesh is weak.' What are its implications?*

Meditate on the direct link between our own human weaknesses and the need for prayer. Consider how we could pray around this particular concept: for example, for the empowerment by the Holy Spirit, or for assistance in setting up boundaries.

Almighty God.

You are so strong!

Thank you that you want to be our strength in times of weakness.

Please help me to recognise my weaknesses; and to call on you to be my strength in all those situations.

Indeed, it is when we learn to depend on you more that we truly become strong.

Fill me afresh with the Holy Spirit.

(Include any additional topics for prayer or thanksgiving, arising from this study)

In Jesus' name.

Amen.

'Doers of the word' (aim): To be prayerfully prepared for times of human weakness.

Is there anything that you think you might find difficult about achieving the aim?

The power of prayer

12th July

There are so many occasions in the Bible when the power of prayer is illustrated in amazing and dramatic ways; including when a group of believers are praying together that God will work in powerful ways in and through them. The result is:

When they had prayed, the place in which they were gathered together was shaken.

(Acts 4:31a)

'My Journal':

- *Think about the fact that God is a powerful God, the God of miracles, and the God who answers prayer in amazing ways. Jot down any thoughts that come to mind during this time.*

Meditate on the concept of perhaps needing to pray more expectantly, for the miraculous to happen - more often than we do.

Lord.

You are a powerful God!

Thank you that prayer is powerful – and that you have given us the wonderful privilege of being able to approach you in this way.

Thank you that when we pray - things happen: positive things for the kingdom.

Please help me to pray with faith and expectation; and not to be afraid to ask for the miraculous.

Help me not to get discouraged, when you say 'no' or 'wait' or answer my prayers in a way that is completely unexpected – because you know best.

(Include any additional topics for prayer or thanksgiving, arising from this study)

In Jesus' name.

Amen.

'Doers of the word' (aim): To experience the power of prayer in all its fullness.

Is there anything that you think you might find difficult about achieving the aim?

Interceding for us

13th July

During those times when prayer seems to be hard and lacking in fluency; or when the situation is so complex or challenging that it seems impossible to know how to pray, or what outcome to pray for; then the Holy Spirit has promised to intercede on our behalf – even expressing those feelings, emotions and concepts that there are no words to express.

Likewise the Spirit helps us in our weakness; for we do not know how to pray as we ought, but that very Spirit intercedes with sighs too deep for words.

(Romans 8:26)

'My Journal':

- *We don't always know how to pray; and we shouldn't beat ourselves up about it – the Holy Spirit has it all in hand! Jot down how that makes you feel.*

Meditate on the knowledge that some things are just too deep or complicated for words to express. The Holy Spirit expresses them in 'sighs' – in other words, something spiritually so much more expressive than language.

Heavenly Father.

The Holy Spirit will intercede for us in prayer!

Thank you that when we really don't know how to express what we want to say to you, or in situations where words just don't seem enough, the Holy Spirit will intercede for us – sometimes, he will not even use words.

Please give me the confidence to allow the Holy Spirit to do this for me.

And to do that, sometimes I will have to admit that I am out of my depth.

(Include any additional topics for prayer or thanksgiving, arising from this study)

In Jesus' name.

Amen.

'Doers of the word' (aim): To experience the Holy Spirit interceding for us, when the words aren't there!

Is there anything that you think you might find difficult about achieving the aim?

Within God's will
14th July

When the Holy Spirit intercedes for us he does so knowing what is in our hearts, and with complete knowledge of the will of God.

And God, who searches the heart, knows what is the mind of the Spirit, because the Spirit intercedes for the saints according to the will of God.

(Romans 8:27)

'My Journal':

- *When the Holy Spirit intercedes for us, he is a link between our hearts and the heart of God – and as he intercedes for us, everything is in complete harmony with the will of God. Jot down your thoughts.*

Meditate on the fact that there may be times when God seems to be a long way away; but, in actual fact, the indwelling Holy Spirit, being part of the Triune God, brings God really close to us. Consider the implications: things like, when we are filled with the power of the Holy Spirit, through being in relationship with Jesus, we are never alone… and we are never left to our own devices in any situation.

Lord God.

We are filled with the indwelling Holy Spirit when we follow Jesus in faith!

Thank you for that; and please help me never to forget that fact – to never feel alone or ever feel left to my own devices.

Encourage me to allow the Holy Spirit to work fully in my life; and to be my help and strength.

Thank you that he is a link between my heart and your heart; and when he intercedes for me, he helps me to pray within your perfect will.

Please help me to be willing to allow that to happen.

(Include any additional topics for prayer or thanksgiving, arising from this study)

In Jesus' name.

Amen.

'Doers of the word' (aim): To pray in harmony with the will of God.

Is there anything that you think you might find difficult about achieving the aim?

Access to God in prayer

15th July

Through Jesus, we have access to God in prayer: we don't have to pay anything, we don't have to go through any kind of telephone exchange or call centre, and we don't have to be vetted in any way... We just need to begin speaking to God; and we have instant access to him!

In whom (Christ Jesus our Lord – verse 11) we have access to God in boldness and confidence through faith in him.

(Ephesians 3:12)

'My Journal':

- *Who is the celebrity with whom you would most like to speak: a film star, a politician, a football player, etc? How difficult would that be to organise? How does it feel knowing that, through Jesus, you can speak to the God who created everything – at any time, from any place, instantly?*

Meditate on what you need to say to God today? Maybe there is something that you have wanted to say to God for a while, but have never said it… Perhaps you have felt that he is not interested or doesn't have the time to listen. He is and he does! You might like to pray it in the prayer time.

Almighty God.

Because of Jesus we have access to you in prayer!

Thank you that we can pray to you from anywhere, at any time, and you hear us - instantly.

Please help me not to waste that opportunity.

Enable me to pray with confidence, boldness and faith – and with expectation!

(Include any additional topics for prayer or thanksgiving, arising from this study)

In Jesus' name.

Amen.

'Doers of the word' (aim): To pray with confidence, boldness and faith – and with expectation!

Is there anything that you think you might find difficult about achieving the aim?

What the Bible says about **prayer**

Pray about anything!
16th July

Paul emphasises the importance and versatility of prayer, when he instructs us to:

Pray without ceasing

(1 Thessalonians 5:17)

'My Journal':

- *For a few minutes try to form a visual image of prayers ascending to God – then sketch it in your journal. Consider the significance of being able to talk to God through prayer - from anywhere, at any time, about anything.*

Meditate on the implications of Paul's instruction to 'pray without ceasing'. Prayer is not just a once a day thing, it should be ongoing as the day progresses. And we should make everything a matter for prayer.

Almighty God.

Thank you that I can bring absolutely everything to you in prayer:

Sharing the good times, but also placing into your hands the difficult times *(bring your prayer requests)*.

Asking for the needs of others, those whom I love, and myself *(bring your prayer requests)*.

And giving thanks to you for all your goodness *(spend some time in thanksgiving)*.

Thank you that I can pray to you from anywhere at any time, and you hear me.

Please grant me the confidence and commitment to come to you in prayer on a regular basis; realising that it is a really important thing to do.

(Include any additional topics for prayer or thanksgiving, arising from this study)

In Jesus' name.

Amen.

'Doers of the word' (aim): To have the confidence to take everything to God in prayer.

Is there anything that you think you might find difficult about achieving the aim?

Listening to God's reply

17th July

A good relationship depends on dialogue: our relationship with God depends on dialogue – us proffering prayer, and then listening to God's response.

Let everyone be quick to listen, slow to speak, slow to anger.

(James 1:19b)

'My Journal':

- *James emphasises just how important it is to listen – I mean: to really listen. How good are you at listening, without interrupting what is being said? Write down some notes about what you think makes a good listener.*

Meditate on the comparison that is drawn between speaking and listening: we are urged to be quick to listen but only slow to speak. Most of us probably get that the wrong way round: that is, we are very quick to express an opinion, but much slower to listen to what others are saying to us.

Loving heavenly Father.

You are an excellent listener!

Thank you that you listen to me when I pray.

Please help me to make the time and the space to listen to you, when you reply to my prayers.

Grant me the understanding of what you say to me.

Help me to be obedient to your will.

And enable me to be patient enough to work within your timing.

(Include any additional topics for prayer or thanksgiving, arising from this study)

In Jesus' name.

Amen.

'Doers of the word' (aim): To really listen to God speaking to us.

Is there anything that you think you might find difficult about achieving the aim?

Pray for each other
18th July

James urges us to pray for each other (especially for our church families): emphasising the power of prayer; particularly in respect to healing - the implication is emotional, mental, physical and spiritual.

Therefore confess your sins to one another, and pray for one another, so that you may be healed. The prayer of the righteous is powerful and effective.

(James 5:16)

'My Journal':

- *What are your own needs for healing, and those of people around you (family, friends, neighbours, colleagues, etc.) – emotional, mental, physical or spiritual?*

Meditate on the different ways in which that healing can be experienced emotionally, mentally, physically and spiritually.

Father God.

You desire that we should pray for one another!

Thank you that prayer is powerful and effective.

Please help me to be disciplined in praying for the needs of others – especially for my church family.

And help me not to be afraid to ask others to pray for me – or to be afraid to pray for myself.

Have your healing hand upon those who suffer from ill health: emotionally, mentally, physically or spiritually.

Let them experience your healing; in whatever form that might be –according to their need.

And let me experience your healing as well *(Give details).*

(Include any additional topics for prayer or thanksgiving, arising from this study)

In Jesus' name.

Amen.

'Doers of the word' (aim): To pray for each other, and ourselves; including prayer for healing.

Is there anything that you think you might find difficult about achieving the aim?

Precious

19th July

All our prayers are so precious to God, that they are placed into golden bowls, in heaven.

When he had taken the scroll, the four living creatures and the twenty-four elders fell before the Lamb, each holding a harp and golden bowls full of incense, which are the prayers of the saints.

(Revelation 5:8)

'My Journal':

- *Consider the significance of prayer being described as incense. It gives a visual image of it rising up to heaven. There is an assurance that our prayers are not lost. They do not just disperse into nothing, as soon as they leave our mouths. They go up into heaven. Jot down your thoughts on this.*

Meditate for a few minutes on the scenario described in Revelation 5:8. Whenever you pray, your prayers go straight up to heaven, and are placed into golden bowls. This may be symbolic, but it still highlights how much God values each prayer that you utter; so much so, that he places them somewhere where they will be safe. Our prayers are so precious to God. How does that make you feel?

Lord.

You value every single prayer we say!

Thank you that none of our prayers are lost, wasted or said in vain.

Thank you that none of my prayers are lost, wasted, or said in vain: wherever I pray from and whenever I pray.

Thank you that all prayers are of equal importance.

Please help me to pray with that assurance in mind.

(Include any additional topics for prayer or thanksgiving, arising from this study)

In Jesus' name.

Amen.

'Doers of the word' (aim): To be assured that God values our prayers.

Is there anything that you think you might find difficult about achieving the aim?

Offered to God

20th July

After our prayers have been received in heaven, they are offered up to God.

Another angel with a golden censer came and stood at the altar; he was given a great quantity of incense to offer with the prayers of all the saints on the golden altar that is before the throne.

(Revelation 8:3)

'My Journal':

- *We might feel privileged to take petitions to our local MP; but how much more privileged we might feel to be able to take petitions to the PM... this verse of scripture promises that we can take our petitions to the Almighty Creator God – How amazing is that?*

Meditate on the fact that this verse gives us the affirmation that we really do have access to God, through prayer.

Almighty God.

You love to hear our prayers!

Thank you that every single prayer that we pray is presented to you in heaven; and that you listen to them, and answer them in the best way possible.

Please help me to be committed to prayer; in the confidence that it will be heard and acted upon, by you.

(Include any additional topics for prayer or thanksgiving, arising from this study)

In Jesus' name.

Amen.

'Doers of the word' (aim): To have confidence that our prayers are presented before God in heaven.

Is there anything that you think you might find difficult about achieving the aim?

11

SERVANTHOOD

Serve with all your heart and with all your soul

21st July

Joshua passes on Moses' commandment to love God, to live in obedience to him, and to serve him – with heart and soul.

'Take good care to observe the commandment and instruction that Moses the servant of the Lord commanded you, to love the Lord your God, to walk in all his ways, to keep his commandments, and to hold fast to him, and to serve him with all your heart and with all your soul."

(Joshua 22:5)

'My Journal':

- *Consider the significance of doing these things with all our hearts: bearing in mind that the heart is central to life itself, and to producing the energy to do things, but it is also associated with deep feelings – love and compassion, in particular. The words commitment and dedication come to mind. Jot down some further thoughts.*

Meditate on the significance of doing these things with all our souls: bearing in mind that the soul is associated with our connection with God, and our spiritual health. Certainly, the basis of living a lifestyle demonstrating servanthood – emulating Jesus – is being in relationship, and in a close daily walk, with the Triune God (God the Father, Jesus the Son, and the Holy Spirit).

Loving heavenly Father.

It is fitting that we should love you and, as an expression of that love, enter into lives of servanthood and obedience to you!

Thank you that you shower us with your unconditional love.

Thank you that your laws are an expression of that love.

Thank for the privilege of being able to serve you, in the work of building your kingdom.

Please help me to love, obey, and serve you – with all my heart, and with all my soul.

(Include any additional topics for prayer or thanksgiving, arising from this study)

In Jesus' name.

Amen.

'Doers of the word' (aim): To serve God with all our hearts, and with all our souls.

Is there anything that you think you might find difficult about achieving the aim?

Me and my household

22nd July

Joshua says, 'Choose.' We are absolutely free to choose whether or not to do things God's way. But look at Joshua's choice at the end of the following verse.

"Now if you are unwilling to serve the Lord, choose this day whom you will serve, whether the Gods your ancestors served in the region beyond the River or the gods of the Amorites in whose land you are living; but as for me and my household, we will serve the Lord."

(Joshua 24:15)

'My Journal':

- *What is your choice, with regards to serving God – in the context, not just of servanthood, but also in terms of total commitment? Remember that there are only two real options: either we serve God completely, or we don't.*

Meditate on what it means, and how it applies to your own situation, when Joshua says, 'As for me and my household, we will serve the Lord'? To what extent do you think it is about using our Christian influence in the home?

Lord.

You give us the opportunity to influence others in our homes, neighbourhoods or work places!

Thank you that we can make a positive difference in those situations, influencing others to do things your way.

Please let me choose to serve you completely; and let my lifestyle reflect that – and help me to be a witness and example to others... especially in my home.

(Include any additional topics for prayer or thanksgiving, arising from this study)

In Jesus' name.

Amen.

'Doers of the word' (aim): To choose to serve the Lord, completely – and to be a good example and influence on others... especially those in the home.

Is there anything that you think you might find difficult about achieving the aim?

I delight to do your will

23rd July

It is easy to have the mind-set that obeying any kind of rules or laws is a chore; but the psalmist speaks about delighting to live according to the will of God, and that God's law is written within his heart.

'I delight to do your will, O my God;
Your law is within my heart.'

(Psalm 40:8)

'My Journal':

- *When we are in a close relationship with someone, generally, we want to share things in common with them – and do things that will please. How does this relate to your relationship with God and delighting to do his will – serving him?*

Meditate on this. When we enter into a personal relationship with Jesus, we are filled with the power of the indwelling Holy Spirit, and reunited with God the Father. The Holy Spirit guides and empowers us to live in obedience to the Father, and to progressively become more Christ like. Using this image, visualise the Holy Spirit metaphorically writing God's law within our hearts.

Heavenly Father.

Your will be done!

Thank you that you have given us your law as a way of revealing your will to us.

Thank you that your law is for our wellbeing; and so that your plans and purposes might be fulfilled.

Thank you for the work of the Holy Spirit.

Please let the Holy Spirit write your law within my heart, and help me to live in obedience to it.

Help me as I seek to serve you: give me a real delight in doing your will.

(Include any additional topics for prayer or thanksgiving, arising from this study)

In Jesus' name.

Amen.

'Doers of the word' (aim): To delight in living according to the will of God.

Is there anything that you think you might find difficult about achieving the aim?

What the Bible says about **servanthood**

Jesus is our example
24th July

We may struggle to be good servants, but Jesus is our perfect example. It was always God's plan that Jesus should take on the nature of a servant at his first coming – born in an animal shelter, that very first Christmas. Isaiah reveals that fact to us, when he speaks about the suffering servant – Jesus.

See, my servant shall prosper;
he shall be exalted and lifted up,
and shall be very high.

(Isaiah 52:13)

'My Journal':

- *As we read about the life, death and resurrection of Jesus, in the gospels, it all speaks of humility, selflessness and suffering – a life of service... serving God, in serving humankind. Such love! Think about that depth of unconditional love for others; and write down your thoughts.*

Meditate on the significance of the various descriptive references to the life of Jesus, in this verse from Isaiah: referring to the nature of his life, his death on the cross, and subsequent resurrection and ascension.

Almighty God.

It was always your plan that Jesus should live a life of servanthood on earth!

Thank you for his demonstration of humility, selflessness and the acceptance of suffering, in order that your greater plans and purposes should be achieved:

Through being lifted up onto the cross - dying to pay the penalty for our sin, rising on the third day, and ascending into heaven – Jesus has been exalted, and has made it possible for us to invest in heavenly treasure and prosperity.

Please help me to have a close daily walk with Jesus, based on my personal relationship with him.

And empower me through the Holy Spirit to follow Jesus' example in being a servant.

(Include any additional topics for prayer or thanksgiving, arising from this study)

In Jesus' name.

Amen.

'Doers of the word' (aim): To understand that servanthood was part of God's plan for Jesus' life on earth, and for our lives on earth; and, as such, that we should follow Jesus' example in serving others.

Is there anything that you think you might find difficult about achieving the aim?

What the Bible says about **servanthood**

The dry ground
25th July

Isaiah gives us an image of Jesus being like a plant growing in the desert: in a spiritual desert. In other words, the mission of Jesus is to bring spiritual life and refreshment to a world that is spiritually barren. And the calling of Jesus' followers to the servant lifestyle is about facilitating others to discover that spiritual life in Jesus.

For he grew up before him like a young plant,
and like a root out of dry ground;
he had no form or majesty that we should look at him,
nothing in his appearance that we should desire him.

(Isaiah 53:2)

'My Journal':

- *Let us note that the implication of this verse is that there is no other source of spiritual nourishment and refreshment available, apart from Jesus. What are the implications to that concept?*

Meditate on the different references made to Jesus' appearance and their implications. As we read the gospels, we understand that Jesus is nearly always surrounded by crowds of people flocking to him for different reasons: something other than physical beauty must be attracting them: things like Jesus' love, compassion, kindness, generosity and the hope that he spreads.

Lord Jesus.

You are the way!

Thank you that you are the way to experience spiritual life and refreshment, in a spiritually barren world.

Please help me to walk closer to you daily; and benefit from that spiritual life and refreshment.

Equip me to facilitate others to discover you in that way.

Thank you that you demonstrate those qualities of beauty that are of real value: things like love, compassion, kindness, generosity and hope.

In a world that is in many ways quite superficial in its judgements, help me to recognise the importance of those qualities evident in your life, and to demonstrate them in my own life.

In your name.

Amen.

'Doers of the word' (aim): To be spiritually nourished and refreshed through a close walk with Jesus; and to demonstrate in our own lives those qualities of inner beauty.

Is there anything that you think you might find difficult about achieving the aim?

Suffering servant

26th July

Serving God, in serving others, doesn't necessarily lead to being accepted or achieve popularity within society. Jesus' life demonstrates that – the suffering servant.

He was despised and rejected by others;
a man of suffering and acquainted with infirmity;
and as one from who others hide their faces
he was despised, and we held him of no account.

(Isaiah 53:3)

'My Journal':

- *The age old question is: Why suffering? During his life, and in his death on the cross, Jesus experiences horrendous suffering; so why do we think that we should be exempt? Prayerfully consider that concept; and jot down anything that God reveals to you.*

Meditate on the fact that as so much detail is contained in the books of the prophets about the life, death, resurrection and second coming of Jesus it would seem to confirm that this is all part of God's amazing, eternal plan. The suffering of Jesus is for the greater good of humankind. Does that alter your view of suffering?

Lord Jesus.

We probably all struggle with the issue of suffering!

Thank you that you suffered and died on the cross, paying the penalty for sin – so that we can all be forgiven, and filled with eternal hope, through a personal relationship with you.

Please help me to endure times of suffering that I meet with in my life; in whatever capacity that might be.

And, where possible, let there be some greater good come from that experience – even if I don't understand what it might be.

Help me to never reject you, in any way.

(Include any additional topics for prayer or thanksgiving, arising from this study)

In your name.

Amen.

'Doers of the word' (aim): To accept that there will be times of suffering, when journeying through the Christian life of servanthood; and not to reject Jesus, as a result.

Is there anything that you think you might find difficult about achieving the aim?

Uniquely equipped to serve

27th July

In one of the parables that Jesus tells, he highlights the fact that everyone of us are given a unique selection of talents and abilities to be used in his service – for the benefit of others.

'For it is as if a man, going on a journey, summoned his slaves and entrusted his property to them; to one he gave five talents, to another two, to another one, to each according to his ability. Then he went away.'

(Matthew 25:14-15)

'My Journal':

- *What talents and abilities do you possess? Make a list. If you struggle to discern this, ask a friend or family member to help. Don't forget those abilities that might easily be overlooked: things like, offering hospitality, doing administration, having practical skills to mend and repair, being an encourager, or having good listening skills.*

Meditate on whether or not you are using those talents and abilities, as you seek to serve Jesus? Prayerfully ask God to reveal any additional ways in which you could use them... or maybe even to reveal talents and abilities to use, that you are not even aware you possess.

Almighty God.

You created us all, in all our uniqueness!

Thank you that you created me with a selection of talents and abilities which I can use in your service.

Please help me to value that combination of skills that makes me completely unique; and encourage me to value this quality in others as well.

Help me to offer those skills up to you to be anointed, as I use them in your service.

Reveal to me, any talents or abilities that I have never used before, and maybe don't even realise that I possess – and give me the confidence to bring them out into the open and begin to use them.

(Include any additional topics for prayer or thanksgiving, arising from this study)

In Jesus' name.

Amen.

'Doers of the word' (aim): To recognise and use our unique combination of talents and abilities, in serving Jesus.

Is there anything that you think you might find difficult about achieving the aim?

What the Bible says about **servanthood**

Accountability
28th July

There will be a time when we are called to account as to how we have used the talents and abilities – and various other resources - that we have been blessed with.

'After a long time the master of those slaves came and settled accounts with them.'

(Matthew 25:19)

'My Journal':

- *Look back at your list of talents and abilities that you wrote yesterday. What would you say about the way in which you have used each of them? Would there be any that you would admit to having wasted?*

Meditate on how you might feel if Jesus returned today, and called you to account? Would there be any regrets; or feelings of 'I wish…'? - Especially with respect to your use of time.

Lord Jesus.

You will return one day!

Thank you for those resources that you have entrusted me with: please help me to not waste them.

Grant me the courage to explore and use all the talents and abilities that you have blessed me with – so I will not be left with feelings of regret.

And guide me in the way that I use other resources you have given to me.

Help me not to repeatedly put off serving you until tomorrow!

(Include any additional topics for prayer or thanksgiving, arising from this study)

In your name.

Amen.

'Doers of the word' (aim): To use our unique selection of talents and abilities (and other resources) as fully as we possibly can.

Is there anything that you think you might find difficult about achieving the aim?

What the Bible says about **servanthood**

Using our talents and abilities for God

29th July

Using our talents and abilities, investing them in living a life of Christian service, will develop and increase them – allowing us to achieve even more, in terms of serving Jesus.

'For to all those who have, more will be given, and they will have an abundance; but from those who have nothing, even what they have will be taken away.'

(Matthew 25:29)

'My Journal':

- *Consider the well-known concept that the more talents or abilities are exercised, the more they develop; and then apply it to your talents and abilities. What conclusions do you come to?*

Meditate on what ways you could be using your talents and abilities more – perhaps with the guidance of a specialist instructor – in order to experience an increase in them? How you could plan to achieve this aim?

Lord God.

You have blessed us all with a unique combination of talents and abilities; and ordained that the more we invest them into our Christian lives of service, the more they will increase.

Thank you for the talents and abilities that I have.

Please help me to use them well.

Grant me the discipline to exercise those talents and abilities in regular service to you – and to prepare and practice as appropriate.

And let me experience that development as a result.

(Include any additional topics for prayer or thanksgiving, arising from this study)

In Jesus' name.

Amen.

'Doers of the word' (aim): To offer our talents up to Jesus; to invest them in Christian service; and to enjoy experiencing an increase.

Is there anything that you think you might find difficult about achieving the aim?

As if we did it for Jesus himself

30th July

Jesus emphasises that whenever we do something good for each other – a simple act of kindness – it is as if we are doing it for him. Equally so, if we miss an opportunity to perform a good deed for someone else, it is as if we have missed an opportunity to perform a good deed for him.

"'For I was hungry and you gave me food, I was thirsty and you gave me something to drink, I was a stranger and you welcomed me, I was naked and you gave me clothing, I was sick and you took care of me, I was in prison and you visited me."'

(Matthew 25:35-36)

'My Journal':

- *Consider the gratitude we feel when someone demonstrates kindness towards another who we are close to: to a good friend or to a family member. Compare this with what Jesus is saying in this verse... but even more so. Make some notes on your thoughts about Jesus' response.*

Meditate on the concept that every time we perform an act of kindness towards another, it is as if we do it for Jesus himself. Will that encourage you to do more? What is your response?

Lord Jesus.

It's as if we have performed that act of kindness for you!

Thank you for those opportunities you set before us, to demonstrate acts of love towards others: opportunities to help them in some way.

Please help me to be willing and decisive enough to take up those opportunities – to do those good deeds as if for you.

(Include any additional topics for prayer or thanksgiving, arising from this study)

In your name.

Amen.

'Doers of the word' (aim): To serve Jesus by serving others.

Is there anything that you think you might find difficult about achieving the aim?

Sharing in everything we do
31st July

We can still be lonely in a crowd, when we are not connecting with anyone. When Jesus promises to be with everyone who follows him, he means that he will share in every experience with us: happiness, sadness, achievement, failure, making a friend, losing a friend, etc.

'And remember, I am with you always, to the end of the age.'

(Matthew 28:20b)

'My Journal':

- *Loneliness can be down to us not allowing other people into our lives: the same principle can apply to our spiritual lives. Jesus wants to be involved with every area of our lives! Make a list of the main ones.*

Meditate on to what extent you actually allow Jesus to participate in your daily activities and share in your feelings. Prayerfully listen to what he reveals to you, and the plan of action.

Lord Jesus.

You will be with me always – if I am prepared to let you into all the areas of my life!

Thank you for the wonderful promise that you will never leave me; but please help me to involve you in everything:

My family life.

My work life.

My social life.

My church life.

The choices and decisions that I make.

The plans that I prepare.

And in all the feelings I experience.

(Include any additional topics for prayer or thanksgiving, arising from this study)

In your name.

Amen.

'Doers of the word' (aim): To include Jesus in everything that we say, do and feel.

Is there anything that you think you might find difficult about achieving the aim?

What the Bible says about **servanthood**

Jesus sets us the example of serving

1st August

Having journeyed by foot – walking on dusty roads, wearing open sandals – I can imagine that it would be quite nice to have your feet washed and dried by a servant... but it is probably not the most enviable task! A true demonstration of servanthood.

Then he (Jesus) poured water into a basin and began to wash the disciples' feet and to wipe them with the towel that was tied around him.

(John 13:5)

'My Journal':

- *You might like to imagine yourself sitting in a comfortable arm chair, with your feet in a bowl of warm soapy water – and someone is gently washing them with a soft sponge. How would you feel if that person was Jesus – God's only Son?*

Meditate on how you might feel if, moments before, you had said, 'You needn't think I am going to wash anyone's dirty feet'. - A little bit guilty, maybe.

Lord Jesus.

You were prepared to wash dirty feet!

Thank you that you love us so much that you took on the nature of a servant – being totally selfless in all respects, including giving your life on the cross, paying the penalty for our sin – so that you might make it possible for us to be forgiven and filled with eternal hope.

Please help me to recognise and value the cost to you; and how privileged I am, to be able to enter into a personal relationship with you… and be spiritually washed clean of my sin.

Grant me faith.

Nurture me to walk closer to you each day – and know you as my risen Lord and Saviour.

(Include any additional topics for prayer or thanksgiving, arising from this study)

In your name.

Amen.

'Doers of the word' (aim): To recognise and respond to Jesus demonstrating the nature of servanthood – and offering spiritual cleansing.

Is there anything that you think you might find difficult about achieving the aim?

Washing each other's feet

2nd August

Jesus calls us, his followers, to emulate him in taking on the nature of servanthood and living it out in our daily lives - metaphorically washing other people's feet.

So if I, your Lord and teacher, have washed your feet, you also ought to wash one another's feet.

(John 13:14)

'My Journal':

- *This time, imagine yourself kneeling on the floor, with someone else's feet in a bowl of warm soapy water – and you are gently washing them with a soft sponge. How would you feel?*

Meditate in the knowledge that service comes in many different forms – according to our abilities, age, health, etc. Consider what you can do to serve others.

Lord Jesus.

You took on the nature of servanthood!

Thank you for doing that for us; and for setting us the example of how we should live our lives.

Please help me to follow that example, as I serve others.

Show me the ways in which I can do this.

And empower me to put this into practice in my own life.

(Include any additional topics for prayer or thanksgiving, arising from this study)

In your name.

Amen.

'Doers of the word' (aim): To emulate Jesus, as we follow his example of servanthood.

Is there anything that you think you might find difficult about achieving the aim?

What the Bible says about **servanthood**

A slave to everyone

3rd August

Slave is quite a strong word, so the connotations in 1 Corinthians 9:19 are of a very selfless form of servanthood – putting the needs of others significantly above those of ourselves – something to which we should aspire.

For though I am free with respect to all, I have made myself a slave to all, so that I might win more of them.

(1 Corinthians 9:19)

'My Journal':

- *List some of the qualities that you associate with selflessness; and include some hypothetical situations involving the outworking of those qualities.*

Meditate on Paul's reference to being free, in this verse. He seems to be referring to not being beholden to anyone – except for God, of course.

Father God.

You long to see people coming into your kingdom!

Thank you for the privilege of being called to be part of that process of winning people over to you.

Please help me, like Paul, to be willing to be a slave to all, for that purpose... In the context of demonstrating such qualities as self-lessness.

Help me to aspire to that level of servanthood; and grant me the empowerment through the Holy Spirit to be a good witness – in every way.

(Include any additional topics for prayer or thanksgiving, arising from this study)

In Jesus' name.

Amen.

'Doers of the word' (aim): To be a slave to all, in the same context as Paul is describing – a deeper level of servanthood.

Is there anything that you think you might find difficult about achieving the aim?

With God, nothing is in vain

4th August

It is easy to feel that, as we seek to serve God, our efforts are sometimes wasted: to feel that nobody notices, nobody cares, or nobody responds. But Paul reassures us that nothing we do for God is ever in vain.

Therefore, my beloved, be steadfast, immovable, always excelling in the work of the Lord, because you know that in the Lord your labour is not in vain.

(1 Corinthians 15:58)

'My Journal':

- *Consider the significance of Paul's words of encouragement in this verse; when he speaks about being 'steadfast, immovable' and 'always excelling in the work of the Lord'. He certainly seems to be saying that we should not give up or be discouraged – instead we should persevere in serving. What are your thoughts?*

Meditate on the significance of Paul's words of assurance in this verse; when he says, 'Your labour is not in vain.' Consider with reference to things like, witnessing, simple acts of love and kindness, encouraging and being a good listener.

Lord.

Nothing that we do for you is in vain!

Thank you that when we include you in everything that we do, you bless people as a result.

Please help me to understand that sometimes I don't see the results of the things I do for you; but that doesn't mean nothing has happened in terms of helping to build your kingdom – a life has been touched in some way with your love.

When I am really busy serving you – or in my eagerness to serve you – don't let me forget to make time to pray; offering my service up to you.

(Include any additional topics for prayer or thanksgiving, arising from this study)

In Jesus' name.

Amen.

'Doers of the word' (aim): To persevere in serving God, in the knowledge that it will not be in vain.

Is there anything that you think you might find difficult about achieving the aim?

What the Bible says about **servanthood**

Do it in love
5th August

Paul is adamant that everything thing we say and do should be motivated by Christ like love… Absolutely everything!

Let all that you do be done in love.

(1 Corinthians 16:14)

'My Journal':

- *There are all kinds of possible motives behind what we do – 'I have to...' 'I ought to...' 'I need to...' 'If I don't do it, no-one else will...' - but love probably isn't always one of them. Sometimes we do things more out of a sense of duty or having to do them. Jot some related thoughts down for prayer.*

Meditate on the unconditional love of God: the nature of unconditional love; and what is means to give love when it is not necessarily returned.

Loving heavenly Father.

You shower us with your unconditional love – all the time!

Thank you that, even though we don't deserve your love, and many people don't return it either, you still pour your love into our lives.

Please help me to understand the nature of your love; even if my historical experience of family love has been lacking.

Let the motivation for everything that I say and do be love.

Fill me with your love to share with others – even when it is not returned.

(Include any additional topics for prayer or thanksgiving, arising from this study)

In Jesus' name.

Amen.

'Doers of the word' (aim): To do everything with the motivation of Christ like love – that includes what we say, as well!

Is there anything that you think you might find difficult about achieving the aim?

Proclaiming Jesus

6th August

Who should get the glory for those acts of kindness we perform? Who is our Christian service all about? To whom should we be signposting through our lives of servanthood? Paul makes it quite clear: it is all about Jesus!

For we do not proclaim ourselves; we proclaim Jesus Christ as Lord and ourselves as your slaves for Jesus' sake.

(2 Corinthians 4:5)

'My Journal':

- *We should be acting as signposts pointing others towards Jesus, because it is God's desire to see people entering into an eternal relationship of incredible blessing, with the Triune God – and it should be our desire as well. How is that achieved?*

Meditate on the fact that Jesus gave his all for us; so we should be prepared to give our all for the benefit of others. Jesus calls us to point them in the direction of receiving salvation, through him – so that they might be forgiven and set free from the consequences of sin.

Risen Lord Jesus.

It is through you that we can receive salvation!

Thank you that you gave your life on the cross, paying the penalty for sin, and rose again, making salvation available to us all – through entering into a personal relationship with you.

Please help me to give sacrificially as I seek to serve you.

Anoint all that I do through the power of the Holy Spirit.

Let me always signpost others towards you, and give God the glory.

But let me be gracious enough to accept appreciation from those with whom I share your love.

(Include any additional topics for prayer or thanksgiving, arising from this study)

In your name.

Amen.

'Doers of the word' (aim): To proclaim Jesus Christ as Lord.

Is there anything that you think you might find difficult about achieving the aim?

Our reward will come

7th August

Let's not forget that, apart from the blessings we receive here on earth, as a result of following Jesus, our eternal reward is the ultimate reward – it does not get any better than that!

Since you know that from the Lord you will receive the inheritance as your reward; you serve the Lord Christ.

(Colossians 3:24)

'My Journal':

- *Think about the 'inheritance' that Paul speaks about. What do you imagine God's heavenly kingdom will be like? There are numerous references in scripture (e.g. Isaiah 25:6-8). It's certainly going to be really good!*

Meditate in the knowledge that in the world as we know it, we are regularly subjected to temptation and the influence of evil… But in God's heavenly kingdom all that will have gone! Think about what that will be like.

Lord Jesus Christ.

Through following you, we inherit the ultimate reward – eternal life in your wonderful heavenly kingdom!

Thank you for making it possible for us to receive the reward that cannot get any better – through following you.

Please help me to be truly committed to being in relationship with you, to following you, and to serving you.

Thank you for all the blessings that you shower upon us in the here and now.

Please help me to always remember to give thanks to you.

(Include any additional topics for prayer or thanksgiving, arising from this study)

In your name.

Amen.

'Doers of the word' (aim): To have the assurance that there will be a wonderful eternal reward for those who follow Jesus.

Is there anything that you think you might find difficult about achieving the aim?

Faith and works

8th August

'Faith without works' is not about earning our way into the kingdom; it is about the evidence of our faith in Jesus being expressed in a life-style demonstrating faith in action.

But someone will say, 'You have faith and I have works.' Show me your faith without works, and I by my works will show you my faith.

(James 2:18)

'My Journal':

- *We cannot be in a relationship with Jesus, based on repentance and in faith, filled with the power of the indwelling Holy Spirit, and not have the drive and motivation to go out and live lives of practical love, compassion and witness – that is the evidence of our faith. Prayerfully consider that; and jot down any thoughts that come to your mind.*

Meditate on the fact that a major part of our witness is how we behave.

Lord Jesus.

Salvation is a free gift from you!

Thank you that we do not need to earn salvation: but we receive it as a result of entering into a personal relationship with you – based on repentance and faith.

Please let that evidence of my faith be seen by others as a witness.

(Include any additional topics for prayer or thanksgiving, arising from this study)

In your name.

Amen.

'Doers of the word' (aim): To live the kind of life that is evidence of our faith in Jesus.

Is there anything that you think you might find difficult about achieving the aim?

Be holy!

9th August

Holiness is not something we speak much about these days – probably not even in the Church. But it is so fundamental to the Christian faith, because holiness is referring to living according to the values of God – it's about not sinning. God instructs us to aspire to holiness.

Instead, as he who called you is holy, be holy yourselves in all your conduct; for it is written, 'You shall be holy, for I am holy.'

(1 Peter 1:15-16)

'My Journal':

- *What does holiness mean to you, in practical terms?*

Meditate for a few minutes on the holiness of the Triune God (God the Father, Jesus the Son, and the Holy Spirit). Be in awe of him and hold him in reverence.

Almighty God.

You are holy!

Thank you that the Bible is full of teaching about how we can live a more holy lifestyle.

Thank you that we have the example of Jesus to follow.

Thank you that when we are in relationship with Jesus, we are filled with the power of the indwelling Holy Spirit.

Please help me to aspire to holiness: in particular, help me to overcome the temptation to continue any areas of ongoing sin, in my life.

Fill me afresh with the Holy Spirit.

Enable me to be a good example to others.

(Include any additional topics for prayer or thanksgiving, arising from this study)

In Jesus' name.

Amen.

'Doers of the word' (aim): To aspire to being holy.

Is there anything that you think you might find difficult about achieving the aim?

What the Bible says about **servanthood**

Be noticed for the right reasons

10th August

What kind of people do we tend to notice in a crowd? Often those who are behaving badly: being rowdy, using bad language, throwing things, breaking windows, etc. As Christians, we should be noticed by others, but for the right reasons.

Conduct yourselves honourably among the Gentiles, so that, though they malign you as evildoers, they may see your honourable deeds and glorify God when he comes to judge.

(1 Peter 2:12)

'My Journal':

- *Think about a time when you were noticed for the wrong reason – it might have been a long time ago, or very recently. How do you feel about it now?*

Meditate on a time when you were noticed for an act of kindness; and how different it felt.

Lord Jesus.

During your life on earth you were always being noticed – for the right reasons.

Thank you that we are able to look at your life on earth, in the scriptures; and learn so much from your amazing example to us.

Please fill me with your love to share with others.

Give me your compassion for those in need.

And help me to perform acts of kindness as a witness.

Let me be noticed for the right reasons – and glorify God.

(Include any additional topics for prayer or thanksgiving, arising from this study)

In your name.

Amen.

'Doers of the word' (aim): To be noticed for the right reasons; as a witness to others.

Is there anything that you think you might find difficult about achieving the aim?

12

THE KINGDOM

What the Bible says about **the Kingdom**

The Kingdom is near

11th August

There should be a sense of urgency to proclaim the good news: that Jesus can set us free from the eternal consequences of sin – because the kingdom is close.

'As you go, proclaim the good news, "The kingdom of heaven has come near."'

(Matthew 10:7)

'My Journal':

- *What might you say to others about your own personal experience of Jesus?*

Meditate on the wording 'as you go'. It suggests living with an ongoing attitude of telling others about Jesus – chatting the gospel. Prayerfully consider how, when and where you are able to do this: for example, opportunities to do this in the home, amongst the extended family, with friends, in your neighbourhoods or amongst work colleagues. The kingdom is near!

Loving heavenly Father.

You want us to tell others about Jesus!

Thank you that through Jesus' life, death and resurrection we have a message of eternal hope to experience ourselves and to share with others – Good News! Brilliant News!

Thank you that the kingdom is near.

Please give me the boldness and confidence to chat the gospel with others.

Help me to make use of the opportunities you set before me.

Fill me afresh with the power of the Holy Spirit; and give me the right words to say – and the actions to go with it.

(Include any additional topics for prayer or thanksgiving, arising from this study)

In Jesus' name.

Amen.

'Doers of the word' (aim): To excitedly tell others about Jesus – as we go - and with a sense of urgency. The kingdom is near!

Is there anything that you think you might find difficult about achieving the aim?

The kingdom will be big!

12th August

Jesus speaks about the kingdom beginning small, but spreading quickly – growing to an unimaginable size. Such growth comes only from God!

He put before them another parable: 'The kingdom of heaven is like a mustard seed that someone took and sowed in his field; it is the smallest of all the seeds, but when it has grown it is the greatest of shrubs and becomes a tree, so that the birds of the air come and make nests in its branches.'

(Matthew 13:31-32)

'My Journal':

- *Even without modern technology, the early Church spread across the world quickly. I was going to say: despite the resistance and opposition - but sometimes persecution motivates. Jot your thoughts down on how that might be the case in today's world.*

Meditate on the fact that Jesus' parable speaks not only about the amount of growth, but also about the strength of what grows – strong enough for the birds to sit on the branches. Consider the strengths of the kingdom: things like, Jesus has already won the victory over sin and evil, the kingdom is based on things like love and honesty, and the Holy Spirit is at work in and through us - Jesus' followers.

Loving heavenly Father.

Your kingdom is big and strong; and it will get bigger!

Thank you that Jesus has already won the victory over sin and evil, through his death on the cross – and resurrection.

Thank you that the kingdom is based on good and lasting values like unconditional love and honesty.

Thank you that the Holy Spirit is at work in and through us – and throughout your kingdom – preparing the way; and guiding and strengthening all of us who follow Jesus.

Please fill me afresh with the power of the Holy Spirit; and help me to play my part in making the kingdom bigger.

Give me a real vision to see the kingdom grow.

(Include any additional topics for prayer or thanksgiving, arising from this study)

In Jesus' name.

Amen.

'Doers of the word' (aim): To help to build the kingdom.

Is there anything that you think you might find difficult about achieving the aim?

The kingdom is the most valuable treasure we could ever gain

13th August

Jesus compares entry into the kingdom with a really valuable treasure: so sought after, that it is worth selling everything, in order to be able to obtain it.

'The kingdom of heaven is like treasure hidden in a field, which someone found and hid; then in his joy he goes and sells all that he has and buys that field.'

(Matthew 13:44)

'My Journal':

- *In this verse, Jesus is saying that our greatest ambition in life should be to gain entry into the kingdom – even if it means sacrificing other more self-centred ambitions. What are your thoughts?*

Meditate on whether or not there is anything in your life that is preventing you from achieving that ambition of entering into the kingdom – or of fully committing to kingdom life. We have to get our priorities right - with God at the top.

Almighty God.

Entry into your kingdom is the most valuable treasure that we could ever acquire!

Thank you that, through our relationships with Jesus, we gain entry into the kingdom.

Please help me to be fully committed to Jesus, the kingdom, and living the kingdom life.

Teach me to get my priorities right – with you at the top.

Grant me the strength of will-power to work out those priorities in practical terms.

Help me to share that priceless treasure with others; by encouraging them to come to know Jesus as their Lord and Saviour.

(Include any additional topics for prayer or thanksgiving, arising from this study)

In Jesus' name.

Amen.

'Doers of the word' (aim): To fully commit to being part of God's kingdom.

Is there anything that you think you might find difficult about achieving the aim?

There is such beauty in the kingdom
14th August

In his parable about a pearl of intense beauty, Jesus describes the nature of the kingdom. None of the kingdoms of this world could come anywhere close to matching the qualities of beauty experienced in God's heavenly kingdom.

'Again the kingdom of heaven is like a merchant in search of fine pearls; on finding one pearl of great value, he went and sold all that he had and bought it.'

(Matthew 13:45-46)

'My Journal':

- *Consider the beauty and wonder of God's creation: things like the intricate beauty of the flowers, trees and shrubs; the complex workings of the body; and the power of nature seen in things like the wind and waves. Make a list of those things that stand out to you.*

Meditate on the qualities associated with inner beauty, demonstrated in the life of someone who had a great influence on your upbringing – similar qualities to those that we see in God himself - things like love, kindness, peace-making, forgiveness, encouragement and generosity.

Almighty God.

Your kingdom is intensely beautiful!

Thank you for the beauty and wonder of your creation – a taster of what is to come.

Thank you that as followers of Jesus we can experience the beauty of your kingdom, in part now, but in full when Jesus returns.

Please help me to walk close to Jesus daily, and, as a result, experience the kingdom.

Help me to experience the things of inner beauty that are so important in the kingdom; and empower me, through the Holy Spirit, to emulate those same qualities of inner beauty in my life – those things that we see so clearly in the life and teaching of Jesus.

When Jesus returns, let me experience your kingdom in all its fullness and beauty.

In his name.

Amen.

'Doers of the word' (aim): To experience the beauty of God's kingdom, in part now, but in full when Jesus returns – through our relationship with him.

Is there anything that you think you might find difficult about achieving the aim?

Enter the kingdom like a child

15th August

To fully understand what Jesus means when he speaks about being like a child, in order to enter the kingdom, we need to differentiate between being childish, and childlike.

He called a child, whom he put among them, and said, 'Truly I tell you, unless you change and become like children, you will never enter the kingdom of heaven.'

(Matthew 18:2-3)

'My Journal':

- *What does it mean to be 'childish' – and there is no harm in being a little bit childish sometimes, even in later life.*

Meditate, in contrast, on what are 'child like' qualities. Things like, unquestioning trust, simple belief, and seeing things in an uncomplicated way come to mind.

Lord.

You don't mind us being a little childish sometimes; but what you really want is for us to be childlike!

Thank you that, when we approach Jesus with those childlike qualities of trust, belief and accepting things in an uncomplicated way, we enter into your kingdom.

Please help me to be a bit more childish sometimes; because I can be very serious about things.

But, most of all, I want to be childlike in my faith.

(Include any additional topics for prayer or thanksgiving, arising from this study)

In Jesus' name.

Amen.

'Doers of the word' (aim): To enter into the kingdom as a child.

Is there anything that you think you might find difficult about achieving the aim?

Wealth can be a problem

16th August

It would appear that the main problem which wealth poses, with regards to entering into the kingdom, isn't so much concerned with having money and possessions, it's more about what our attitude might be towards them. The love of money is a barrier!

'Again I tell you, it is easier for a camel to go through the eye of a needle than for someone who is rich to enter the kingdom of God.'

(Matthew 19:24)

'My Journal':

- *Making money can become the only focus in life; it can lead to becoming very selfish; it can lead to dishonesty; and money and possessions can end up in becoming more like a god. Make some notes on why you think this is a barrier with regards to entering the kingdom.*

Meditate on the analogy here. There is some debate as to whether or not the reference of the camel and the eye of the needle is meant to be taken literally or not. But let's not worry too much about that: the gist is, Jesus is highlighting that it is extremely difficult, or even an impossible task to do – just so, for someone who is rich to enter into the kingdom of God. But a couple of verses later Jesus tells us that with God 'all things are possible'. Consider how we can use wealth and possessions in ways that are glorifying to God – with his help.

Lord Jesus.

Wealth can make it very difficult for us to really connect with you!

Thank you for your ongoing provision to us.

Thank you that, with God, all things are possible.

Please help me to have a healthy attitude towards wealth and possessions: whether it be in acquiring them or in possessing them.

Help me to use the resources, with which I have been blessed, in ways that are glorifying to you – with your guidance.

In your name.

Amen.

'Doers of the word' (aim): To use any wealth that we possess in ways that are glorifying to God; and even if we haven't any, sometimes the desire for wealth can be a problem, that needs dealing with!

Is there anything that you think you might find difficult about achieving the aim?

What the Bible says about **the Kingdom**

17th August

Telling the story

Once more Jesus spoke to them in parables, saying: 'The kingdom of heaven may be compared to a king who gave a wedding banquet for his son. He sent his slaves to call those who had been invited to the wedding banquet, but they would not come. Again he sent other slaves, saying, "Tell those who have been invited: Look, I have prepared my dinner, my oxen and my fat calves have been slaughtered, and everything is ready; come to the wedding banquet." But they made light of it and went away, one to his farm, another to his business, while the rest seized his slaves, maltreated them, and killed them.

The king was enraged. He sent his troops, destroyed those murderers, and burned their city. Then he said to his slaves, "The wedding is ready, but those invited were not worthy. Go therefore into the main streets, and invite everyone you find to the wedding banquet." Those slaves went out into the streets and gathered all whom they found, both good and bad; so the wedding hall was filled with guests.

But when the king came in to see the guests, he noticed a man there who was not wearing a wedding robe, and he said to him, "Friend, how did you get in here without a wedding robe?" And he was speechless. Then the king said to the attendants, "Bind him hand and foot, and throw him into the outer darkness, where there will be weeping and gnashing of teeth." For many are called, but few are chosen.'

(Matthew 22:1-14)

…to be looked at over the next seven days.

Lord God.
Thank you for the truth of scripture, and that it is relevant to every generation.
Thank you for this passage of scripture that speaks about the kingdom.
Please help me to understand what I have just read; and to meditate upon it daily.
(Include any additional topics for prayer or thanksgiving, arising from this study)
In Jesus' name.
Amen.

Like a wonderful banquet!

18th August

The kingdom is compared with a great banquet on numerous occasions in the Bible: amazing food and drink – the opportunity to be spiritually nourished and refreshed by God, in his eternal kingdom.

'The kingdom of heaven may be compared to a king who gave a wedding banquet for his son.'

(Matthew 22:2)

'My Journal':

- *Think about an amazing meal that you have enjoyed with family or friends, at some point in your life – it could have been at a wedding. Consider the whole experience, including the choice of good food and drink, the fellowship enjoyed with other guests, and having your hunger and thirst satisfied. Meditate on this in a spiritual context; and jot some notes down on your thoughts.*

Meditate on the fact that the feast has been prepared for you! Consider the love that has been put into its preparation. Realise that we can enter into the kingdom here and now, experiencing it in part to start with; but when Jesus returns, we will experience the kingdom in all its fullness, for eternity.

Almighty God.

You have prepared a spiritual banquet for us all: full of good things, to nourish and refresh for eternity!

Thank you that, through having a personal relationship with Jesus, we can all enjoy and benefit from those things – the offer is open to everyone.

Please help me to walk very closely with Jesus on a daily basis.

(Include any additional topics for prayer or thanksgiving, arising from this study)

In Jesus' name.

Amen.

'Doers of the word' (aim): To enjoy and benefit from that which God has prepared for us.

Is there anything that you think you might find difficult about achieving the aim?

Refusing your invitation!
19th August

Why would anyone turn down the offer of being in God's wonderful eternal kingdom? But they do!

'He sent his slaves to call those who had been invited to the wedding banquet, but they would not come.'

(Matthew 22:3)

'My Journal':

- *I am sure that we have all turned down an invitation to an event, at some point during our lives: maybe because of illness, another commitment, or simply, because we didn't want to go. Consider and make notes on reasons why people in modern society might chose not to be part of God's kingdom.*

Meditate on what your eternal future looks like.

Heavenly Father.

You have given us all an amazing invitation that will make us safe for eternity!

Thank you for that invitation.

Please help us to accept that invitation; and not allow things like fears or busyness to lead us to turn it down.

Help me to have the assurance of a safe eternal future through being in a personal relationship with Jesus, and as a result, being part of the kingdom.

(Include any additional topics for prayer or thanksgiving, arising from this study)

In Jesus' name.

Amen.

'Doers of the word' (aim): To accept God's invitation to be part of the kingdom; and to have a secure eternal future.

Is there anything that you think you might find difficult about achieving the aim?

Making excuses

20th August

We love to make excuses: but there are some things that we should never make excuses for – including the refusal to respond positively to God's invitation to enter into his kingdom.

'But they made light of it and went away, one to his farm, another to his business.'

(Matthew 22:5)

'My Journal':

- *What kind of excuses do you make; for what situations; and why? Jot down some thoughts, and then prayerfully meditate on them – see what God says to you.*

Meditate on the concept that things like work can be fundamentally good; but the problems occur when we get our priorities wrong. An example of wrong priorities is when work takes over from family life or prevents us from giving God the time and commitment that is rightfully his.

Lord.

We should never make excuses to you!

Thank you that you really want to be part of our lives; and it is your desire for us to be part of your kingdom.

Please help me not to make excuses regarding why I can't be fully committed to being part of your kingdom – or to make excuses in response to you calling me to do something, as I seek to serve you.

Grant me a willingness to respond to you; and help me to get my priorities right.

(Include any additional topics for prayer or thanksgiving, arising from this study)

In Jesus' name.

Amen.

'Doers of the word' (aim): To not make excuses – especially with God!

Is there anything that you think you might find difficult about achieving the aim?

It's an open invitation!

21st August

People sometimes speak to me about feeling unworthy of being a Christian: but Jesus highlights that the invitation into the kingdom is open to absolutely everyone!

'"Go therefore into the main streets, and invite everyone you find to the wedding banquet."'

(Matthew 22:9)

'My Journal':

- *There is a double challenge of this verse. It states that the kingdom is open to everyone; which is a real challenge for those who are still resisting. It is also a challenge that, for those of us who are Christians, our witness should not exclude anyone. Jot down your response.*

Meditate on the fact that those who might feel ostracised from society, perhaps because of some kind of vulnerability, God wants to include in the kingdom! This would include people who live with mental health issues or disabilities; those who are victims of abuse; and many more.

Lord God.

Your kingdom is for absolutely everyone!

Thank you that even those who feel unworthy, ostracised or vulnerable are welcome.

Please help me to act upon the knowledge that the kingdom is for everyone.

Help me to fully commit myself.

Enable me to reach out to as many people as possible, as I witness.

And prevent me from demonstrating any kind of prejudice or discrimination.

(Include any additional topics for prayer or thanksgiving, arising from this study)

In Jesus' name.

Amen.

'Doers of the word' (aim): To act upon the kingdom being open to absolutely everyone – including the vulnerable.

Is there anything that you think you might find difficult about achieving the aim?

The clothes are provided!

22nd August

The essence of this parable is that the clothes are provided; so there is no excuse for the man not to be dressed correctly. Through Jesus we can be clothed in righteousness.

'But when the king came in to see the guests, he noticed a man there who was not wearing a wedding robe, and he said to him, "Friend, how did you get in here without a wedding robe?" And he was speechless.'

(Matthew 22:11-12)

'My Journal':

- *Jesus died on the cross, paying the penalty for our sin, so that through a personal relationship with him – based on repentance and faith – we are clothed in his righteousness and made fit to enter into the kingdom. Jot down your response.*

Meditate on the spiritual significance of the clothes being provided.

Lord Jesus.

You have provided the clothes to wear – your righteousness!

Thank you that you gave your life on the cross; paying the penalty for sin – and rose again.

Thank you that through entering into a relationship with you – based on repentance and faith – we are clothed in your righteousness, and made fit to enter into the kingdom for eternity.

Please help me to willingly wear those clothes.

Let others make that same choice, to wear what has been provided.

(Include any additional topics for prayer from your journal)

In your name.

Amen.

'Doers of the word' (aim): To wear the metaphorical clothes that have been provided.

Is there anything that you think you might find difficult about achieving the aim?

There are consequences
23rd August

Most people probably like to believe in heaven, because it is a wonderful place; but not so many people want to consider that there is an alternative for those who chose to turn their backs on God – somewhere that is not a nice place to be, because God's presence will not be experienced there.

'Then the king said to the attendants, "Bind him hand and foot, and throw him into the outer darkness, where there will be weeping and gnashing of teeth."'

(Matthew 22:13)

'My Journal':

- *The Bible is quite explicit that there is an alternative to heaven – one name for it is hell. There are consequences if we turn our backs on God! Write down your thoughts.*

Meditate on the consequences of the most important choice we will ever make in our lives: to enter into the kingdom – or not to enter into the kingdom.

Our loving heavenly Father.

There is a choice – and there are consequences to what we choose!

Thank you that we are all free to choose to be part of your eternal kingdom.

Please help me to make the right choice; and encourage others to do the same.

Thank you that when we do make that choice to do things your way, in faith (Hebrews 11:1), we can have sure and certain hope of our eternal futures.

(Include any additional topics for prayer or thanksgiving, arising from this study)

In Jesus' name.

Amen.

'Doers of the word' (aim): To recognise that there is an alternative to God's eternal kingdom – and to accept the consequences of our choice.

Is there anything that you think you might find difficult about achieving the aim?

Few are chosen

24th August

Though the invitation into the kingdom is for everyone, Jesus makes the point that many will fail to make a positive response to that invitation – and thus will not be chosen to enter into the kingdom.

'For many are called, but few are chosen.'

(Matthew 22:14)

'My Journal':

- *Consider what those who fail to make a positive response to God's invitation are missing out on – maybe you have friends or members of your family who are in that group. Write down what God says to you during this time.*

Meditate on ways in which you could encourage others to make a positive response to the invitation to enter into God's kingdom.

Loving heavenly Father.

It is our choice!

Thank you that you have given us the choice as to how we respond to your invitation.

Please let people choose to enter into your kingdom.

Help me to witness to those in my family and my friends, who still haven't made that decision.

Help me to overcome the obstacles.

And grant me courage.

(Include any additional topics for prayer or thanksgiving, arising from this study)

In Jesus' name.

Amen.

'Doers of the word' (aim): To prayerfully encourage others to respond positively to God's invitation.

Is there anything that you think you might find difficult about achieving the aim?

What the Bible says about **the Kingdom**

The secrets are revealed

25th August

The parables of Jesus are such that there is layer upon layer of teaching about the kingdom within them; and the more we prayerfully explore them, the deeper we are able to go.

He said, 'To you it has been given to know the secrets of the kingdom of God; but to others I speak in parables, so that

"looking they may not perceive,
and listening they may not understand."'

(Luke 8:10)

'My Journal':

- *On their most superficial level, the parables of Jesus are earthy stories that his listeners find easy to associate with: for example, stories about setting seeds; building houses on firm foundations; or helping our neighbour. But on a deeper level there is so much more – wonderful teaching about the kingdom. Jot down your thoughts and responses.*

Meditate prayerfully on the fact that it is only as a result of Jesus' revelation to us, through the Holy Spirit, that we can peel back the layers of the parables, and understand their deeper truths.

Lord Jesus.

It is your intention that we should discover those hidden lessons, contained within your parables!

Thank you that there is such a wealth of teaching in each one of your amazing parables, that we read in the Bible.

Please fill me afresh with the Holy Spirit, and grant me understanding of the hidden truths, as I peel back the different layers.

(Include any additional topics for prayer or thanksgiving, arising from this study)

In your name.

Amen.

'Doers of the word' (aim): To discover those lessons concealed in the parables of Jesus.

Is there anything that you think you might find difficult about achieving the aim?

Proclaim the kingdom

26th August

When the Bible speaks about Jesus sending out the twelve to proclaim the kingdom of God, there is the suggestion of it being a very active response to the need for people to hear it. There is still that same need in the world around us today. Let's approach it with that same frame of mind.

And he sent them out to proclaim the kingdom of God and to heal.

(Luke 9:2)

'My Journal':

- *Proclaiming the kingdom, telling the Good News, witnessing and sharing testimony all constitute us going out into the world – amongst our friends, biological families, church families, neighbourhoods, work places and those we socialise with – demonstrating a positive approach to outreach. Prayerfully consider that, and jot down anything that God reveals to you.*

Meditate on the fact that Jesus instructs the twelve to 'proclaim the kingdom' and to 'heal'. Jesus wants them to demonstrate God's power as they share his message. I wonder if we are as expectant, as we should be today, of God still performing miracles through us and in response to our prayers. Maybe you have experienced a miracle recently.

Almighty God.

We have an amazing message of hope to proclaim; and you are still the God of miracles!

Thank you that you are at work in our lives, when we follow Jesus; you are at work in the world in which we live; and you are preparing for our eternal futures.

Please empower and motivate me to proclaim the message of hope through the kingdom; and also to have the faith and expectation, when I pray, to ask for the miraculous to happen.

Your will be done.

(Include any additional topics for prayer or thanksgiving, arising from this study)

In Jesus' name.

Amen.

'Doers of the word' (aim): To proclaim the kingdom; and also to pray with faith and expectation that God will still work miracles in the 21st century world around us.

Is there anything that you think you might find difficult about achieving the aim?

What the Bible says about **the Kingdom**

Don't look back

27th August

Following Jesus means that when the going gets tough, or we get tired or tempted by distractions, we do not give up – hankering after our old way of life, once again – or lose our focus on Jesus.

Jesus said to him, 'No-one who puts a hand to the plough and looks back is fit for the kingdom of God.'

(Luke 9:62)

'My Journal':

- *Jot down some examples of things that might encourage us to become distracted, discouraged or even pine after our old way of life.*

Meditate on what is needed at those times, to help you to remain focused on Jesus: things like, speaking with a close Christian friend; spending time in prayer and Bible study; resting in God's arms, allowing him to offer encouragement and healing; and when a door closes, to watch out for God to open a window of new opportunity.

Lord.

You have called us to take part in the spiritual harvest: to sow seed, to care for and nurture the young plants, and to help to bring in the harvest!

Thank you that, as your followers, we have entered into a new, joyful lifestyle that is full of peace and hope – but it is not without its difficulties and discouragements.

Please equip me to face up to those difficulties, distractions, disappointments and discouragements – whatever they might be – and help me to remain focused on you and your will.

Strengthen, encourage and uplift me to be ready for the next new opportunity that you set before me.

(Include any additional topics for prayer or thanksgiving, arising from this study)

In Jesus' name.

Amen.

'Doers of the word' (aim): To keep moving forward in our Christian walk and calling.

Is there anything that you think you might find difficult about achieving the aim?

Strive for the kingdom

28th August

Jesus encourages us to get our focus` right: to be focused on the Triune God (God the Father, Jesus the Son, and the Holy Spirit), and the things of the kingdom.

'Instead, strive for his kingdom, and these things will be given to you as well.'

(Luke 12:31)

'My Journal':

- *Jesus assures us of God's continued provision to us, in these comforting words. Write down your thoughts.*

Meditate on the challenge that Jesus' words offer in this verse. It's all about where we place our focus in life: on the things of God, or the things of the material world.

Almighty God.

You know that there are certain physical things that we need: like food, drink, shelter, warmth and clothing.

Thank you that you want to give us the assurance that when we focus on you and the kingdom, other things will fall into place – you will provide for us.

Please grant me the faith to believe that, and act upon it in my focus in life – whilst still living in a responsible manner.

(Include any additional topics for prayer or thanksgiving, arising from this study)

In Jesus' name.

Amen.

'Doers of the word' (aim): To be focused on God and the Kingdom; and to trust in God's provision.

Is there anything that you think you might find difficult about achieving the aim?

What the Bible says about **the Kingdom**

It is the Father's pleasure!

29th August

God offers us the kingdom freely and joyfully.

'Do not be afraid, little flock, for it is your Father's good pleasure to give you the kingdom.'

(Luke 12:32)

'My Journal':

- *How does it feel when a gift is given to you begrudgingly? With the giving, comments may be made about how much it has cost; or how difficult it has been to find the right size, colour or model. Jot down some feelings.*

Meditate in the knowledge that it is God's 'good pleasure' to give us the kingdom. How does that make you feel?

Gracious God.

You love to give us good gifts; and you take great pleasure in giving us the kingdom!

Thank you that you want us to be part of the kingdom.

Please help me to appreciate the spirit in which you offer me a place in your kingdom – and your pleasure in my acceptance.

As I share the knowledge of your kingdom with others, help me to pass on something of that pleasure that you feel.

(Include any additional topics for prayer or thanksgiving, arising from this study)

In Jesus' name.

Amen.

'Doers of the word' (aim): To appreciate the spirit in which the kingdom has been given to us.

Is there anything that you think you might find difficult about achieving the aim?

The kingdom is among you

30th August

Jesus makes the very significant point that the kingdom of God is something that we can experience now.

Once Jesus was asked by the Pharisees when the kingdom of God was coming, and he answered. 'The kingdom of God is not coming with things that can be observed; nor will they say, "Look, here it is!" or "There it is!" For, in fact, the kingdom of God is among you.'

(Luke 17:20-21)

'My Journal':

- *The kingdom is something that we can experience in part now, and in full when Jesus returns – when it will reach its ultimate fulfilment. How does that make you feel?*

Meditate on the significance of the kingdom being among us now: things like, highlighting the importance of how we live our lives here and now; and not to end up just living for the future.

Lord Jesus.

The kingdom is here – now!

Thank you that one day we will be able to experience your kingdom in all its fullness – when you return – but until then we are still living in your kingdom, when we are in a relationship with you.

Please help me to live my life as someone who is already in the kingdom; according to kingdom values and aims.

(Include any additional topics for prayer or thanksgiving, arising from this study)

In your name.

Amen.

'Doers of the word' (aim): To act upon the importance of how we live our lives here and now, because the kingdom is here.

Is there anything that you think you might find difficult about achieving the aim?

There is power in the kingdom!

31st August

Talk is easy; but when it is just talk, it is empty. There is no place for empty words in kingdom living; the power of God should shine through all that we do and say – and all that we are.

For the kingdom of God depends not on talk but on power.

(1 Corinthians 4:20)

'My Journal':

- *God's power is available to us all, through the indwelling Holy Spirit – a free gift to all followers of Jesus. Have you experienced that power in your own life?*

Meditate on what it means to profess faith in Jesus in empty words only: things like, lacking in belief, faith, commitment or active response to Jesus. We should be feeling God's power at work in our lives, daily!

Almighty God.

We can all experience your power at work in our lives!

Thank you that when we enter into a personal relationship with Jesus, we are filled with your power, through the indwelling Holy Spirit.

Please fill me afresh with the Holy Spirit; and let the words I speak proclaiming my faith, be evidenced by my active response to the Bible, my commitment to serving Jesus, and my lifestyle in general.

Let people see your power at work in my life.

(Include any additional topics for prayer or thanksgiving, arising from this study)

In Jesus' name.

Amen.

'Doers of the word' (aim): To demonstrate God's power at work in our everyday lives.

Is there anything that you think you might find difficult about achieving the aim?

13

HARVEST

Promises fulfilled

1st September

The whole process of seedtime and harvest demonstrates that's God's promises will be fulfilled: it highlights his constancy, faithfulness and provision.

'As long as the earth endures,
seedtime and harvest, cold and heat,
summer and winter, day and night,
shall not cease.'

(Genesis 8:22)

'My Journal':

- *How do you think the process of seedtime and harvest demonstrates the constancy, faithfulness and provision of God – and the fact that he always fulfils his promises?*

Meditate on the fact that temperature, changing seasons, different weather, and light and dark are all part of the process of the growth of a plant; which demonstrates the completeness of God's provision to us, as he provides the means for his promises to be fulfilled.

Lord God.

You always fulfil your promises!

Thank you for all the promises in scripture – most, if not all of them of them, with eternal significance, and based on our relationship with Jesus.

Please help me to trust that you will fulfil those promises.

Let my relationship with Jesus be an ever closer one.

(Include any additional topics for prayer or thanksgiving, arising from this study)

In Jesus' name.

Amen.

'Doers of the word' (aim): To trust in God's promises.

Is there anything that you think you might find difficult about achieving the aim?

What the Bible says about **seedtime and harvest**

Shouts of joy

2nd September

The psalmist speaks about crying as we go out to plant the seed, and shouting with joy as we gather in the crops: highlighting the hardships of planting and harvesting – both physically and spiritually – but of the joy experienced, when all is safely gathered in.

May those who sow in tears
reap with shouts of joy.

(Psalm 126:5)

'My Journal':

- *Consider the concept of sowing in tears, in a spiritual context, and make some notes: things like facing opposition, being persecuted, dealing with frustrations, coping with disappointments, and also feeling that deep down sadness that so many people are still struggling on without knowing God – and without having eternal hope. Make a note of your thoughts.*

Meditate on God's sadness, that so many turn their backs on him in the modern world; and his joy when people choose to come into the kingdom.

Loving God.

You celebrate when someone enters into the kingdom, through faith in Jesus!

Thank you that it is your will for us all to be part of your kingdom; and that, through Jesus' death and resurrection, you made it possible.

Please help me to plant and harvest spiritually – in the power of the Holy Spirit.

(Include any additional topics for prayer or thanksgiving, arising from this study)

In Jesus' name.

Amen.

'Doers of the word' (aim): To plant spiritual seed, and harvest spiritual crops.

Is there anything that you think you might find difficult about achieving the aim?

What the Bible says about **seedtime and harvest**

Order in God's creation
3rd September

The writer of Ecclesiastes tells us that there is a time for everything: including for planting and reaping – physically and spiritually.

For everything there is a season, and a time for every matter under heaven:

a time to be born, and a time to die;
a time to plant, and a time to pluck up what is planted.

(Ecclesiastes 3:1-2)

'My Journal':

- *Consider for a few minutes the fact that God is a God of order. His plans and purposes are precisely and carefully thought out – even down to times and dates. Jot down your thoughts.*

Meditate on the significance of God's timing being perfect: we should never get impatient and try to hurry him.

Almighty God.

Your timing is absolutely perfect; but my patience can be a problem!

Thank you that you are organised; and within your creation is planning, order, and a right time for everything.

Please help me to be more patient: to be prepared to wait for your timing on all things.

(Include any additional topics for prayer or thanksgiving, arising from this study)

In Jesus' name.

Amen.

'Doers of the word' (aim): To always wait for God's perfect timing.

Is there anything that you think you might find difficult about achieving the aim?

What the Bible says about **seedtime and harvest**

4th September

Telling the story

'Listen! A sower went out to sow. And as he sowed, some seed fell on the path, and the birds came and ate it up. Other seed fell on rocky ground, where it did not have much soil, and it sprang up quickly, since it had no depth of soil. And when the sun rose, it was scorched; and since it had no root, it withered away. Other seed fell among thorns, and the thorns grew up and choked it, and it yielded no grain. Other seed fell into good soil and brought forth grain, growing up and increasing and yielding thirty and sixty and a hundredfold.' And he said, 'Let anyone with ears to hear listen!'

(Mark 4:3-8)

When he was alone, those who were around him along with the twelve asked him about the parables. And he said to them, 'To you has been given the secret of the kingdom of God, but for those outside, everything comes in parables; in order that

"they may indeed look, but not perceive,
and may indeed listen, but not understand;
so that they may not turn again and be forgiven."'

And he said to them, 'Do you not understand this parable? Then how will you understand all the parables? The sower sows the word. These are the ones on the path where the word is sown: when they hear, Satan immediately comes and takes away the word that is sown in them. And these are the ones sown on rocky ground: when they hear the word, they immediately receive it with joy. But they have no root, and endure only for a while; then, when trouble or persecution arises on account of the word, immediately they fall away. And others are those sown among the thorns: these are the ones who hear the word, but the cares of the world, and the lure of wealth, and the desire for other things come in and choke the word, and it yields nothing. And these are the ones sown on the good soil: they hear the word and accept it and bear fruit, thirty and sixty and a hundredfold.'

(Mark 4:10-20)

...to be looked at over the next five days.

Lord God.

Thank you for the truth of scripture, and that it is relevant to every generation.

Thank you for this passage of scripture that looks at one of your parables.

Please help me to understand what I have just read; and to meditate upon it today.

(Include any additional topics for prayer or thanksgiving, arising from this study)

In Jesus' name.

Amen.

What the Bible says about **seedtime and harvest**

Spiritual seed
5th September

Jesus explains that the spiritual seed is the message about the kingdom – God's word. This parable is about how people respond to that message... and to Jesus himself.

'The sower sows the word.'

(Mark 4:14)

'My Journal':

- *How have responded to the message about the kingdom: in terms of things like belief, commitment, making a positive response, and producing spiritual fruit?*

Meditate on your response to Jesus, in terms of the relationship you have with him.

Lord Jesus.

Your parables have such a depth of teaching about the kingdom!

Thank you that you teach us in 'bite sized pieces': very down to earth stories, but with huge spiritual significance.

Please help me to open up the parables.

Grant me the understanding of what they mean, and how they apply to my life – and my eternal future.

Let me make a positive response to them – and you!

(Include any additional topics for prayer or thanksgiving, arising from this study)

In your name.

Amen.

'Doers of the word' (aim): To understand that there are a variety of different responses to the spiritual seed – but only one that produces a harvest.

Is there anything that you think you might find difficult about achieving the aim?

Hard hearts

6th September

The hearts of some people are so hardened against anything to do with God, that it is as if they don't even hear what he is saying to them.

'These are the ones on the path where the word is sown: when they hear, Satan immediately comes and takes away the word that is sown in them.'

(Mark 4:15)

'My Journal':

- *It is not just that the seed falls somewhere where it is unable to grow satisfactorily; the seed is immediately snatched away by the birds. Jesus speaks about Satan snatching away the spiritual seed. Consider what that means in practical terms, and make a note of your thoughts.*

Meditate on any occasions in your own life, when you have been met with hostile responses after mentioning Christian things to someone. Consider the need in modern society to make time to listen to words of testimony; despite the many distractions.

Heavenly Father.

Your plans and purposes include blessing for us all!

Thank you that you are more powerful than Satan.

Please soften hardened hearts, and help us all to be open to you – and help me not to rob you of the time that is rightfully yours in my life.

Empower me to resist distractions.

Help me to listen to you.

Help others to listen to you.

(Include any additional topics for prayer or thanksgiving, arising from this study)

In Jesus' name.

Amen.

'Doers of the word' (aim): To pray against the work of Satan, as he tries to defeat the plans and purposes of God... And to not be that person who is hardened to the things of God.

Is there anything that you think you might find difficult about achieving the aim?

What the Bible says about **seedtime and harvest**

When the novelty wears off

7th September

Some people enter into the Christian faith with such enthusiasm, but there is no real commitment; so, when difficulties arise – particularly in terms of facing opposition – instead of being a source of strength, their faith is the first thing to go.

And these are the ones sown on rocky ground: when they hear the word, they immediately receive it with joy. But they have no root, and endure only for a while; then, when trouble or persecution arises on account of the word, immediately they fall away.

(Mark 4:16-17)

'My Journal':

- *In what way does your relationship with Jesus enhance your life; strengthening you in good times and bad?*

Meditate on your daily walk with Jesus; prayerfully allowing the Holy Spirit to come into your life afresh.

Lord.

You want to be our strength, especially during difficult times!

Thank you that you fill us with the power of the Holy Spirit when we are in relationship with you.

Please let my relationship with you be based on a genuine commitment… and, as such, be my strength in life.

Help me to draw even closer to you in those difficult times.

(Include any additional topics for prayer or thanksgiving, arising from this study)

In Jesus' name.

Amen.

'Doers of the word' (aim): To be truly committed to following Jesus, and to be strengthened by the Holy Spirit through that relationship.

Is there anything that you think you might find difficult about achieving the aim?

Wrong priorities
8th September

There's a saying, 'we make the time to do what we want to do.' Maybe that is not always completely accurate, but following Jesus can get so easily get pushed out by the busyness of life.

'And others are those sown among the thorns; these are the ones who hear the word, but the cares of the world, and the lure of wealth, and the desire for other things come in and choke the word, and it yields nothing.'

(Mark 4:18-19)

'My Journal':

- *List your priorities in life.*

Meditate on the priorities you believe God wants you to base your life on: to include things like, setting aside time to spend with him, and making time to serve Jesus in the ways to which he has called you. Do they match up with those ones on your list? Or are you sometimes too busy for God?

Almighty God.

Our priorities should always focus on you!

Thank you that you know what is best.

Please help me to look to you as I set my priorities.

Give me the strength of character to make the time to do those things that are important in your eyes.

Help me not to allow the busyness of life to push you out.

(Include any additional topics for prayer or thanksgiving, arising from this study)

In Jesus' name.

Amen.

'Doers of the word' (aim): To be able to set and follow God given priorities.

Is there anything that you think you might find difficult about achieving the aim?

What the Bible says about **seedtime and harvest**

A true commitment

9th September

Some people make a true commitment to being part of God's kingdom, and live in an appropriate way: it is their strength during difficult times, and their priority during the busyness of life.

'And these are the ones sown on the good soil: they hear the word and accept it and bear fruit, thirty and sixty and a hundred fold.'

(Mark 4:20)

'My Journal':

- *The crux of this parable is that there will be a spiritual harvest! In other words, there will be people who make a real, lasting and productive commitment to following Jesus. How does that make you feel?*

Meditate on what the spiritual harvest consists of, in your life. Does it include things like a lifetime of actively serving Jesus, enjoying a close daily walk with him, and an eternal future filled with blessing?

Lord Jesus.

You want us to have a real and lasting relationship with you – enabling us to produce a spiritual harvest in our lives!

Thank you that, through responding positively to you and the teaching of the Bible, we can do that.

Please help me to be spiritually fruitful in my life; through walking close to you daily, being filled with the Holy Spirit, and as I strive to live in obedience to the Father.

(Include any additional topics for prayer or thanksgiving, arising from this study)

In your name.

Amen.

'Doers of the word' (aim): To produce a spiritual harvest in our lives.

Is there anything that you think you might find difficult about achieving the aim?

What the Bible says about **seedtime and harvest**

The seed needs to die
10th September

Jesus explains the need for him to die on the cross, in terms of a seed effectively having to die, in order for it to germinate, and for the new plant to grow.

'Very truly, I tell you, unless a grain of wheat falls into the earth and dies, it remains just a single grain; but if it dies, it bears much fruit.'

(John 12:24)

'My Journal':

- Consider the concept of losing the seed in order to gain the plant. You might actually like to focus on some seeds while you do this. Make a note of what comes in to your mind – maybe a picture, a word, or a verse of scripture.

Meditate on Jesus sacrificially giving his life on the cross; in order that the kingdom might grow, and that we could have eternal life.

Lord Jesus.

You were prepared to die on the cross, in order that the kingdom might grow; and that we all might have eternal life!

Thank you for your amazing sacrificial act of love.

Please help me to recognise, believe, and make a positive response to that act of love and self-sacrifice.

Thank you that you rose from the dead, and are alive today.

Please be present in my life on a daily basis.

(Include any additional topics for prayer or thanksgiving, arising from this study)

In your name.

Amen.

'Doers of the word' (aim): To accept the risen Jesus needed to die on the cross, in order that the kingdom might grow.

Is there anything that you think you might find difficult about achieving the aim?

What the Bible says about **sowing and reaping (Harvest)**

Harvesting trouble
11th September

In the book of Job, Eliphaz speaks about his life experience being that those who 'plough iniquity and sow trouble' will 'reap the same'. Certainly, there are consequences to the way in which we behave.

'As I have seen, those who plough iniquity
and sow trouble reap the same.'

(Job 4:8)

'My Journal':

- *We know from the story of Job that Eliphaz's statement, though largely true, is not completely true, in the broken world in which we live. There are times when trouble comes our way through no fault of our own. Consider how you deal with those times – drawing on God's help. Jot down your thoughts.*

Meditate on the fact that modern society often seems to imagine that we can do just as we like, with no negative consequences; but of course, that is not true. Think of some hypothetical scenarios illustrating that point.

Lord God.

There are consequences to our choices, decisions and actions!

Thank you that when we live our lives – here and now – according to your will, then our eternal future is safe in your hands.

Please strengthen us to cope with those times of trouble that come our way – even when we have done nothing to bring that situation onto ourselves.

Help me to live life your way - including in the choices and decisions I make.

(Include any additional topics for prayer or thanksgiving, arising from this study)

In Jesus' name.

Amen.

'Doers of the word' (aim): To live life with a continual awareness that our choices, decisions and actions have consequences – particularly in an eternal context.

Is there anything that you think you might find difficult about achieving the aim?

What the Bible says about **sowing and reaping (Harvest)**

All relative

12th September

At the risk of stating the obvious, Paul points out to us the more seed that is planted, the greater the harvest will be. In other words, the more of our various resources we are prepared to invest, in helping to build God's kingdom, the greater the results will be!

The point is this: the one who sows sparingly will also reap sparingly, and the one who sows bountifully will also reap bountifully.

(2 Corinthians 9:6)

'My Journal':

- *The more resources we invest into building the kingdom, the greater the spiritual harvest will be - and we all have something to invest. Make a note of your thoughts on this statement.*

Meditate on the resources that you have; and then ask yourself: What am I prepared to invest in the kingdom?

Risen Lord Jesus.

You invested your life for the kingdom – when you died on the cross!

Thank you that you love us so much, that you were prepared to invest so heavily.

Please help me to invest all that I have, and all that I am, into helping to build the kingdom: my wealth, my talents and abilities, and my time.

(Include any additional topics for prayer or thanksgiving, arising from this study)

In your name.

Amen.

'Doers of the word' (aim): To invest all that we have and are into the kingdom.

Is there anything that you think you might find difficult about achieving the aim?

What the Bible says about **sowing and reaping (Harvest)**

Filled with the Spirit
13th September

The ultimate harvest, of living a Spirit filled, fruitful life, is eternal life in God's wonderful heavenly kingdom.

Do not be deceived; God is not mocked, for you reap whatever you sow. If you sow to your own flesh, you will reap corruption from the flesh; but if you sow to the Spirit, you will reap eternal life from the Spirit.

(Galatians 6:7-8)

'My Journal':

- *Who is steering your life: is it you, or is it the Holy Spirit?*

Meditate on what it means to allow the Holy Spirit to be in control of our lives; following entering into a personal relationship with Jesus.

Lord Jesus.

You fill us with the Holy Spirit when we are in a relationship with you!

Thank you for the gift of the Holy Spirit.

Please fill me afresh.

And help me to allow the Holy Spirit full control of my life – allowing him to do the steering!

Empower me to be the person you would have me be.

Grant me the assurance that I will spend eternity in your presence.

(Include any additional topics for prayer or thanksgiving, arising from this study)

In your name.

Amen.

'Doers of the word' (aim): To live a life in which the Holy Spirit has full control – and to be assured of eternal life.

Is there anything that you think you might find difficult about achieving the aim?

What the Bible says about **spiritual fruitfulness (Harvest)**

Growing by the stream

14th September

What a wonderful picture the psalmist paints when he describes a close walk with God as being like a tree growing by the stream – nourished, refreshed and fruitful.

They are like trees
planted by streams of water,
which yield their fruit in its season,
and their leaves do not wither.
In all that they do, they prosper.

(Psalm 1:3)

'My Journal':

- *Consider the image, in a spiritual context: through a close relationship with the Triune God, we are able to receive spiritual nourishment and refreshment - and be fruitful. Jot down your thoughts, or even sketch the image that this verse instils into your mind.*

Meditate on the different components necessary for you to be spiritually nourished and refreshed – beginning with a close relationship with Jesus and being filled with the Holy Spirit.

Almighty God.

Through a personal relationship with Jesus, we can be spiritually nourished!

Thank you for the Bible, prayer, worship, praise, the opportunity to have fellowship with other Christians and with you – ways of receiving spiritual nourishment.

Please help me to walk closely with Jesus each day.

Fill me afresh with the Holy Spirit.

Grant me the enablement to live in obedience to the Father.

And help me to always make time to be in your presence, and to do those things that will nourish, refresh and equip.

(Include any additional topics for prayer from your journal)

In Jesus' name.

Amen.

'Doers of the word' (aim): To grow by the metaphorical stream, and be nourished.

Is there anything that you think you might find difficult about achieving the aim?

What the Bible says about **spiritual fruitfulness (Harvest)**

Still fruitful in later life

15th September

There is no age limit to being spiritually fruitful; illustrated by the psalmist describing trees that are still being healthy and fruitful, even when they are old.

In old age they still produce fruit;
they are always green and full of sap.

(Psalm 92:14)

'My Journal':

- *How old do you feel?*

Meditate on those things that determine how old you feel: maybe things like health and mobility, interests, looks, how other people treat you, whether or not you are retired, feeling that you are slowing down or no longer useful, or just the numerical age that you are actually. But you are not too old to still be spiritually fruitful!

Loving heavenly Father.

You can still use us in your service as we journey through later life!

Thank you that we can be useful whatever age we might be; and whatever state of health and mobility we are experiencing.

You can use us in your service, whether we are young, middle aged or in later life.

Please help me to feel useful and continue to serve you.

But help me to take on those roles that are suited to my age and fitness: maybe do something less energetic when I become less fit and mobile – or as I tire more quickly.

I know that I am useful!

(Include any additional topics for prayer or thanksgiving, arising from this study)

In Jesus' name.

Amen.

'Doers of the word' (aim): To continue to produce spiritual fruit whatever age we might be.

Is there anything that you think you might find difficult about achieving the aim?

What the Bible says about **spiritual fruitfulness (Harvest)**

True repentance
16th September

True repentance is more than just saying 'Sorry!' It involves a change of actions. Jesus effectively challenges us with: 'Let me see the change in your lives.'

Bear fruit worthy of repentance.

(Matthew 3:8)

'My Journal':

- *In the power of the Holy Spirit, the change in our lives isn't just about becoming less sinful... it is also about being more positively Christ like, in the context of doing good. Make a note of your thoughts and response.*

Meditate for a few minutes on anything in your life of which you need to be repentant.

Lord Jesus.

You died on the cross so that we might be forgiven for our sin!

Thank you for your offer of forgiveness.

Please forgive me for those occasions when I still fall short of your standards; and help me to be seen to change my actions for the better.

Help me to be less sinful.

And help me to demonstrate your love in action more and more.

(Include any additional topics for prayer or thanksgiving, arising from this study)

In your name.

Amen.

'Doers of the word' (aim): To be truly repentant in our lives.

Is there anything that you think you might find difficult about achieving the aim?

What the Bible says about **spiritual fruitfulness (Harvest)**

Pleasing God
17th September

Paul highlights that those acts of practical Christ like love both honour God and are pleasing to him.

So that you may lead lives worthy of the Lord, fully pleasing to him, as you bear fruit in every good work and as you grow in the knowledge of God.

(Colossians 1:10)

'My Journal':

- *Love is one of those things that was never intended to be kept to ourselves. Love is meant for sharing in caring and practical ways. And when we do that it brings pleasure to God. Be encouraged in that knowledge; and make some notes on your thoughts.*

Meditate on what 'every good work' constitutes in practical terms, in your life. It could be a case of: Who can you help, and in what ways? How can you demonstrate kindness or generosity towards others? And in what ways can you experience more of God, by living according to his will?

Loving God.

When we live lives of love in action, doing good works, it is pleasing to you!

Thank you that when we are in relationship with Jesus, you fill us with your love to share with others.

Please help me to live the kind of life that is fruitful in good works and pleasing to you.

(Include any additional topics for prayer or thanksgiving, arising from this study)

In Jesus' name.

Amen.

'Doers of the word' (aim): To be fruitful and please God.

Is there anything that you think you might find difficult about achieving the aim?

What the Bible says about **the spiritual harvest (Harvest)**

The workers are few
18th September

Jesus highlights the need for workers in the spiritual harvest field: to witness in word and deed – and to gently nurture and encourage people into the kingdom (through Jesus, of course).

Then he said to his disciples, 'The harvest is plentiful, but the labourers are few; therefore ask the Lord of the harvest to send out labourers into his harvest.'

(Matthew 9:37-38)

'My Journal':

- *Jot down some notes about a time when you were shorthanded at work. How did it feel? What was your response at the time? Consider your response to the need that Jesus highlights, for more workers to help gather in the spiritual harvest.*

Meditate on what the job description for this role might include: things like witnessing in words and actions, praying with people, or being an encourager.

Lord.

The harvest is plentiful but the workers are few!

Thank you that there is a plentiful spiritual harvest to be gathered in.

Please help me to be willing to play an active part in gathering in that harvest.

Help me to commit to serving in this way.

(Include any additional topics for prayer or thanksgiving, arising from this study)

In Jesus' name.

Amen.

'Doers of the word' (aim): To serve in the spiritual harvest field.

Is there anything that you think you might find difficult about achieving the aim?

What the Bible says about **the spiritual harvest (Harvest)**

The harvest is ready

19th September

Jesus urges us not to be complacent: the harvest (spiritual) is ready now, and it is at risk of being lost. We need to have a sense of urgency as we witness to others.

'Do you not say, "Four months more, and then comes the harvest"? But I tell you, look around you, and see how the fields are ripe for harvesting.'

(John 4:35)

'My Journal':

- *Consider the analogy. The crux is that the harvest is at the point of being at risk of getting wasted, if it is not gathered in quickly. Try to feel that urgency. Make some notes on your thoughts.*

Meditate on the readiness of the spiritual harvest; and prayerfully feel the sadness in God's heart at the thought of any of the harvest being lost.

Lord.

The spiritual harvest is ready now!

Thank you that the harvest is ripe.

Please give me a real sense of urgency; to help gather it in, before it is wasted.

Help me to remember that this is all about people's eternal wellbeing.

Lead me to those whose lives I can touch with your love and the message of salvation through Jesus – and help me to achieve those things.

Let others come forward to help in the harvest.

(Include any additional topics for prayer or thanksgiving, arising from this study)

In Jesus' name.

Amen.

'Doers of the word' (aim): To feel that sense of urgency, and respond positively to it.

Is there anything that you think you might find difficult about achieving the aim?

What the Bible says about **the spiritual harvest (Harvest)**

Celebrating together
20th September

When the spiritual harvest has been gathered in, there will be a time of celebration for the workers – those who have served Jesus.

The reaper is already receiving wages and is gathering fruit for eternal life, so that sower and reaper may rejoice together.

(John 4:36)

'My Journal':

- *Consider the great celebration when the harvest has been gathered in. What a joy it will be, to be part of that occasion. Indeed, we should celebrate each and every person that we see enter into a personal relationship with Jesus. How does that make you feel?*

Meditate on the significance of the reference to the reaper 'receiving wages' and 'gathering fruit for eternal life'. Being part of bringing in the spiritual harvest is an eternal investment – for ourselves and others - one which we cannot afford to miss.

Loving God.

You are the God of salvation!

Thank you that as we help in the process of gathering in the harvest, we are investing in our eternal future – as well as that of other people.

Thank you that, as such, we will share in the celebrations when the spiritual harvest has been gathered in safely.

Please help me to feel your joy every time I see someone enter into a personal relationship with Jesus.

(Include any additional topics for prayer or thanksgiving, arising from this study)

In Jesus' name.

Amen.

'Doers of the word' (aim): To be part of God's eternal celebration.

Is there anything that you think you might find difficult about achieving the aim?

What the Bible says about **the spiritual harvest (Harvest)**

Responsibility through example
21st September

Paul highlights, not only the importance of setting a good example for others to follow; but he also emphasises the responsibility we carry when someone follows a bad example we have set.

So by your knowledge those weak believers for whom Christ died are destroyed.

(1 Corinthians 8:11)

'My Journal':

- *The Bible quotation concerns doing something that might not be fundamentally wrong, but could lead an onlooker astray. Consider how this might apply in everyday situations; and make some notes.*

Meditate on the importance of being aware of the needs and vulnerability of others, and act in a way that will build up and encourage them in their spiritual journey; and not be destructive.

Lord Jesus.

You are our perfect example in all things!

Thank you that we are able to look to you in this way.

Please help me to be sensitive to the needs of others; help me to have an awareness of any areas of vulnerability; and enable me set an example that is helpful and constructive.

(Include any additional topics for prayer or thanksgiving, arising from this study)

In your name.

Amen.

'Doers of the word' (aim): To be aware of the example we are setting to others; and endeavour to make it a helpful one.

Is there anything that you think you might find difficult about achieving the aim?

What the Bible says about **the spiritual harvest (Harvest)**

Perseverance

22nd September

Paul urges us not to give up serving Jesus, in being a servant to others.

So let us not grow weary in doing what is right, for we will reap at harvest time, if we do not give up.

(Galatians 6:9)

'My Journal':

- *Think about those things that could lead us to give up serving Jesus. Maybe one of the main causes is discouragement: when after years of working in the Church, little or no significant results might have been seen, from your labours. Jot down your thoughts.*

Meditate on the concept, and its significance in your life, of God seeing what we don't always see; in terms of the results of our service.

Lord God.

You urge us not to give up on doing your will!

Thank you that you offer us encouragement in so many different ways.

Please help me not to become discouraged in serving you; but grant me perseverance.

(Include any additional topics for prayer or thanksgiving, arising from this study)

In Jesus' name.

Amen.

'Doers of the word' (aim): To demonstrate perseverance in our lives of Christian service.

Is there anything that you think you might find difficult about achieving the aim?

What the Bible says about **the spiritual harvest (Harvest)**

The book of life
23rd September

We are told that the names of all Jesus' followers will be written down in the book of life.

If you conquer, you will be clothed like them in white robes, and I will not blot your name out of the book of life; I will confess your name before my Father and before his angels.

(Revelation 3:5)

'My Journal':

- *What are some of the achievements you have made in your life, which have been recorded in writing?*

Meditate on what the risen Jesus achieved for us when he gave his life on the cross. Consider the significance of wearing 'white robes': being clothed in the righteousness of Christ, through his death on the cross – paying the penalty for sin.

Risen Lord Jesus.

You have achieved the ultimate achievement for us!

Thank you for giving your life on the cross for us, paying the penalty for sin – Our sin... My sin!

Thank you that you rose again, and are alive today – and through entering into a personal relationship with you, we are metaphorically clothed in your righteousness, and made fit to spend eternity in your heavenly kingdom – that our names are recorded in the book of life.

Please help me, whatever I have or haven't achieved, to realise and accept that this really is something that I am not able to achieve for myself.

Help me to walk close to you each day; to strive to live according to the Father's will; to allow the Holy Spirit to work freely in my life; and to rely on what you have achieved for me.

(Include any additional topics for prayer or thanksgiving, arising from this study)

In your name.

Amen.

'Doers of the word' (aim): To be clothed in the righteousness of Christ.

Is there anything that you think you might find difficult about achieving the aim?

Final judgement

24th September

Paul speaks about the final judgement being based on whether or not our names have been written in the book of life.

And I saw the dead, great and small, standing before the throne, and books were opened. Also another book was opened, the book of life. And the dead were judged according to their works, as recorded in the books.

(Revelation 20:12)

'My Journal':

- *What kind of physical and material investments give reassurance for our futures?*

Meditate on the eternal investment described in this verse; having our names written in the book of life, through our personal relationship with Jesus – evidenced in good works.

Lord Jesus.

There will be a day of judgement!

Thank you that we can be confident at that time; through our relationship and daily walk with you.

Please help me to have a close relationship with you; and a close daily walk with you... and, as a result, help me to be confident on the day of judgement.

(Include any additional topics for prayer or thanksgiving, arising from this study)

In your name.

Amen.

'Doers of the word' (aim): To be confident on the day of judgement.

Is there anything that you think you might find difficult about achieving the aim?

What the Bible says about **thanksgiving (Harvest)**

'Make known his deeds'

25th September

The writer of Chronicles links together thanksgiving, with telling others about all the amazing things that God has done for us.

O give thanks to the Lord, call on his name,
make known his deeds among peoples.

(1 Chronicles 16:8)

'My Journal':

- *What are some of the amazing things that God does for us on a daily basis?*

Meditate on things to thank God for, in your life.

Almighty God.

You are a great and generous God!

Thank you for every blessing that you shower upon me.

Please grant me the boldness and courage to tell others about what an amazing God you are; and what a difference you have made to my life.

(Include any additional topics for prayer or thanksgiving, arising from this study)

In Jesus' name.

Amen.

'Doers of the word' (aim): To tell other people what a great God we have!

Is there anything that you think you might find difficult about achieving the aim?

What the Bible says about **thanksgiving (Harvest)**

Everything belongs to God

26th September

The psalmist points out a very important, significant and fundamental principle, that everything, including ourselves, belong to God.

The earth is the Lord's and all that is in it,
the world, and those who live in it.

(Psalm 24:1)

'My Journal':

- *Everything and everyone belongs to God - that includes all that we have and are; and the world in which we live. How does that make you feel?*

Meditate on how that knowledge should affect the way in which we live our lives: for example, we have a duty to take care of the world, because it is not ours; and we are but stewards of our so called possessions and resources, so they come with responsibilities. Those resources include our talents, abilities and time.

Creator God.

You created everything and everyone: that is why it all belongs to you!

Thank you for your amazing creation, of which we are part; and that you have entrusted to us, to make use of in our lives.

Thank you that we are yours, and you want to be in relationship with us all.

Please help me to be a good steward of all that you have entrusted to me.

I give you all that I have and am, to be used in your service.

(Include any additional topics for prayer or thanksgiving, arising from this study)

In Jesus' name.

Amen.

'Doers of the word' (aim): To be good stewards of those things with which God has entrusted us.

Is there anything that you think you might find difficult about achieving the aim?

What the Bible says about **thanksgiving (Harvest)**

Be thankful
27th September

Maybe, in modern society, there is not as much emphasis placed on saying 'please' and 'thank you' – sadly. The psalmist urges us to enter into God's presence with thanksgiving and praise.

Enter his gates with thanksgiving,
and his courts with praise.
Give thanks to him, bless his name.
For the Lord is good;
his steadfast love endures forever,
and his faithfulness to all generations.

(Psalm 100:4-5)

'My Journal':

- *Consider, God's blessings, his goodness, his love, and his faithfulness – all demonstrated in so many different ways. Make a list of what some of those ways are.*

Meditate on God's blessings to you. Enter into his presence today in an attitude of thanksgiving and praise.

Almighty God.

We have so much for which we should thank and praise you!

Thank you for your blessings...

Thank you for your goodness...

Thank you for your love...

Thank you for your faithfulness...

Thank you for eternal hope, through Jesus.

Please help me to live in an attitude of praise and thanksgiving.

(Include any additional topics for prayer or thanksgiving, arising from this study)

In Jesus' name.

Amen.

'Doers of the word' (aim): To enter God's presence in an attitude of thanksgiving and praise – on a regular basis.

Is there anything that you think you might find difficult about achieving the aim?

What the Bible says about **thanksgiving (Harvest)**

God's unending love and faithfulness

28th September

Our experience of life, in the 'here and now', is that so much seems to be transient – even our own physical lives. But the love and faithfulness of God – and all that entails – is steadfast and eternal.

Praise the Lord, all you nations!
Extol him, all you peoples!
For great is his steadfast love towards us,
and the faithfulness of the Lord endures forever.
Praise the Lord!

(Psalm 117:1-2)

'My Journal':

- *Consider a love that is unconditional, completely dependable, and it lasts forever – that's God's love! Jot down your thoughts.*

Meditate on God's faithfulness. He will never let us down. He will never let you down! How does that feel?

Heavenly Father.

Your love and faithfulness are unending!

Thank you that your love is unconditional, completely dependable, and it lasts forever.

Thank you that your faithfulness means that you will never let us down.

Please help me to accept your love, and be assured by your faithfulness – despite having been let down in the past by people, and having experienced transience in different situations.

(Include any additional topics for prayer or thanksgiving, arising from this study)

In Jesus' name.

Amen.

'Doers of the word' (aim): To fully experience God's unconditional love and his faithfulness – forever.

Is there anything that you think you might find difficult about achieving the aim?

Jesus gives thanks for the wine

29th September

So often, in the Gospels, we read that Jesus gives thanks to God before a meal; and it is right that we should show our appreciation in that same way. But, at what we call the Last Supper, when Jesus gives thanks for the wine, there is a huge spiritual significance – predicting his death and resurrection, and the opportunity for us to receive salvation as a result.

Then he took a cup, and after giving thanks he said, 'Take this and divide it among yourselves... And he did the same with the cup after supper, saying, 'This cup that is poured out for you is the new covenant in my blood.'

(Luke 22:17 and 20)

'My Journal':

- *It is a good routine to get into, to give thanks to God before a meal. That means, we are thinking about, and responding with thanksgiving to God's provision to us, maybe three times a day. Jot down some thoughts.*

Meditate on this thought. When we share the bread and the wine together at church, again we should give thanks; but for the spiritual significance of that simple meal. Consider the love, mercy, grace and desire to forgive, made possible through the death and resurrection of Jesus… and think about the promise of this verse.

Almighty God.

You are the God of salvation!

Thank you that, through Jesus' death and resurrection, we have the opportunity to be forgiven; and set free from the consequences of sin.

Please help me to fully appreciate your provision to me of physical food and drink; but thank you particularly for the huge significance contained within the simple meal of the Communion/ Sacrament.

Help me not to devalue the significance of Jesus' death and resurrection.

(Include any additional topics for prayer or thanksgiving, arising from this study)

In Jesus' name.

Amen.

'Doers of the word' (aim): To give thanks for our meals, and for the greater significance of the bread and wine in celebrating Communion/ the Sacrament.

Is there anything that you think you might find difficult about achieving the aim?

What the Bible says about **thanksgiving (Harvest)**

Jesus gives thanks for the bread
30th September

Jesus predicts his body being broken on the cross, as he breaks the bread and gives thanks to God for it, at what we call the Last Supper. The crucifixion is to be such an amazing demonstration of love!

Then he took a loaf of bread, and when he had given thanks, he broke it and gave it to them, saying, 'This is my body, which is given for you. Do this in remembrance of me.'

(Luke 22:19)

'My Journal':

- *Think about the degree of selfless, unconditional love Jesus goes on to demonstrate on the cross – feel that love! Write down your thoughts.*

Meditate on Jesus' words: 'This is my body, which is given for you.' Replace the word 'you' with your own name, making it really personal. How does that make you feel?

Lord Jesus.

Such love!

Thank you for your demonstration of selfless, unconditional love on the cross.

Please help me to make an ongoing, positive response to that love.

(Include any additional topics for prayer or thanksgiving, arising from this study)

In your name.

Amen.

'Doers of the word' (aim): To feel the love of Jesus, demonstrated on the cross – and respond positively to it.

Is there anything that you think you might find difficult about achieving the aim?

14

THE LAW

God's word

1st October

As an introduction to the Ten Commandments, we are told that they are from God - they are his laws; and each one is an expression of his love and values.

Then God spoke all these words.

(Exodus 20:1)

'My Journal':

- *What is the significance of the fact that the Ten Commandments are from God?*

Meditate on the concept that there is something very decisive about God speaking things out: it reminds us of the account of creation, where God speaks out, and it comes about (Genesis 1:1 – 2:3).

Lord God.

You have spoken the Ten Commandments!

Thank you for your law: full of truth, relevant to every generation, and an expression of your love and values.

Please help me to recognise that these are commandments and not guidelines; and they are from you...

And help me to live in obedience to them.

Fill me afresh with the power of the indwelling Holy Spirit.

(Include any additional topics for prayer or thanksgiving, arising from this study)

In Jesus' name.

Amen.

'Doers of the word' (aim): To recognise the importance of the Ten Commandments: to follow and to respond accordingly.

Is there anything that you think you might find difficult about achieving the aim?

What the Bible says about **the law**

Remember (Commandment number 1a)
2nd October

We forget God's goodness, faithfulness and provision to us, so quickly and easily! Before giving the Ten Commandments, God reminds the Israelites of his faithfulness and provision to them in the past.

I am the Lord your God, who brought you out of the land of Egypt, out of the house of slavery.

(Exodus 20:2)

'My Journal':

- *In a general sense, what might God remind us of today, concerning his faithfulness and provision to us?*

Meditate on ways in which God has demonstrated his goodness, faithfulness and provision specifically to you, in the last week.

Almighty God.

Your goodness, faithfulness and provision are amazing!

Thank you for all the ways in which you bring blessing to us.

Please help me to remember all that you have done for me; and respond by living in an attitude of obedience to you.

(Include any additional topics for prayer or thanksgiving, arising from this study)

In Jesus' name.

Amen.

'Doers of the word' (aim): To remember God's goodness, faithfulness and provision.

Is there anything that you think you might find difficult about achieving the aim?

Be faithful (Commandment number 1b)

3rd October

God is not prepared to share his position of being in first place in our lives.

You shall have no other Gods before me.

(Exodus 20:3)

'My Journal':

- *Consider what it means to put God in his rightful place, in our lives – getting our priorities right; with God at the top! Jot down any difficulties with doing that in your life.*

Meditate on what some of the other gods are, that we could be tempted to worship and serve: gods like, wealth and the pursuit of it, the acquisition of possessions, different types of addictions, or holding people in great esteem for their beauty or celebrity status.

Almighty God.

We should place you first in our lives!

Thank you that you are worthy of being in that place.

Please help me not to have any other gods apart from you.

Help me to make you the main focus and priority in my life.

Grant me the discernment to recognise those things that are in competition with you.

And teach me to put aside those aspects of my busyness or focus that prevent you from being given that rightful place.

(Include any additional topics for prayer or thanksgiving, arising from this study)

In Jesus' name.

Amen.

'Doers of the word' (aim): To not have any other gods; apart from God himself.

Is there anything that you think you might find difficult about achieving the aim?

Do not make idols (Commandment number 2a)

4th October

Humankind has a habit of sometimes creating its own traditions, ceremonies and even laws within the Church – ones that do not have Biblical support.

You shall not make for yourself an idol, whether in the form of anything that is in heaven above, or that is on the earth beneath, or that is in the water under the earth.

(Exodus 20:4)

'My Journal':

- *There is something quite deliberate, inferred to in this verse: 'You shall not make...' It feels as if it is aimed at very deliberate moves against God and his will. What do you think?*

Meditate on this. The reference to 'in heaven above' would seem to imply that people are misrepresenting something of eternal spiritual significance; and the reference to the 'earth beneath' or the 'water under the earth' to be trying to limit the things of God to the transient nature of the physical world.

Lord God.

You don't want us to create our own idols: focuses for our worship – in whatever form they might take - made by human beings.

Thank you that we don't need to do that.

Please help me to restrain from creating such things.

Teach me to always focus my worship on you.

(Include any additional topics for prayer or thanksgiving, arising from this study)

In Jesus' name.

Amen.

'Doers of the word' (aim): To not create our own human based focuses for our worship, which distract from God.

Is there anything that you think you might find difficult about achieving the aim?

Do not worship idols (Commandment number 2b)

5th October

Only God is worthy of our worship.

You shall not bow down to them or worship them; for I the Lord your God am a jealous God, punishing children for the iniquity of parents, to the third and fourth generation of those who reject me.

(Exodus 20:5)

'My Journal':

- *To where, to what, or to whom should our worship be directed towards? - Because that is what this commandment is about... And if it is not directed solely to God, then we are getting it wrong. Jot down your thoughts.*

Meditate on the concept that even within the Church, we can fall into the trap of focusing our worship more on the rituals, traditions and ceremonies, than God. And that can apply to any denomination or style of worship.

Almighty God.

You command us to worship you alone!

Thank you that you are worthy of our worship.

Please help me to only worship you.

Don't let me be tempted to worship any idols; in whatever form they might appear – intentionally or unintentionally.

(Include any additional topics for prayer or thanksgiving, arising from this study)

In Jesus' name.

Amen.

'Doers of the word' (aim): Not to worship idols.

Is there anything that you think you might find difficult about achieving the aim?

Experiencing the fullness of God's love (Commandment number 2c)

6th October

Amongst the Ten Commandments Jesus pops a real 'gem' about his love: there is a link between experiencing God's love in all its fullness, and living in an attitude of obedience to him.

But showing steadfast love to the thousandth generation of those who love me and keep my commandments.

(Exodus 20:6)

'My Journal':

- *God's love is showered upon us all unconditionally; but we only experience it in all its fullness, when it is linked with a relationship with him: I guess it is about being receptive to what God is offering us. What are your thoughts?*

Meditate on what it means to experience the steadfast love of God, in respect to it being unconditional, uncontainable, all encompassing, dependable, faithful, hopeful and eternal.

Loving God.

You love us all unconditionally!

Your love is steadfast: it is dependable; we experience your faithfulness through it; it brings hope; and it is eternal.

Please help me to be in the kind of relationship with you, that will facilitate that love being released and fully experienced in my life – and that I might spread it to others.

Help me to live in obedience to you.

(Include any additional topics for prayer or thanksgiving, arising from this study)

In Jesus' name.

Amen.

'Doers of the word' (aim): To experience God's steadfast love in all its fullness.

Is there anything that you think you might find difficult about achieving the aim?

Blaspheme (Commandment number 3)

7th October

We are told in no uncertain terms that we should not use language that is blasphemous against God.

You shall not make wrongful use of the name of the Lord your God, for the Lord will not acquit anyone who misuses his name.

(Exodus 20:7)

'My Journal':

- *How often in the course of a week, a day, an hour, or even minute by minute, do you hear the names of the Triune God misused? It is all too frequently that we hear those names used in mocking, flippant, careless, thoughtless, disrespectful and contemptuous ways. Jot down your responses.*

Meditate for a few moments why we, as followers of Jesus, so infrequently challenge such blasphemous use of language on such a regular basis – especially on TV.

Lord.

You are worthy of our respect at all times!

Thank you that you are such a great God.

Why do people blaspheme about you so much, by misusing your names?

Please help me to be strong enough to stop myself from doing that; and to have the confidence to confront those who are.

Forgive me for the times when I have failed to do those things.

(Include any additional topics for prayer or thanksgiving, arising from this study)

In Jesus' name.

Amen.

'Doers of the word' (aim): To not misuse the names of God; and to be bold enough to begin to challenge those who do misuse them.

Is there anything that you think you might find difficult about achieving the aim?

Time set apart (Commandment number 4a)

8th October

In the Ten Commandments we are reminded of the importance of rest, refreshment, family time, and time set apart to spend with God.

Remember the Sabbath day, and keep it holy.

(Exodus 20:8)

'My Journal':

- *'Remember the Sabbath Day' is about taking time out from the busyness of everyday life for self-care. In my childhood, most things used to stop on a Sunday; making it a day when people were encouraged to rest, relax, spend time with the family, go to church, etc. Now, it is very difficult to find any kind of natural break in modern society. Jot down some notes about your own experience.*

Meditate on the fact that we are reminded to set time apart to spend with God in the words: 'keep it holy'. And that is probably the bit that really does get left out.

Lord God.

You know what we need for our self-care!

You know that we need rest, refreshment, family time and time for you.

Thank you that all those things are available, but we do need to take the time, space and stillness to do them.

Please help me to be disciplined with my self-care.

(Include any additional topics for prayer or thanksgiving, arising from this study)

In Jesus' name.

Amen.

'Doers of the word' (aim): To set aside time to rest, relax, spend time with the family and have quality time with God.

Is there anything that you think you might find difficult about achieving the aim?

You shall not do any work (Commandment number 4b)

9th October

God spells out to us the pattern to follow with regards to work and time out. It is not just a casual thought; it is our creator's commandment to us – we should be disciplined enough to take time out from work, with strict boundaries!

For six days you shall labour and do all your work. But the seventh day is a sabbath to the Lord your God; you shall not do any work – you, your son or your daughter, your male or female slave, your livestock, or the alien resident in your towns.

(Exodus 20:9-10)

'My Journal':

- *How good are you at taking time out from work: self-care time, in terms of rest, refreshment, family time and God time? Make some notes on what you think about the God given proportions in this verse.*

Meditate on the references to having an onus of responsibility with regards to encouraging and enabling our families, employees and even working animals to take that time out from work.

Lord God.

You have set us a timetable to follow regarding taking time off from work; and you have set us the responsibility not only to take time out for ourselves, but also to encourage, and where we can to facilitate, others to do the same!

Complete time out, from any form of work!

Thank you for your concern that we take that time out, which we need from the busyness, not just of work, but of life in general.

Please help me to respond positively to those responsibilities.

(Include any additional topics for prayer or thanksgiving, arising from this study)

In Jesus' name.

Amen.

'Doers of the word' (aim): To be disciplined enough to take time out from work for self-care; and to encourage and facilitate those within our authority or influence to do the same.

Is there anything that you think you might find difficult about achieving the aim?

<u>Ordained by God (Commandment number 4c)</u>

10th October

We are told that God himself ordained this pattern of work: that we should take time out for rest, refreshment and time with God. We read about this in the account of Creation (Genesis 1 and 2).

For in six days the Lord made heaven and earth, the sea, and all that is in them, but rested on the seventh day; therefore the Lord blessed the sabbath day and consecrated it.

(Exodus 20:11)

'My Journal':

- *Consider the significance of God setting this precedent of taking time out from the busyness – for us to follow. Jot down some thoughts.*

Meditate on what this verse has to say about having a good work ethic: that is, we were created to work; but not necessarily paid work – consider within this context, Christian service.

Creator God.

Even you took time out, after your amazing work of creation!

Thank you that you have set us a pattern of work to follow - including a good work ethic.

Please help me to follow your example; including, entering into a life of Christian service.

(Include any additional topics for prayer or thanksgiving, arising from this study)

In Jesus' name.

Amen.

'Doers of the word' (aim): To follow God's example to us, concerning a work ethic; and also of taking time out for self-care and being with God.

Is there anything that you think you might find difficult about achieving the aim?

Respect for elders (and listen to them) (Commandment number 5)

11th October

We are instructed to honour our parents: to treat them with respect and listen to what they say. The implication is that we should extend that to our elders in a more general sense, as well.

Honour your father and your mother, so that your days may be long in the land that the Lord your God is giving you.

(Exodus 20:12)

'My Journal':

- *Respecting our elders, is about wisdom being passed down through the generations; having role models to follow; and simply demonstrating gratitude to those who have brought us up and provided care and instruction for us in our youth. Consider those who have been your key role models and mentors. Jot down some names of those people, to thank God for, in the prayer.*

Meditate on the other side of the coin: Are you worthy of that honour yourself – to be a key role model and mentor for young people - as a parent, grandparent, aunt or uncle, etc? What are your thoughts?

Our loving heavenly Father.

You are the perfect parent!

Thank you for all those people in my life who have been – and those who still are - good examples, role models and mentors.

Please help me to respect them, learn from them, and appreciate what they have done for me.

Enable me to be a good example, role model, and mentor to the young people that I have influence over.

(Include any additional topics for prayer or thanksgiving, arising from this study)

In Jesus' name.

Amen.

'Doers of the word' (aim): To respect and listen to our elders; and to be worthy of 'honour' from our children, grandchildren, etc.

Is there anything that you think you might find difficult about achieving the aim?

Do not harm others (in fact, do good to them) (Commandment number 6)

12th October

Commandment number six simply tells us not to murder; but I am sure that the wider implication is that we should not do any kind of physical harm to others.

You shall not murder.

(Exodus 20:13)

'My Journal':

- *Think about taking a holistic approach to this commandment. Why stop at not doing any kind of physical harm to others? Let us not do any kind of harm to others: physical, mental, emotional, or spiritual. Make a note of your thoughts.*

Meditate on the outworking of this holistic approach: what kind of weapons do we sometimes more subtly attack others with? - Things like unkind or critical words; being controlling or manipulative; or unfaithfulness in relationships.

Our loving heavenly Father.

You are a God of love and compassion!

Thank you that your plan for our lives is for our good, and not for harm (Jeremiah 29:11).

Please strengthen me, helping me to avoid doing anything to harm others: physically, mentally, emotionally or spiritually.

(Include any additional topics for prayer or thanksgiving, arising from this study)

In Jesus' name.

Amen.

'Doers of the word' (aim): To not harm others.

Is there anything that you think you might find difficult about achieving the aim?

What the Bible says about **the law**

Be faithful in relationships (including with God) (Commandment number 7)
13th October

Jesus picks up the next commandment in his Sermon on the Mount: expanding it to be a warning against either making a mentally or physically adulterous response to someone (Matthew 5:27-28).

You shall not commit adultery.

(Exodus 20:14)

'My Journal':

- *Consider the importance of relationships in general, in society; and being faithful within those relationships. Make a note of your thoughts.*

Meditate on this verse in a spiritual context: that is, being faithful in our relationship with God. What are the implications?

Lord God.

You are always faithful to us; and it is your desire that we should be faithful to you!

Thank you that we can depend on you.

Please help me to be faithful in all my relationships; especially in my relationship with you.

(Include any additional topics for prayer or thanksgiving, arising from this study)

In Jesus' name.

Amen.

'Doers of the word' (aim): To be faithful in relationships; especially in our relationship with God.

Is there anything that you think you might find difficult about achieving the aim?

What the Bible says about **the law**

Do not steal (Commandment number 8)
14th October

The eighth commandment appears to be very self-explanatory: it's about not taking things that belong to someone else.

You shall not steal.

(Exodus 20:15)

'My Journal':

- *Spend a few minutes considering the more obvious applications of this commandment. Make a list.*

Meditate on less obvious forms of stealing, of which you might be guilty: for example, it is so easy to misuse the time or resources that rightfully belong to God, our family, or our partners.

Almighty God.

You created us in your image: to relate to you, and to spend time with you!

Thank you that, through Jesus, we can all be in a relationship with you and spend time with you.

Please help me not to steal the time – or other resources - which rightfully belong to you, to my family, or to my partner.

(Include any additional topics for prayer or thanksgiving, arising from this study)

In Jesus' name.

Amen.

'Doers of the word' (aim): To not steal: including to not steal the time that rightfully belongs to someone else – including God.

Is there anything that you think you might find difficult about achieving the aim?

Be honest (Commandment number 9)

15th October

Complete honesty is commanded.

You shall not bear false witness against your neighbour.

(Exodus 20:16)

'My Journal':

- *What is complete honesty; and how wide reaching is it?*

Meditate on some of the repercussions of dishonesty; especially when we tell untruths or half truths about other people, or fail to volunteer the truth when the opportunity arises.

Lord Jesus.

You set us the example of being completely honest!

Thank you for your perfect example in all things.

Please help me to be honest in all my dealings with other people on a day to day basis.

Help me not to tell half-truths.

Encourage me to volunteer the truth when the opportunity arises.

And let me be completely honest in all things.

(Include any additional topics for prayer or thanksgiving, arising from this study)

In your name.

Amen.

'Doers of the word' (aim): To be completely honest.

Is there anything that you think you might find difficult about achieving the aim?

Jealousy and envy (Commandment number 10)

16th October

Jealousy and envy can eat away at us, leading to all kinds of unhealthy emotions and actions. The last of the Ten Commandments is quite explicit, when it instructs that we should not 'covet' anything that belongs to someone else.

You shall not covet your neighbour's house; you shall not covet your neighbour's wife, or male or female slave, or ox, or donkey, or anything that belongs to your neighbour.

(Exodus 20:17)

'My Journal':

- *Coveting is about wanting something that doesn't belong to us; envying the fact that someone else has something that we cannot afford or can never be ours for another reason. What might that lead to in practical terms?*

Meditate, prayerfully, on whether or not there is jealousy or envy evident in your life. What is the evidence, and what needs to be done?

Our loving heavenly Father.

It is not your will for us to be jealous or envious of each other: wanting the things that they possess, including relationships!

Thank you that you are a generous God, who has blessed us with your amazing love.

Please help me to be content with those things you have blessed me with; and not to want those things that I can't have.

(Include any additional topics for prayer or thanksgiving, arising from this study)

In Jesus' name.

Amen.

'Doers of the word' (aim): To not be jealous or envious of things that belong to someone else.

Is there anything that you think you might find difficult about achieving the aim?

What the Bible says about **the law**

Understand and absorb the law
17th October

The Bible highlights how all-encompassing God's law should be in our lives.

This book of the law shall not depart out of your mouth; you shall meditate on it day and night, so that you may be careful to act in accordance with all that is written in it. For then you shall make your way prosperous, and then you shall be successful.

(Joshua 1:8)

'My Journal':

- *Think about exactly what this verse is saying concerning the place of God's law in our lives: that is, we should prayerfully read and understand it, feed on it, and receive nourishment from it; we should constantly think about it; and we should put it into practice in our everyday lives. It is the key to true prosperity and success. Jot down your thoughts.*

Meditate on how this description of prosperity and success may differ from that of society.

Lord God.

You have given us your law, so that we might be successful and prosperous!

Thank you for your law.

Please help me to spend time prayerfully reading the scriptures.

Grant me understanding of what your law means.

Help me to accumulate a knowledge of the law; and the wisdom to know how to apply it.

And please empower me to live it out on a daily basis, in my life.

(Include any additional topics for prayer or thanksgiving, arising from this study)

In Jesus' name.

Amen.

'Doers of the word' (aim): To read, understand, absorb and put into practice, the teaching of God's law.

Is there anything that you think you might find difficult about achieving the aim?

What the Bible says about **the law**

Obey the law

18th October

We are told in the book of Joshua, not only that we should observe God's law, but it is emphasised that it is not negotiable.

Therefore be very steadfast to observe and do all that is written in the book of the law of Moses, turning aside from it neither to the right nor to the left.

(Joshua 23:6)

'My Journal':

- *We should turn aside from God's law 'neither to the right nor to the left'. Make some notes about your conclusions, giving actual or hypothetical examples.*

Meditate on this concept in the light of compromise.

Lord God.

Your values do not change!

Your nature is unchanging!

Thank you that we can depend on the constancy of your law.

Please help me to adhere to your laws; and not to bend and twist them to suit my own desires or weaknesses.

(Include any additional topics for prayer or thanksgiving, arising from this study)

In Jesus' name.

Amen.

'Doers of the word' (aim): To obey God's law, without trying to adapt it to suit ourselves.

Is there anything that you think you might find difficult about achieving the aim?

What the Bible says about **the law**

The benchmark for sin

19th October

The Bible makes us face the harsh reality that we do not have the capacity within ourselves to earn salvation though obedience to the law: on the contrary, it is God's law that defines every one of us as sinners.

And again,

For 'no human being will be justified in his sight' by deeds prescribed by the law, for through the law comes the knowledge of sin.

(Romans 3:20)

'My Journal':

- *The starting point of our journey, to experience salvation, is recognising that we have all fallen short of God's standards, and that we do not have the capacity within ourselves to be set free from the consequences of sin. How does that feel?*

Meditate on what sin really is. It's all about not achieving a metaphorical pass mark in our lives - whether it be by 1% or by 30% - and it's about not managing to keep God's law. As far as the consequences for sin are concerned, they are the same for all sin.

Risen Lord Jesus.

Your mission is to sinners (Luke 19:7)!

Thank you that though we have all sinned; and we are not able to free ourselves from the consequences of sin, in our own capacity; it is not the end, because your mission is to sinners (Luke 19:10)!

Please help me to recognise my own sinfulness, and my need to experience salvation through you.

(Include any additional topics for prayer or thanksgiving, arising from this study)

In your name.

Amen.

'Doers of the word' (aim): To recognise and own, the fact that we have all sinned, and face the eternal consequences of sin; and we do not have the capacity within ourselves to put it right.

Is there anything that you think you might find difficult about achieving the aim?

The law and grace

20th October

Grace is all about being given what we don't deserve, by God – through his love for us. Salvation is not earned; it is by grace!

But law came in, with the result that the trespass multiplied; but where sin increased, grace abounded all the more.

(Romans 5:20)

'My Journal':

- *Think about the implications of the first half of the saying, 'Where sin increased, grace abounded all the more.' As humankind's focus becomes less and less centred on God, and more and more centred on living self-centred ways of life in collusion with Satan, so sin increases in the world. How does that make you feel?*

Meditate on the nature of God's grace: no sin is too big for God to forgive, through Jesus.

Father God.

Your grace is limitless!

As sin increases, your grace abounds all the more.

Thank you that there is no sin that your grace cannot cover.

Please cover my sin with your grace; through my personal relationship with Jesus.

(Include any additional topics for prayer or thanksgiving, arising from this study)

In his name.

Amen.

'Doers of the word' (aim): To understand and experience God's grace.

Is there anything that you think you might find difficult about achieving the aim?

What the Bible says about **the law**

Justified
21st October

Paul tells us in Galatians that the law has been leading us to the coming of Christ; at which time we would be able to be justified through faith.

Therefore the law was our disciplinarian until Christ came, so that we might be justified by faith

(Galatians 3:24)

'My Journal':

- *What do you think the word 'justified' means; in the context of God's law and sin?*

Meditate on the concept of justification. It has been said that justification means that it is just as if we had never sinned – in other words, we have been set free from sin's consequences. Justification by faith is about entering into a personal relationship with Jesus – based on faith. It is not about earning forgiveness, and freedom from sin's consequences; it is about believing and trusting in Jesus.

Lord Jesus.

It is only through faith in you that we can be justified: made just as if we had never sinned!

Thank you that you died on the cross, paying the penalty for all sin – and you rose again.

Thank you that you died on the cross, paying the penalty for my sin – and you are alive today.

Please increase my faith in you; forgive me and grant me the assurance of my salvation through you.

(Include any additional topics for prayer or thanksgiving, arising from this study)

In your name.

Amen.

'Doers of the word' (aim): To be justified, through faith.

Is there anything that you think you might find difficult about achieving the aim?

15

THE LORD

Risen Lord

22nd October

Jesus is alive today!

But for ours also. It will be reckoned to us who believe in him who raised Jesus our Lord from the dead.

(Romans 4:24)

'My Journal':

- *Jesus is alive today. We follow a risen Lord and Saviour! Make a note of your thoughts.*

Meditate on the fact that Jesus was raised from the dead. One of the greatest fears, and biggest hurdles to jump over, is physical death... but Jesus' resurrection demonstrates that death is not the end!

Jesus.

You have risen, and are alive today!

Thank you that you are a risen Lord and Saviour; and that I can have a close relationship with you.

Thank you that you are with me all the time, through having that relationship (Matthew 28:20b).

Please help me to walk closely to you each day.

Fill me with eternal hope; in the knowledge that death is not the end for your followers.

(Include any additional topics for prayer from your journal)

In your name.

Amen.

'Doers of the word' (aim): To follow the risen Jesus; and be filled with eternal hope.

Is there anything that you think you might find difficult about achieving the aim?

Reconciled by the Lord

23rd October

Reconciliation is a lovely concept, in a world where so many people seem to be falling out with each other: it suggests the healing of relationships and a bringing together.

But more than that, we even boast in God through our Lord Jesus Christ, through whom we have now received reconciliation.

(Romans 5:11)

'My Journal':

- *Consider the concept: 'we have now received reconciliation' through Jesus. In other words, we have been given reconciliation - like a gift – through our relationship with Jesus. It highlights that we need a stronger power than we possess to enable reconciliation to happen. Jot down some thoughts.*

Meditate on what the process of reconciliation includes. Initially it refers to being reconciled with the Triune God, which includes being in a close relationship; but it should follow on, that then, we strive for reconciliation with those around us – and that is a matter for prayer.

Lord Jesus.

You give us the gift of reconciliation; when we follow you in faith!

Thank you that you enable us to be reconciled with you, the Father and the Holy Spirit... and with each other.

Please let me experience your reconciliation in my life; and for eternity.

Let there be forgiveness and healing with any broken relationships in my life – especially in the Church.

(Include any additional topics for prayer or thanksgiving, arising from this study)

In your name.

Amen.

'Doers of the word' (aim): To receive the gift of reconciliation, through Jesus.

Is there anything that you think you might find difficult about achieving the aim?

Eternal life, through the Lord

24th October

The Bible gives us a simple choice: sin leads to spiritual death but a relationship with Jesus leads to eternal spiritual life – a free gift from God.

For the wages of sin is death, but the free gift of God is eternal life in Christ Jesus our Lord.

(Romans 6:23)

'My Journal':

- *Think about the concept of 'wages'; and link it with the verse. It's primarily about there being consequences, or a payback, for living a sinful life – receiving what is earned or deserved. Make a note of your thoughts.*

Meditate on the concept of receiving a free gift, as opposed to receiving wages; and link it with the verse. It is saying that the reward spoken about (eternal life) is undeserved and unearned – it is by the grace of God.

Loving God.

Eternal life is a free gift from you: made possible through Jesus – by grace!

Thank you that Jesus paid the penalty for sin, when he died on the cross.

Thank you that Jesus paid the penalty for my sin, when he died on the cross.

Thank you that Jesus rose again, and is alive today – and that entering into a personal relationship with him results in receiving eternal life.

Please give me the assurance of receiving eternal life; as a result of my daily walk with Jesus.

(Include any additional topics for prayer or thanksgiving, arising from this study)

In Jesus' name.

Amen.

'Doers of the word' (aim): To receive the free gift of eternal life through Jesus.

Is there anything that you think you might find difficult about achieving the aim?

Inseparable from God's love, through the Lord

25th October

Absolutely nothing can separate us from God's love.

For I am convinced that neither death, nor life, nor angels, nor rulers, nor things present, nor things to come, nor powers, nor height, nor depth, nor anything else in all creation, will be able to separate us from the love of God in Christ Jesus our Lord.

(Romans 8:38-39)

'My Journal':

- *Think about the fact that death cannot separate us from God's love; and its significance. Make a note of your thoughts.*

Meditate on Paul's words, when he refers to 'powers' not being able to overcome God's love or our experience of it. We are in a spiritual battle, surrounded by powers of evil, but God – and his love - is more powerful than any of them.

Loving God.

Nothing can separate us from your love!

Thank you that through my personal relationship with Jesus, I will experience your love in my life for ever.

Please immerse me in your love, and give me that assurance.

(Include any additional topics for prayer or thanksgiving, arising from this study)

In Jesus' name.

Amen.

'Doers of the word' (aim): To receive the love of God, to trust in his power, and to be part of his eternal heavenly kingdom.

Is there anything that you think you might find difficult about achieving the aim?

Saved, through the Lord

26th October

Paul passes on to us some wonderful words of assurance, when he says:

Because if you confess with your lips that Jesus is Lord and believe in your heart that God raised him from the dead, you will be saved.

(Romans 10:9)

'My Journal':

- *Do you know Jesus as your Risen Lord? Is that the basis of your relationship with him? If so, Paul gives you the assurance by concluding: 'You will be saved.' Think about those words of promise and hope; and make a note of your thoughts.*

Meditate on the fact that there is nothing in this verse about having to earn our salvation: it is a gift from God. Consider the significance of this: the penalty for sin is something that none of us are able to afford to pay (Romans 3:9-18).

Risen Lord Jesus.

You are alive today!

Thank you that you died on the cross, paying the penalty for sin: something that none of us can afford to pay ourselves.

Thank you that I can be assured of my own salvation; when I know you as my risen, Lord and Saviour.

Please help me to know you in this way.

(Include any additional topics for prayer or thanksgiving, arising from this study)

In your name.

Amen.

'Doers of the word' (aim): To know that you are saved by the risen, Lord Jesus.

Is there anything that you think you might find difficult about achieving the aim?

Belonging to the Lord
27th October

Paul speaks about what it means to be in relationship with Jesus: belonging to the Lord in life and in death – what a wonderfully reassuring thought.

If we live, we live to the Lord, and if we die, we die to the Lord; so then, whether we live or whether we die, we are the Lord's.

(Romans 14:8)

'My Journal':

- *When we are in a personal relationship with the Lord Jesus, we are his for ever: in terms of being in his presence, being in his love, being in his safe keeping, and being in fellowship with the Triune God. How does that make you feel?*

Meditate on the significance of living our lives for the Lord: walking with Jesus daily; and when we die, spending eternity with the Lord, in God's heavenly kingdom.

Living Lord Jesus.

We can be yours in life and in death!

Thank you that when we enter into a relationship with you; it is eternal – it is a 'for ever' relationship.

Please help me to walk closely to you, now and for always.

(Include any additional topics for prayer or thanksgiving, arising from this study)

In your name.

Amen.

'Doers of the word' (aim): To belong to the Lord Jesus, in life and death.

Is there anything that you think you might find difficult about achieving the aim?

Boast in the Lord

28th October

We are told in Corinthians that, if we are going to boast about our achievements, then let us *boast in the Lord* – because he is our enablement, through the Holy Spirit.

In order that, as it is written, 'Let the one who boasts, boast in the Lord.'

(1 Corinthians 1:31)

'My Journal':

- *Thinking about, and then make a list of, all your achievements that are worthy of boasting.*

Meditate on the part that the Triune God played in all those achievements in your list: for example, all our talents and abilities are God given; the love which we share with others is the love of God within us; and so the list goes on.

Lord.

We should boast in you!

Thank you that you equip us to serve you, through the Holy Spirit.

Thank you for all the talents and abilities with which you have blessed me.

Thank you for filling me with your love and compassion, to share with others.

And thank you for giving me the right words to say to people about you.

Please fill me afresh with the Holy Spirit.

Help me to serve you more.

Give me more boldness and courage.

Help me to boast in you.

(Include any additional topics for prayer or thanksgiving, arising from this study)

In Jesus' name.

Amen.

'Doers of the word' (aim): To boast in the Lord.

Is there anything that you think you might find difficult about achieving the aim?

Victory, through the Lord

29th October

The victory over sin and evil is one in which we can all share, through following Jesus.

But thanks be to God, who gives us the victory through our Lord Jesus Christ.

(1 Corinthians 15:57)

'My Journal':

- *The victory is a spiritual one over sin and evil; and we share that victory through being in a relationship with the Lord Jesus Christ. How does that feel?*

Meditate on the privilege of sharing that victory.

Lord Jesus.

You have won the victory over sin and evil!

Thank you that when you return, that victory will find its ultimate fulfilment.

Thank you that we can all share in that victory; and all that it entails.

Please let me be part of your victory, through a close daily walk with you.

(Include any additional topics for prayer or thanksgiving, arising from this study)

In your name.

Amen.

'Doers of the word' (aim): To share in the victory that Jesus has won for us over sin and evil.

Is there anything that you think you might find difficult about achieving the aim?

Confess Jesus is Lord

30th October

We are all called to make a confession of faith – that Jesus is Lord.

And every tongue should confess
that Jesus Christ is Lord,
to the glory of God the Father.

(Philippians 2:11)

'My Journal':

- *This verse has an implication that we should not, and cannot, have a secret faith in Jesus. As well as being called to make a confession of faith in Jesus, on the day of judgement, this also feels like an encouragement to make a public declaration of following Jesus here and now. What do you think?*

Meditate on what is meant by confessing that 'Jesus Christ is Lord': things like recognising and acknowledging Jesus' right to rule and acceptance of that rule in our lives.

Risen Jesus.
You are Lord!
Thank you that you are worthy to rule.
Please help me to accept that rule in my life; willingly and in love.
(Include any additional topics for prayer from your journal)
In your name.
Amen.

'Doers of the word' (aim): To confess Jesus as Lord.

Is there anything that you think you might find difficult about achieving the aim?

The Lord is near
31st October

The writer of Philippians shares words of great comfort, when he speaks about the Lord being 'near'.

Let your gentleness be known to everyone. The Lord is near.

(Philippians 4:5)

'My Journal':

- *The image in this verse is of Jesus being within metaphorical touching distance. We can imagine being able reach out our arms, and Jesus is there. Think about this, and jot down some notes on your thoughts.*

Meditate on the fact that this concept of Jesus being near is linked, in its context, with rejoicing, not worrying, praying and being at peace (Philippians 4:4-7). How does that make you feel?

Lord Jesus.

You are near!

Thank you that you are within metaphorical touching distance; and that through reaching out to you I can rejoice, be at peace, and need not be worried.

Please help me to prayerfully come to you.

(Include any additional topics for prayer or thanksgiving, arising from this study)

In your name.

Amen.

'Doers of the word' (aim): To live as someone who knows that the Lord is near.

Is there anything that you think you might find difficult about achieving the aim?

16

REMEMBRANCE

What the Bible says about **peace (Remembrance)**

A place of safety

1st November

The psalmist speaks about sleeping in peace, and lying down in safety: what a lovely image! He links it with being in relationship with the Lord.

I will both lie down and sleep in peace;
for you alone, O Lord, make me lie down in safety.

(Psalm 4:8)

'My Journal':

- *For a few moments, consider the image that the psalmist has created in this verse, as you close your eyes and picture it in your mind. Write down your thoughts about the link between relationship, safety and peace.*

Meditate on what kind of things make you feel safe.

God our heavenly Father.

In you we can experience peace and safety!

Thank you that through being in a personal relationship with you, we enter into a place of eternal safety and find inner peace.

Please help me to know that safety and peace, as I walk close to Jesus daily.

(Include any additional topics for prayer or thanksgiving, arising from this study)

In Jesus' name.

Amen.

'Doers of the word' (aim): To feel at peace, in a place of safety, through being n relationship with God.

Is there anything that you think you might find difficult about achieving the aim?

What the Bible says about **peace (Remembrance)**

Seek and pursue peace

2nd November

The Bible tells us that peace is something to be sought and pursued. It is a lifestyle choice: to live a peaceful life and to be a peacemaker, or not to live a peaceful life and not to be a peacemaker.

Depart from evil, and do good;
seek peace, and pursue it.

(Psalm 34:14)

'My Journal':

- *Consider the significance of the words 'seek' and 'pursue' linked with 'peace' in this verse: for example, these are two quite strong words which suggest actively striving to live a life radiating peace, and of being a peacemaker. Write down your conclusions.*

Meditate on the fact that Jesus came to the earth to bring peace (Luke 2:13-14).

Lord Jesus.

You came to the earth to bring peace to humankind!

Thank you that, through your death and resurrection, you have made it possible for us to be filled with an inner spiritual peace.

Please fill my life with your peace.

Help me to create an atmosphere of peace through living a peaceful lifestyle.

And enable me to be a peacemaker in troubled situations.

(Include any additional topics for prayer or thanksgiving, arising from this study)

In your name.

Amen.

'Doers of the word' (aim): To experience God's peace, to live a peaceful life, and to be a peacemaker.

Is there anything that you think you might find difficult about achieving the aim?

What the Bible says about **peace (Remembrance)**

Righteousness and peace

3rd November

The psalmist speaks about key elements for us individually, and as church congregations, to experience spiritual refreshment and revival from God. And he creates a wonderful image of the close links between them.

Steadfast love and faithfulness will meet;
righteousness and peace will kiss each other.

(Psalm 85:10)

'My Journal':

- *Picture in your mind's eye how you could symbolically paint or draw love and faithfulness meeting; and then jot down some notes, or do a quick sketch.*

Meditate on the image of righteousness and peace kissing each other; remembering that Jesus' death and resurrection enable us to be made righteousness (2 Corinthians 5:21) and be filled with peace (John 14:27).

Lord Jesus.

Through our relationship with you, we experience the love and faithfulness of God; and through being filled with your righteousness, we experience your peace in our lives.

Thank you that through that love, faithfulness, righteousness and peace, we experience spiritual refreshment and revival in our personal lives, and our church congregations.

Please grant me, and the church congregation to which I belong, a fresh experience of all these things.

(Include any additional topics for prayer or thanksgiving, arising from this study)

In your name.

Amen.

'Doers of the word' (aim): To benefit from refreshment and revival, through receiving a fresh experience of God's love, faithfulness, righteousness and peace.

Is there anything that you think you might find difficult about achieving the aim?

What the Bible says about **peace (Remembrance)**

No peace for the wicked

4th November

The only way to experience inner peace is through approaching Jesus with repentance and in faith, entering into a relationship with him, and experiencing his forgiveness for sin.

'There is no peace', says the Lord, 'for the wicked.'

(Isaiah 48:22)

'My Journal':

- *Consider that, unless we deal with the sin in our lives, we will never experience inner peace. Make some notes about how you see the issue of sin: things like, accepting that we have all sinned (Romans 3:23); accepting that sin leads to destruction (Genesis 3:17-19); and accepting that Jesus is the only answer (John 14:6).*

Meditate on the nature of true repentance; that it should be evidenced by an appropriate change in our actions (Luke 3:8a).

Lord Jesus.

Your mission is to sinners (Luke 19:7, 10)!

Thank you that you are the way to be forgiven, and you are the way to be set free from sin's consequences.

Please help me to be truly repentant; grant me faith; and help me to behave in a way that is fitting of that repentance.

(Include any additional topics for prayer or thanksgiving, arising from this study)

In your name.

Amen.

'Doers of the word' (aim): To approach Jesus with repentance and in faith.

Is there anything that you think you might find difficult about achieving the aim?

What the Bible says about **peace (Remembrance)**

The path of peace
5th November

When Zechariah speaks out prophetic words about his son, at the birth of John the Baptist, he describes him as guiding our feet into the *way of peace* – referring to him preparing the way for Jesus' ministry. As followers of Jesus, our calling is to be his witnesses, also pointing others towards him.

To give light to those who sit in darkness and in the shadow of death,
to guide our feet into the way of peace.

(Luke 1:79)

'My Journal':

- *Consider ways in which we can witness to others, helping to lead them towards Jesus, so that they may experience the inner peace that he offers: for example, we can chat to others about the Bible; we can speak words of testimony; or we can lead through example. Make a note of your thoughts.*

Meditate for a moment on the analogy of guiding feet along a pathway. Life is a journey; we have choices, and we can choose to walk along that pathway of peace with Jesus – or not.

Lord Jesus.

You are the light in the darkness of sin and evil!

And you are the peace in a world where there is so much discord!

Thank you that as we follow you, we are on that *way of peace*.

Please help me to walk along that pathway; and to be a signpost pointing others towards it.

(Include any additional topics for prayer or thanksgiving, arising from this study)

In your name.

Amen.

'Doers of the word' (aim): To walk along the pathway of peace with Jesus, ourselves; and to point others towards finding that pathway as well.

Is there anything that you think you might find difficult about achieving the aim?

What the Bible says about **peace (Remembrance)**

The gift of inner peace

6th November

Jesus speaks about leaving his peace with us, as a gift; he then high-lights that his peace is an inner peace, when he implores us not to allow our hearts to be troubled or fearful.

Peace I leave with you; my peace I give to you. I do not give to you as the world gives. Do not let your hearts be troubled, and do not let them be afraid.

(John 14:27)

'My Journal':

- *Consider the concept of the inner peace that Jesus gives - a peace that combats things like stress, anxiety, guilt and fear. Make some notes on your experience of that kind of peace, in your life – or its absence.*

Meditate on the peace that Jesus gives; and then draw a comparison with what you think the world's view of peace is all about – and what it offers.

Risen Lord Jesus.

You give us the gift of your peace.

Thank you that the peace you give is spiritual and eternal.

Thank you for peace within.

Please fill me full of the peace that reduces stress and anxiety, takes away the guilt and helps me to control the fears.

(Include any additional topics for prayer or thanksgiving, arising from this study)

In your name.

Amen.

'Doers of the word' (aim): To receive the gift of Jesus' inner peace.

Is there anything that you think you might find difficult about achieving the aim?

What the Bible says about **peace (Remembrance)**

Peace with God
7th November

We are told in scripture that justification by faith leads to being at peace with God.

Therefore, since we are justified by faith, we have peace with God through our Lord Jesus Christ.

(Romans 5:1)

'My Journal':

- *Consider for a few moments the nature of faith (Hebrews 11:1), and how it relates to our relationships with Jesus. Write down your thoughts.*

Meditate on this fact. Justification is forgiveness from God that is so complete; it is just as if we have never sinned. Consider its relevance to being at peace with God - beginning with being set free from the consequences of sin.

Almighty God.

You are the great creator God!

Thank you that through faith in Jesus we can be made just as if we have never sinned – set free from the consequences of sin – and be at peace with you.

Please grant me more faith in my relationship with Jesus.

Help me to know your forgiveness and the justification that Paul speaks about.

And let me be at peace with you.

(Include any additional topics for prayer or thanksgiving, arising from this study)

In Jesus' name.

Amen.

'Doers of the word' (aim): To be justified through faith in Jesus and be at peace with God.

Is there anything that you think you might find difficult about achieving the aim?

What the Bible says about **peace (Remembrance)**

Living in peace with everyone

8th November

It is quite a challenge – to say the least – when Paul instructs us to live in peace with everyone.

If it is possible, so far as it depends on you, live peaceably with all.

(Romans 12:18)

'My Journal':

- *Think about the words 'so far as it depends on you'. Obviously there are two sides to living in peace; we are responsible for our side. Make some notes on how we can promote that peacefulness between ourselves and others.*

Meditate on the enormity of this instruction 'live peaceably with all'. Prayerfully think about those with whom you find that really easy, and also, those with whom you find that a constant struggle.

Our loving heavenly Father.

It is your desire that we should live at peace with one another!

Thank you that you can equip us to achieve our part in this.

Please fill me afresh with the Holy Spirit.

Help me, in my dealings with others, to demonstrate qualities like respect, honesty, tolerance, humility and love – equipped through the indwelling Holy Spirit.

(Include any additional topics for prayer from your journal)

In Jesus' name.

Amen.

'Doers of the word' (aim): To live peaceably with all.

Is there anything that you think you might find difficult about achieving the aim?

What the Bible says about **peace (Remembrance)**

Kingdom values
9th November

God's kingdom is not based on the physical; but on the spiritual.

For the kingdom of God is not food and drink but righteousness and peace and joy in the Holy Spirit.

(Romans 14:17)

'My Journal':

- *What kind of things make our connection with the physical world as strong as it is?*

Meditate on the characteristics of the kingdom mentioned in this verse: 'righteousness and peace and joy in the Holy Spirit'. These are things that we cannot achieve for ourselves – only through the Triune God.

Lord Jesus.

It is only through you that we can be made righteous, experience inner peace, and be filled with joy!

Thank you that you long to have a relationship with each one of us.

Please help me to walk close to you each day; to allow the Holy Spirit to work fully in my life; and to be obedient to the Father's will.

Help me, through that, to know righteousness, inner peace and joy in my life.

(Include any additional topics for prayer or thanksgiving, arising from this study)

In your name.

Amen.

'Doers of the word' (aim): To hold the things of the physical world lightly; and focus on the characteristics of the kingdom.

Is there anything that you think you might find difficult about achieving the aim?

What the Bible says about **peace (Remembrance)**

Peace ruling in our hearts

10th November

The Bible speaks about allowing Jesus' peace to rule in our hearts: there is so much need for that in the modern world!

And let the peace of Christ rule in your hearts, to which indeed you were called in the one body. And be thankful.

(Colossians 3:15)

'My Journal':

- *There is a lot in this short verse. It speaks about peace ruling in our hearts; being part of the body of Christ* (1 Corinthians 12:12); and thankfulness. Consider the significance of these things in terms of our relationship with Jesus; and make some notes.

Meditate on the words: 'Let the peace of Christ rule in your hearts' – and make a mental note of anything God says to you about it. They set us a real challenge. It is urging us to allow Jesus' peace to rule how we live our lives: it should be fundamental to our behaviour, reactions, decisions, hopes, relationships, ambitions, etc.

Lord Jesus.

Your desire is to bring peace to the world!

Thank you for your peace.

Please let your peace rule in my heart – through my relationship with you.

Thank you that as a follower of you, I am part of your body: help me to play my part as a team player.

Help me to express my thankfulness to you at all times; and to live a thankful lifestyle.

(Include any additional topics for prayer or thanksgiving, arising from this study)

In your name.

Amen.

'Doers of the word' (aim): To let the peace of Christ rule in our hearts; to be part of the body of Christ; and to be thankful.

Is there anything that you think you might find difficult about achieving the aim?

What the Bible says about **peace (Remembrance)**

Complete in everything good

11th November

In Hebrew's, Paul links together the God of peace with the enablement for us to be made *complete in everything good*: preparing us to do his will.

Now may the God of peace, who brought back from the dead our Lord Jesus, the great shepherd of the sheep, by the blood of the eternal covenant, make you complete in everything good so that you may do his will, working among us that which is pleasing in his sight, through Jesus Christ, to whom be the glory for ever and ever, Amen.

(Hebrews 13:20-21)

'My Journal':

- *Think about the connection between God being 'the God of peace', Jesus' death and resurrection, the 'eternal covenant', salvation and the enablement to please God. Make some notes.*

Meditate on the significance of the phrase: 'complete in everything good' - that is, through Jesus' death and resurrection, we experience the ultimate blessing, empowerment and the potential to please God.

God of peace.

Your nature, plans and purposes all include peace!

Thank you that you offer your peace to us – through Jesus.

Please make me complete in everything good, equipping me to please you.

(Include any additional topics for prayer or thanksgiving, arising from this study)

In Jesus' name.

Amen.

'Doers of the word' (aim): To be made complete in everything good; through the God of peace.

Is there anything that you think you might find difficult about achieving the aim?

17

WILDERNESS EXPERIENCES

What the Bible says about **wilderness experiences**

12th November

Telling the story

Ahab told Jezebel all that Elijah had done, and how he had killed all the prophets with the sword. Then Jezebel sent a messenger to Elijah, saying, 'So may the gods do to me, and more also, if I do not make your life like the life of one of them by this time tomorrow.' Then he was afraid; he got up and fled for his life, and came to Beer-sheba, which belongs to Judah; he left his servant there.

But he himself went a day's journey into the wilderness, and came and sat down under a solitary broom tree. He asked that he might die: 'It is enough; now, O Lord, take away my life, for I am no better than my ancestors.' Then he lay down under the broom tree and fell asleep. Suddenly an angel touched him and said to him, 'Get up and eat.' He looked, and there at his head was a cake baked on hot stones, and a jar of water. He ate and drank, and lay down again. The angel of the Lord came a second time, touched him, and said, 'Get up and eat, otherwise the journey will be too much for you.' He got up, and ate and drank; then he went in the strength of that food for forty days and forty nights to Horeb the mount of God. At that place he came to a cave, and spent the night there.

(1 Kings 19:1-9a)

... to be looked at over the next three days.

Lord God.

Thank you for the truth of scripture, and that it is relevant to every generation.

Thank you for this passage of scripture that speaks about wilderness experiences.

Please help me to understand what I have just read; and to meditate upon it today.

(Include any additional topics for prayer or thanksgiving, arising from this study)

In Jesus' name.

Amen.

What the Bible says about **wilderness experiences**

Afraid and depressed
13th November

Depression and anxiety can strike anyone, at any time, from any background. Sometimes there is an obvious reason for it; but often there is not. It is not about lacking in faith or being a 'bad' Christian.

But he himself went a day's journey into the wilderness, and came and sat down under a solitary broom tree. He asked that he might die: 'It is enough; now, O Lord, take away my life, for I am no better than my ancestors.'

(1 Kings 19:4)

'My Journal':

- *Living with severe depression, feeling anxious, facing repeated discouragements, or simply that feeling of nothing seems to be working out, amongst other things, could be referred to as wilderness experiences. It's like a feeling of being stuck in some way. Maybe that sounds familiar to you at this time. Jot down some notes about your personal experiences of such things.*

Meditate on the knowledge that when everything seems to be hopeless, we are able to draw on hope from God (Psalm 42:5).

Almighty God.

You are the God of hope!

Thank you that whatever is happening in our lives, we can draw hope from you, through our relationship with Jesus.

Please help me to keep trusting in you; and not to stop moving forwards in my life - even when I am feeling at rock bottom.

And at those times, stop me from being made to feel guilty by others, for feeling discouraged, depressed or anxious – because I am doing my best.

(Include any additional topics for prayer or thanksgiving, arising from this study)

In Jesus' name.

Amen.

'Doers of the word' (aim): To seek help and support (particularly from the God of hope) during those times when we might be feeling depressed, anxious, discouraged or when nothing seems to be working out – and not be made to feel guilty by others for feeling that way.

Is there anything that you think you might find difficult about achieving the aim?

Cared for by God when we are at our lowest

14th November

God never stops caring about us, and God never leaves us, when we are in a relationship with him, through Jesus. We don't always attribute that care to him, because he often sends one of his people to deliver that care for him – or maybe even an angel.

Then he lay down under the broom tree and fell asleep. Suddenly an angel touched him and said to him, 'Get up and eat.' He looked, and there at his head was a cake baked on hot stones, and a jar of water. He ate and drank, and lay down again.

(1 Kings 19:5-6)

'My Journal':

- *Think about the quality of the care that God sends to Elijah at this time of fear, depression and discouragement. Freshly baked bread and a jar of clean water... And the angel wakes Elijah with just a touch, not a poke or a violent shake... Maybe God is caring for you in some way at the present time. Jot down some notes.*

Meditate on the fact that God knows what Elijah needs at this precise moment in time: it is not prayer or a time of studying the scriptures, it is physical food and drink. What do you particularly need at this time? Is it spiritual input, or is it more towards practical care… or both?

Almighty God.

You are a God of compassion and you care for us all – especially when we are hurting in some way!

Thank you that, when we are in a relationship with Jesus, you never leave us.

Thank you for those of your people, whom you place around us, who help us during those wilderness experiences in our lives.

Please help me to graciously receive your care during those times in my life.

(Include any additional topics for prayer or thanksgiving, arising from this study)

In Jesus' name.

Amen.

'Doers of the word' (aim): To receive God's care.

Is there anything that you think you might find difficult about achieving the aim?

What the Bible says about **wilderness experiences**

Restored and refreshed by God
15th November

God sends his angel for a second time to Elijah. After eating, the prophet is restored and refreshed, ready to continue his journey.

The angel of the Lord came a second time, touched him, and said, 'Get up and eat, otherwise the journey will be too much for you.' He got up, and ate and drank; then he went in the strength of that food for forty days and forty nights to Horeb the mount of God.

(1 Kings 19:7-8)

'My Journal':

- *What is God is showing you, to be the next stage of your life's journey; and how he is preparing and refreshing you now, in readiness for it?*

Meditate on how you could help to bring restoration and refreshment to others who are feeling vulnerable and hurting at this time; and help them to be ready to move forwards in their lives.

Loving heavenly Father.

You restore us and refresh us for the next stage of our journeys with you!

Thank you that you know what we need, and when we need it – and you provide it.

Please restore me when I get tired and maybe discouraged, in preparation for the next chapter in my life – whatever that might be.

When the time is right, reveal to me what that is.

(Include any additional topics for prayer or thanksgiving, arising from this study)

In Jesus' name.

Amen.

'Doers of the word' (aim): To be restored and refreshed by God; ready for the next step in our lives.

Is there anything that you think you might find difficult about achieving the aim?

What the Bible says about **wilderness experiences**

16th November
Telling the story

Then the word of the Lord came to him, saying, 'What are you doing here, Elijah?' He answered, 'I have been very zealous for the Lord, the God of hosts; for the Israelites have forsaken your covenant, thrown down your altars, and killed your prophets with the sword. I alone am left, and they are seeking my life, to take it away.'

He said, 'Go out and stand on the mountain before the Lord, for the Lord is about to pass by.' Now there was a great wind, so strong that it was splitting mountains and breaking rocks in pieces before the Lord, but the Lord was not in the wind; and after the wind an earthquake, but the Lord was not in the earthquake; and after the earthquake a fire, but the Lord was not in the fire; and after the fire a sound of sheer silence. When Elijah heard it, he wrapped his face in his mantle and went out and stood at the entrance of the cave. Then there came a voice to him that said, 'What are you doing here, Elijah?'
(1 Kings 19:9b-13)

... to be looked at over the next four days.

Lord God.

Thank you for the truth of scripture, and that it is relevant to every generation.

Thank you for this passage of scripture that talks about wilderness experiences.

Please help me to understand what I have just read; and to meditate upon it today.

(Include any additional topics for prayer or thanksgiving, arising from this study)

In Jesus' name.

Amen.

Discouraged
17th November

Life can appear to be unfair, and discouraging at times; especially when we have really strived to build up our relationship with God, and do his will – and it doesn't feel as if it has worked out. It probably sounds a bit flippant to say what I am about to say, but it is true: Living in the here and now, we don't see the eternal picture.

He answered, 'I have been very zealous for the Lord, the God of hosts; for the Israelites have forsaken your covenant, thrown down your altars, and killed your prophets with the sword. I alone am left, and they are seeking my life, to take it away.'

(1 Kings 19:10)

'My Journal':

- *Obviously, our main focus will tend to be on the present physical world in which we live - and it is a very important part of God's plan for us – however, it is actually only a tiny part of our eternal existence. Sketch a picture or diagram that might help you to grasp hold of that concept, a little better.*

Meditate on why our lives in the present, physical world in which we live are so important. Include things like, we face the choice of whether or not to do things God's way, we are able to influence others in a positive way as they face that choice, and it is an opportunity to get to know God better.

Almighty God.

You can see everything there is to see of the eternal picture!

Thank you that there is an eternal picture, it is a good one, and we can all be part of it, through following Jesus.

Please help me to walk closely to Jesus; and in so doing, to do things your way.

Grant me the ability to see something of the eternal picture - just as much as I need to see now.

But, help me to also appreciate the importance of how I live my life in the 'here and now': to make the right choices – and to build up my relationship with you.

(Include any additional topics for prayer or thanksgiving, arising from this study)

In Jesus' name.

Amen.

'Doers of the word' (aim): To try to grasp onto the eternal picture more, but without losing sight of the importance of our lives, here and now, and what we do with them.

Is there anything that you think you might find difficult about achieving the aim?

What the Bible says about **wilderness experiences**

A powerful God

18th November

God has so many different aspects to his character and nature. He is certainly a powerful God; and the God who created and sustains the world in which we live. And so it would not be unreasonable to expect God to appear to Elijah in some earth shattering way – but not this time!

He said, 'Go out and stand on the mountain before the Lord, for the Lord is about to pass by.' Now there was a great wind, so strong that it was splitting mountains and breaking rocks in pieces before the Lord, but the Lord was not in the wind; and after the wind an earthquake, but the Lord was not in the earthquake.

(1 Kings 19:11)

'My Journal':

- *Consider the power of God for a few minutes: his power to create, sustain, provide and control; but also remember the power of his love to positively transform lives in countless different ways. Make a note of your thoughts.*

Meditate on how people might expect God to 'pass by' in the 21st Century western world. Do they sometimes miss him as a result of having wrong preconceptions?

Almighty God.

You are so powerful!

You are the great Creator God.

You are the God who sustains that which you have created.

You are the God who provides for your creation.

You are the God who is in control of that which you have created.

But you are also a personal God, who constantly demonstrates to us, the power of your love.

Thank you that your power is demonstrated in these and many other ways.

Please help me to share your love with others.

(Include any additional topics for prayer or thanksgiving, arising from this study)

In Jesus' name.

Amen.

'Doers of the word' (aim): To recognise the different aspects of God's power.

Is there anything that you think you might find difficult about achieving the aim?

A refining God

19th November

God is the God of salvation. Through our relationship with Jesus, he cleanses, refines, restores and makes us ready to spend eternity in his presence. But God does not appear to Elijah in this way, on this occasion!

And after the earthquake a fire, but the Lord was not in the fire.

(1 Kings 19:12a)

'My Journal':

- *God is the God of salvation: through Jesus he forgives, restores, cleanses and refines. We have eternal hope through the salvation God offers. How does that make you feel?*

Meditate on some of the ways in which God refines us – and strengthens us: things like, those difficult choices we have to make, experiencing trying circumstances in our lives, or even those times of failure.

Almighty God.

You are the God of salvation, the God who refines, and the God who gives hope!

Thank you that through Jesus, we can experience all those things.

Please strengthen me, and help me to face up to and endure any difficulties and hardships I am facing at the present time – and use those situations for your glory and purposes.

(Include any additional topics for prayer or thanksgiving, arising from this study)

In Jesus' name.

Amen.

'Doers of the word' (aim): To endure that process of refinement; by the God of Salvation, who gives us hope.

Is there anything that you think you might find difficult about achieving the aim?

Gentle encouragement

20th November

God meets us in the way that is appropriate to us at the time: in power; testing or refining… or in gentleness, stillness and 'sheer silence'.

And after the fire a sound of sheer silence.

(1 Kings 19:12b)

'My Journal':

- *How do you need to meet with God at this time? Or to look at it another way, how God is choosing to appear to you at this time? Do you need to experience him in his power? Do you need to undergo his testing or refining? Or do you need to feel his gentle touch, and encouragement, in the stillness and silence?*

Meditate on what is meant by the 'sound of sheer silence'. I guess we do hear silence, in the context of being able to experience it through our senses – and absorb it into our whole being. The use of the word 'sheer' emphasises the completeness of the silence – something which is often so very difficult to discover in the busy world in which we live.

Gracious God.

You meet with us in the way that we need to meet with you: sometimes it is in power; sometimes it is to test and refine; but other times it is in a gentle way, in stillness and silence!

Thank you that you know what we need; and meet with us in that way.

Please help me to recognise you, in whatever way you meet with me... and enable me to find that stillness and silence in my life, when that is how you want to do it.

(Include any additional topics for prayer or thanksgiving, arising from this study)

In Jesus' name.

Amen.

'Doers of the word' (aim): To experience God in whatever way he might appear to us – even in the silence and stillness.

Is there anything that you think you might find difficult about achieving the aim?

18

WITNESSING

What the Bible says about **witnessing**

True or false witnesses

21st November

As witnesses for Jesus; the evidence that we give has to be honest.

Whoever speaks the truth gives honest evidence,
but a false witness speaks deceitfully.

(Proverbs 12:17)

'My Journal':

- *We are probably all familiar with witnesses in court making an oath to tell the truth. This verse reinforces the essential quality of a good witness being honesty: speaking about their own personal experience truthfully and openly. Consider the fact that we, as Christians, are called to speak honestly and openly about our personal experience of being in relationship, and in a close daily walk, with Jesus. What is your response to this challenge?*

Meditate on what you might say to someone when witnessing to them about Jesus.

Lord Jesus.

It is your will for us to be your witnesses, telling others about our personal experience of being in relationship with you, and of walking daily with you!

Thank you that I have a wonderful story to tell; even though at times there have been difficulties.

A story involving love, forgiveness and hope.

Please help me to be a good witness: to be open and honest.

(Include any additional topics for prayer or thanksgiving, arising from this study)

In your name.

Amen.

'Doers of the word' (aim): To speak truthfully and openly to others, about Jesus.

Is there anything that you think you might find difficult about achieving the aim?

What the Bible says about **witnessing**

Called to witness
22nd November

Just as the Israelites were called to be a witnessing nation; all followers of Jesus are called to be his witnesses – as part of our lives of service.

You are my witnesses, says the Lord,
and my servant whom I have chosen,
so that you may know and believe me
and understand that I am he.
Before me no god was formed,
nor shall there be any after me.

(Isaiah 43:10)

'My Journal':

- *What qualities do you think are required to fulfil Jesus' calling to be his witnesses? Honesty is certainly one of them.*

Meditate on what makes a close daily walk with Jesus: things like, faith, prayer, Bible study, worship, praise and obedience.

Risen Lord Jesus.

As your followers, we all have a testimony to tell!

Thank you that we can all have a relationship with you – for eternity.

And when we do: it gives us a wonderful, inspirational story to share.

Please grant me the honesty, obedience, courage, boldness and trust to fulfil the calling – to be your witness.

(Include any additional topics for prayer or thanksgiving, arising from this study)

In your name.

Amen.

'Doers of the word' (aim): To fulfil the calling to be a witness of Jesus.

Is there anything that you think you might find difficult about achieving the aim?

What the Bible says about **witnessing**

Tell the full story
23rd November

We are told that when we witness to others about Jesus, and what he has done for us, not to hold back – but to tell the whole story!

'Go, stand in the temple and tell the people the whole message about this life.'

(Acts 5:20)

'My Journal':

- Consider what Jesus has done for us when he gave his life on the cross, paying the penalty for our sin, rose again, and is alive today – offering us all salvation! Make a note of how that makes you feel.

Meditate on how Jesus has worked in your life, since you met him as your Lord and Saviour... and then be prepared to tell the whole story!

Risen, living Lord Jesus.

It is because of you that we have an amazing story to tell – The Good News!

Thank you for dying on the cross, paying the penalty for sin; that you rose again, and are alive today... and through repentance and faith in you we can all be forgiven, set free from sin's consequences, and filled with eternal hope... and I have a testimony to share.

Please give me confidence, boldness and sensitivity – and help me to share the whole story!

(Include any additional topics for prayer or thanksgiving, arising from this study)

In your name.

Amen.

'Doers of the word' (aim): To not hold back when we are sharing the message of Jesus with others; and as we speak out our personal testimony.

Is there anything that you think you might find difficult about achieving the aim?

Testimony: what you have seen and heard

24th November

To my understanding, the challenge a witness faces is that they give evidence from their own personal experience of a particular incident – primarily, what they have seen and heard.

For you will be his witness to all the world of what you have seen and heard.

(Acts 22:15)

'My Journal':

- *What is your personal experience of Jesus? In what ways is Jesus at work in your life?*

Meditate on how we can hear Jesus speak into our lives today. Include through scripture, through the words of wise Christian friends and teachers, through circumstances, through that inner voice that says 'yes' or 'no', or through doors which open or close.

Loving Lord Jesus.

You are my friend, my Lord and my Saviour!

Thank you for all the different ways in which I experience you in my life on a daily basis.

Thank you that you speak to me in different ways.

Please help me to tell others what I have 'seen and heard'.

(Include any additional topics for prayer or thanksgiving, arising from this study)

In your name.

Amen.

'Doers of the word' (aim): To tell the world about our personal experience of Jesus: what we have seen and heard.

Is there anything that you think you might find difficult about achieving the aim?

Relying on God's power when we witness

25th November

What a comfort it is, that when we witness, we are not reliant on our own strength.

My speech and my proclamation were not with plausible words of wisdom, but with a demonstration of the Spirit and of power, so that your faith might rest not on human wisdom but on the power of God.

(1 Corinthians 2:4 and 5)

'My Journal':

- *Remember the fact that when we are prepared to be used by God, in his service and to further the kingdom, we do it in the power of the indwelling Holy Spirit – in God's power! Make some notes about how that makes you feel.*

Meditate in the knowledge that even though the Holy Spirit never leaves us, we need to welcome him afresh into our lives every day... allowing him complete freedom to work within us.

Almighty God.

You are a powerful God!

Thank you that when we serve you: it is in your power that we do so.

Please fill me afresh with the indwelling Holy Spirit: empowering and enabling me in all that I do for you.

Help me to rely on you.

(Include any additional topics for prayer or thanksgiving, arising from this study)

In Jesus name.

Amen.

'Doers of the word' (aim): To rely on God's power, as we serve and witness.

Is there anything that you think you might find difficult about achieving the aim?

Given the words to speak

26th November

There is no need for us to be anxious about what we are going to say, as we witness to others; as long as we trust that the Holy Spirit will give us the right words.

And we speak of these things in words not taught by human wisdom but taught by the Spirit, interpreting spiritual things to those who are spiritual.

(1 Corinthians 2:13)

'My Journal':

- *Consider the significance of God providing us with the right words to say, when we witness, through the power of his indwelling Holy Spirit. Jot down your thoughts.*

Meditate on the fact that 'we speak of these things in words not taught by human wisdom'. Let's not try to use our own wisdom as we speak up for Jesus.

Almighty God.

You will provide us with the words for us to say, when we witness!

Thank you for the power of the indwelling Holy Spirit.

Please fill me afresh with the Holy Spirit today.

Help me to depend on your wisdom – and not look to my own.

Let me have the right words as I speak to others about Jesus, and my faith.

(Include any additional topics for prayer or thanksgiving, arising from this study)

In Jesus' name.

Amen.

'Doers of the word' (aim): To allow God to provide us with the right words to say, when we witness – through the indwelling Holy Spirit.

Is there anything that you think you might find difficult about achieving the aim?

Chatting the gospel

27th November

In Ephesians, we see a lovely picture painted of living a life of continuous praise, worship and thanksgiving to the Triune God: where everything that we say and do is part of that process; and at the same time, talking to others about Jesus also becomes really natural and spontaneous – chatting the gospel!

As you sing psalms and hymns and spiritual songs among yourselves, singing and making melody to the Lord in your hearts, giving thanks to God the Father at all times and for everything in the name of our Lord Jesus Christ.

(Ephesians 5:19-20)

'My Journal':

- *What does it mean, to make everything you say and do into an act of praise, worship and witness? – Everything!*

Meditate on what it means to sing and make melody 'to the Lord in your hearts': the concept of having such a deep down inner joy and peace, through knowing Jesus as our Lord and Saviour, and being reunited with the Triune God, that our whole being wants to shout out about Jesus – chatting the gospel! Is that how you feel?

Loving heavenly Father, Jesus and Holy Spirit.

You are worthy of our praise, worship and thanksgiving!

Thank you that through being in relationship with you, through Jesus, we experience that wonderful deep down inner joy and peace – right down in our hearts.

Please help me to allow that feeling of joy and peace to shine out, finding its natural expression, in witnessing to others.

(Include any additional topics for prayer or thanksgiving, arising from this study)

In Jesus' name.

Amen.

'Doers of the word' (aim): To make everything that we say or do into an act of praise, worship and thanksgiving to the Triune God – chatting the gospel.

Is there anything that you think you might find difficult about achieving the aim?

Do not be ashamed to share

28th November

The Bible speaks about there being persecution: but that is no reason to be ashamed to share our testimony with others – we should do it anyway!

Do not be ashamed, then, of the testimony about our Lord or me his prisoner, but join with me in suffering for the gospel, relying on the power of God.

(2 Timothy 1:8)

'My Journal':

- *Consider the different themes in this short verse: not being ashamed to speak openly about Jesus, persecution and suffering for the sake of our faith, and relying on God's power in all that we say and do. Make a note of your responses.*

Meditate on how you might feel, if a really close friend of yours were so ashamed of you, that they never spoke about you to anyone else. How do you think Jesus feels if we are ashamed to talk to others about him?

My Lord and Saviour, Jesus Christ.
You have given me such an amazing testimony to share!
Thank you for the empowerment of the Holy Spirit.
Please help me never to be ashamed to tell my testimony to others.
Strengthen me in times of persecution and suffering.
Grant me boldness and confidence.
(Include any additional topics for prayer or thanksgiving, arising from this study)
In your name.
Amen.

'Doers of the word' (aim): To not be ashamed to share words of testimony.

Is there anything that you think you might find difficult about achieving the aim?

Be prepared to give an answer

29th November

Are you ready to answer, when someone asks you about your faith?

But in your hearts sanctify Christ as Lord. Always be ready to make your defence to anyone who demands from you an account of the hope that is in you.

(1 Peter 3:15)

'My Journal':

- *Consider the words 'always be ready'. We need to be in a permanent state of readiness to answer people, when they question us about our faith – and the basis of our eternal hope. Remember that God will give us the words when we look to him! Jot down your thoughts.*

Meditate on the verse talking about making our 'defence'. We will be under attack. We are in a spiritual battle. But though we are still in the conflict at the present time, Jesus has won the victory over sin and evil; and that will find its ultimate fulfilment when he returns.

Lord Jesus.

You are Lord!

Thank you that you gave your 'everything', so that we might be saved, and filled with eternal hope.

Please help me to be ready and willing to defend my faith, at all times.

Fill me afresh with the Holy Spirit.

Help me to remember that we are in a spiritual battle: strengthen and protect me.

(Include any additional topics for prayer or thanksgiving, arising from this study)

In your name.

Amen.

'Doers of the word' (aim): To be ready – and willing – to answer people, when they challenge us to defend our faith.

Is there anything that you think you might find difficult about achieving the aim?

The gospel is universal
30th November

The gospel message is for everyone!

Then I saw another angel flying in mid-heaven, with an eternal gospel to proclaim to those who live on the earth – to every nation and tribe and language and people.

(*Revelation 14:6*)

'My Journal':

- *Consider the universal nature of the message of salvation through Jesus - referred to in this verse. What does that mean in practical terms?*

Meditate on the fact that the message has eternal significance to us all.

Loving heavenly Father.

The message of salvation, through Jesus, is for all people.

Thank you that, through being in a personal relationship with Jesus, based on repentance and faith, we are filled with eternal hope.

This message is available to everyone.

Please help me to proclaim such a message, as universally as I can... and to encourage people to respond positively to it.

(Include any additional topics for prayer or thanksgiving, arising from this study)

In Jesus' name.

Amen.

'Doers of the word' (aim): To proclaim an inclusive message.

Is there anything that you think you might find difficult about achieving the aim?

19

ADVENT & CHRISTMAS

What the Bible says about **the birth of Jesus (Advent and Christmas)**

1st December

Telling the story

Now the birth of Jesus the Messiah took place in this way. When his mother Mary had been engaged to Joseph, but before they lived together, she was found to be with child from the Holy Spirit. Her husband Joseph, being a righteous man and unwilling to expose her to public disgrace, planned to dismiss her quietly. But just when he had resolved to do this, an angel of the Lord appeared to him in a dream and said, 'Joseph, son of David, do not be afraid to take Mary as your wife, for the child conceived in her is from the Holy Spirit. She will bear a son, and you are to name him Jesus, for he will save his people from their sins. All this took place to fulfil what had been spoken by the Lord through the prophet:

'Look, the virgin shall conceive and bear a son,
And they shall name him Emmanuel',

which means, 'God is with us.' When Joseph awoke from sleep, he did as the angel of the Lord commanded him; he took her as his wife, but had no marital relations with her until she had borne a son; and he named him Jesus.

(Matthew 1:18-25)

... to be looked at over the next six days.

Lord God.

Thank you for the truth of scripture, and that it is relevant to every generation.

Thank you for this passage of scripture that leads into the Christmas Story.

Please help me to understand what I have just read; and to meditate upon it today.

(Include any additional topics for prayer or thanksgiving, arising from this study)

In Jesus' name.

Amen.

What the Bible says about **the birth of Jesus (Advent and Christmas)**

God speaks to Joseph
2nd December

The angel appears to Joseph in a dream to explain God's plan to him: because God wants Joseph to be part of that plan.

But just when he had resolved to do this, an angel of the Lord appeared to him in a dream, and said.

(Matthew 1:20a)

'My Journal':

- *Consider what a privilege it is, to be called to be part of God's plan. Having said that, we all have a part to play in the wider plan. How do you feel about that?*

Meditate on what difference that makes to how you live your life on a daily basis? Maybe you are a little more aware of your behaviour, spend more time in Bible study, or pray lots.

Lord.

Thank you that you have a plan for your creation; and you want us all to be part of that plan!

Thank you that you want me to be part of your plan.

I really do feel privileged *(speak about how you feel).*

Please help me to be willing to serve you in this way, and enable me to successfully complete those things to which I am called.

(Include any additional topics for prayer or thanksgiving, arising from this study)

In Jesus' name.

Amen.

'Doers of the word' (aim): To be willing to be part of God's plan.

Is there anything that you think you might find difficult about achieving the aim?

What the Bible says about **the birth of Jesus (Advent and Christmas)**

Jesus really is the Son of God

3rd December

Through the Holy Spirit, God makes an intervention into the history of the world; and does something that is not within the natural order of his creation.

'Joseph, son of David, do not be afraid to take Mary as your wife, for the child conceived in her is from the Holy Spirit.'

(Matthew 1:20b)

'My Journal':

- *The birth of Jesus is the result of no ordinary conception. Matthew makes it clear that Jesus is conceived by the Holy Spirit – he is God's Son. Consider the significance of that: Jesus is both divine and human. Make some notes of your thoughts.*

Meditate on the facts that we can learn so much about God, from Jesus; and Jesus understands those human emotions that we go through. Spend some time thinking about what the implications are concerning these things. What is your response to God's Son? - To be in a personal relationship and daily walk with the Triune God through Jesus; or not.

Father God.

Jesus is your Son!

Thank you that you sent your Son Jesus into the world that first Christmas: to live amongst us, teaching us more about you and about the kingdom; and to give humankind a second chance – that includes me.

Thank you that you love me that much!

Please help me to grasp onto the significance of you sending your Son Jesus into the world; and make a positive response to him.

Let the whole world recognise that Christmas is all about the birth of your Son.

(Include any additional topics for prayer or thanksgiving, arising from this study)

In Jesus' name.

Amen.

'Doers of the word' (aim): To recognise who Jesus is; and make a positive response to him.

Is there anything that you think you might find difficult about achieving the aim?

What the Bible says about **the birth of Jesus (Advent and Christmas)**

God has a plan for our salvation
4th December

Sin is an issue, because it creates a barrier between us and God: but Christmas is all about God's plan to break down that barrier.

'She will bear a son, and you are to name him Jesus, for he will save his people from their sins.'

(Matthew 1:21)

'My Journal':

- *Salvation could be referred to as a jargon word, even though it is used a lot in Christian circles, but there is no other word that means the same thing. Consider what it means to be saved from our sins, and their consequences - and jot down some notes.*

Meditate on the fact that God's plan for salvation includes everyone: have you accepted that salvation for yourself, and are you witnessing to others? - Speaking to others about what the Bible says concerning salvation, and about your own personal experience of being in relationship with Jesus – filling you with eternal hope.

God our heavenly Father.

You are the God of salvation!

Thank you that on that first Christmas, you had a plan for our salvation that involved your Son, Jesus being born as a baby.

Thank you that Jesus was prepared to die on the cross, paying the penalty for our sin – for my sin! - and that he rose again, and is alive today.

Thank you that through entering into a personal relationship with him, I am forgiven for my sin; I am made blameless for the day of judgement; and filled with eternal hope.

Please help to lead others towards discovering salvation through Jesus, for themselves.

(Include any additional topics for prayer or thanksgiving, arising from this study)

In Jesus' name.

Amen.

'Doers of the word' (aim): To experience God's salvation for ourselves; and to help lead others to discover it for themselves.

Is there anything that you think you might find difficult about achieving the aim?

What the Bible says about **the birth of Jesus (Advent and Christmas)**

God is working his plan out
5th December

So many of our own plans never work out: but God's plans do!

'All this took place to fulfil what had been spoken by the Lord through the prophet.'

(Matthew 1:22)

'My Journal':

- *Think about promise for a few minutes. The prophets passed on God's promise concerning the birth of Jesus; and it happens, just as it had been prophesised. God's promise will always be fulfilled – consider the significance of that to your life. Jot down some notes.*

Meditate on trust. Has your trust been damaged over the years, through life experiences? - Things like being let down by other people - maybe by earthly parents - who have broken promises they have made to you. God is the perfect parent and will not let us down: Do you believe that?

Almighty God.

Your promises never fail!

Thank you that the Christmas story is the fulfilment of generations of prophecy.

Thank you that you are a God of promise; and that the Bible is full of amazing, eternal promises – all of which will be fulfilled.

Thank you that following Jesus opens up all those promises to us.

Please help me to walk closely to Jesus daily, in faith *(talk about any aspects of your daily walk with Jesus that you struggle with – it might be trust).*

(Include any additional topics for prayer or thanksgiving, arising from this study)

In Jesus' name.

Amen.

'Doers of the word' (aim): To trust in the promises of God.

Is there anything that you think you might find difficult about achieving the aim?

What the Bible says about **the birth of Jesus (Advent and Christmas)**

God is with us

6th December

We never need to be alone, or even feel alone, because God is with us: and wants to be in an eternal relationship with each one of us.

'And they shall name him Emmanuel', which means, 'God is with us.'

(Matthew 1:23b)

'My Journal':

- *Consider the implications of the deity of Jesus - God living on earth. The great creator God wants to communicate with us; and to enter into a personal relationship with everyone. How does that make you feel?*

Meditate on what an amazing opportunity and privilege it is to know God. There are fundamentally two different aspects to knowing God: he is the Creator God - all powerful, all knowing and all seeing; but he is also a God who we can get to know personally – a loving parent!

Creator God.

You came down to earth to live amongst us!

Thank you that you came into the world as a helpless baby that first Christmas.

Thank you that your desire is to communicate with us all – and to enter into a personal relationship with us individually.

Please help me to listen to what you are saying to me; and to make a positive response to being in relationship with you – through Jesus.

(Include any additional topics for prayer or thanksgiving, arising from this study)

In Jesus' name.

Amen.

'Doers of the word' (aim): To respond positively to the great Creator God reaching out to us; and to get to know him as a personal God.

Is there anything that you think you might find difficult about achieving the aim?

What the Bible says about **the birth of Jesus (Advent and Christmas)**

A message for Joseph
7th December

Joseph listens, understands, believes and acts upon the message which the angel brings from God.

When Joseph awoke from sleep, he did as the angel of the Lord commanded him; he took her as his wife.

(Matthew 1:24)

'My Journal':

- How might you discover what God is saying to you through his Son, Jesus? Make some notes.

Meditate on what our response should be to the things that God says to us: for example, making an immediate response of obedience.

Lord.

You communicate to us through Jesus!

Thank you that you speak to us in so many different ways: for example, through the Bible, through the words of wise Christian friends, through circumstances and situations, through doors opening or closing, and through the life and teaching of Jesus – and being in a prayerful relationship with him…

Please help me to listen to you; to understand the significance of how those things apply to my life; to believe everything that you say; and to act upon it.

Fill me afresh with the power of the indwelling Holy Spirit; and make me a 'doer' of your word *(ask for any necessary qualities that you feel you lack)*!

(Include any additional topics for prayer or thanksgiving, arising from this study)

In Jesus' name.

Amen.

'Doers of the word' (aim): To listen to God speak – especially through Jesus; and respond with obedience.

Is there anything that you think you might find difficult about achieving the aim?

What the Bible says about **the birth of Jesus (Advent and Christmas)**

8th December
Telling the story

In those days a decree went out from Emperor Augustus that all the world should be registered. This was the first registration and was taken while Quirinius was governor of Syria. All went to their own towns to be registered. Joseph also went from the town of Nazareth in Galilee to Judea, to the city of David called Bethlehem, because he was descended from the house and family of David. He went to be registered with Mary, to whom he was engaged and who was expecting a child. While they were there, the time came for her to deliver her child. And she gave birth to her first born son and wrapped him in bands of cloth, and laid him in a manger, because there was no place for them in the inn.

(Luke 2:1-7)

... to be looked at over the next four days.

Lord God.

Thank you for the truth of scripture, and that it is relevant to every generation.

Thank you for this passage of scripture that leads up to the birth of Jesus.

Please help me to understand what I have just read; and to meditate upon it today.

In Jesus' name.

Amen.

What the Bible says about **the birth of Jesus (Advent and Christmas)**

God's guidance: not coincidence
9th December

The Emperor Augustus is used by God to bring Mary and Joseph to the right place for Jesus' birth.

In those days a decree went out from Emperor Augustus that all the world should be registered.

(Luke 2:1)

'My Journal':

- *The Christmas story illustrates that with God, nothing is by chance. Spend some time meditating on that; and jot down some notes about your thoughts.*

Meditate on another favourite Bible story; and the way in which a series of events has to happen, in order for God's plan to be fulfilled – but not by coincidence!

Almighty God.

Nothing is impossible for you!

Thank you that you are a powerful God – your hand is at work all around us… and nothing is by coincidence with you.

Thank you that you work out your plans and purposes; however long the chain of events necessary for that to take place.

Please help me to recognise your power at work in this way.

(Include any additional topics for prayer or thanksgiving, arising from this study)

In Jesus' name.

Amen.

'Doers of the word' (aim): To recognise God's hand at work, guiding and enabling his plans and purposes to be fulfilled.

Is there anything that you think you might find difficult about achieving the aim?

What the Bible says about **the birth of Jesus (Advent and Christmas)**

Feeling unnoticed

10th December

The donkey often appears on Christmas cards, but it doesn't get a mention - or even implied - in the scriptural accounts. But it is imagined, and quite possible, that a donkey carries the mother of God's Son at what is probably her most vulnerable time.

He went to be registered with Mary, to whom he was engaged and who was expecting a child.

(Luke 2:5)

'My Journal':

- *Sometimes we might feel unnoticed in our lives of service; but we are never unnoticed by God. God knows and values what we are doing for him. Jot down your thoughts as you think about that fact.*

Meditate on the knowledge that, whatever your job is in your church congregation, it is of importance to its overall ministry.

Heavenly Father.

You notice everything that we do to further your plans and purposes!

Thank you that we can all be involved in furthering your kingdom; and what we do to that end is of equal importance in your eyes.

Please help me to work hard and conscientiously at those things to which you have called me; and anoint them with the Holy Spirit.

Bless the ministry of the church congregation to which I belong – and of the wider Church.

(Include any additional topics for prayer or thanksgiving, arising from this study)

In Jesus' name.

Amen.

'Doers of the word' (aim): To know that God is noticing what you do for him.

Is there anything that you think you might find difficult about achieving the aim?

What the Bible says about **the birth of Jesus (Advent and Christmas)**

God reaches out

11th December

The Baby Jesus is God reaching out into a broken and damaged world – unable to save itself – but so many are not listening.

And she gave birth to her firstborn son and wrapped him in bands of cloth, and laid him in a manger.

(Luke 2:7a)

'My Journal':

- *Make a list of the characteristics of a broken and damaged world.*

Meditate on the nature and extent of the Triune God's unconditional love: that he would enter into such a world – to save humankind from that brokenness.

Lord Jesus.

You entered into a broken and damaged world, in order to bring healing from that brokenness!

Thank you for your birth, life, death and resurrection; and the salvation that you made possible, as a result.

Please let people respond positively to your offer of eternal hope.

Help me to spread the Good News of that offer.

(Include any additional topics for prayer or thanksgiving, arising from this study)

In your name.

Amen.

'Doers of the word' (aim): To respond positively to God reaching out to us, through the Baby Jesus.

Is there anything that you think you might find difficult about achieving the aim?

What the Bible says about **the birth of Jesus (Advent and Christmas)**

No room for Jesus
12th December

The innkeeper is always in the nativity play; even though he doesn't actually get a mention in the Bible either – all it says is that the inn is full.

Because there was no place for them in the inn.

(Luke 2:7b)

'My Journal':

- *Jesus wants to be in all our lives: to be included and involved in everything we say and do. Make a list of the different areas of your life, in which Jesus wants to be part.*

Meditate on ways in which we can end up in saying 'No-room!' to Jesus: for example, in the busyness of work, social lives, family lives or hobbies; or we can be so focused on things like self-centred ambitions, our own plans or gaining wealth and possessions, that there is just no room left in our focus for Jesus.

Lord Jesus.

You want to be involved in our lives – in a big way!

Thank you that you want to play a big part in my life.

In everything that I say and do.

Please help me to make room for you in my busyness and focus.

And never be guilty of effectively saying, 'No room!'

(Include any additional topics for prayer or thanksgiving, arising from this study)

In your name.

Amen

'Doers of the word' (aim): To always make room for Jesus, in our lives.

Is there anything that you think you might find difficult about achieving the aim?

What the Bible says about **the birth of Jesus (Advent and Christmas)**

13th December
Telling the story

In that region there were shepherds living in the fields, keeping watch over their flock by night. Then an angel of the Lord stood before them, and the glory of the Lord shone around them, and they were terrified. But the angel said to them, 'Do not be afraid; for see – I am bringing you good news of great joy for all the people: to you is born this day in the city of David a Saviour, who is the Messiah, the Lord. This will be a sign for you: you will find a child wrapped in bands of cloth and lying in a manger. And suddenly there was with the angel a multitude of the heavenly host, praising God and saying,

'Glory to God in the highest heaven,
and on earth peace among those whom he favours.'

When the angels had left them and gone into heaven, the shepherds said to one another, 'Let us go now to Bethlehem and see this thing that has taken place, which the Lord has made known to us.' So they went with haste and found Mary and Joseph, and the child lying in the manger. When they saw this, they made known what had been told them about this child; and all who heard it were amazed at what the shepherds told them. But Mary treasured all these words and pondered them in her heart. The shepherds returned, glorifying and praising God for all they had heard and seen, as it had been told them.

(Luke 2:8-20)

... to be looked at over the next six days.

Lord God.

Thank you for the truth of scripture, and that it is relevant to every generation.

Thank you for this passage of scripture that describes the Good News being announced to the shepherds.

Please help me to understand what I have just read; and to meditate upon it today.

(Include any additional topics for prayer or thanksgiving, arising from this study)

In Jesus' name.

Amen.

What the Bible says about **the birth of Jesus (Advent and Christmas)**

The shepherds hear the message

14th December

The birth of God's Son is announced to 'ordinary' people – not royalty, dignitaries, church leaders or celebrities.

In that region there were shepherds living in the fields, keeping watch over their flock by night. Then an angel of the Lord stood before them...

(Luke 2:8-9a)

'My Journal':

- *We think of royal princes and princesses being born in splendour, and surrounded by security. But there are no airs and graces about the birth of Jesus – God's Son. The angelic appearance is to a group of shepherds on the hillside. God wants us to understand that Jesus is approachable, so that we can all easily connect with him. Think about the significance of that for a few minutes; and jot down some notes.*

Meditate on what it would be like to be in the shepherds' shoes: having your work interrupted by an angelic appearance.

Loving heavenly Father,

Thank you that you gave the whole of humankind the most precious gift that you could ever give, that first Christmas – the gift of your Son Jesus!

Thank you that you wanted him to be approachable, so that we could get to know him as a friend – and through him, get to know you better.

This Christmas time, please help me to really get to know Jesus – maybe to meet with him for the very first time – and to be able to get to know you as a loving parent.

(Include any additional topics for prayer or thanksgiving, arising from this study)

In Jesus' name.

Amen.

'Doers of the word' (aim): To realise that the message of that first Christmas is for everyone.

Is there anything that you think you might find difficult about achieving the aim?

What the Bible says about **the birth of Jesus (Advent and Christmas)**

Good news!
15th December

The angel proclaims good news from God.

But the angel said to them, 'Do not be afraid; for see – I am bringing you good news of great joy for all the people.

(Luke 2:10)

'My Journal':

- *In the modern world, people seem to focus primarily on bad news – Why is that? The news that the angel has come to announce is good news; and it still applies to the world today! Jot down your thoughts.*

Meditate on the angel's news: 'I am bringing you good news of great joy for all people.' How does that feel?

Almighty God.

Your message to us is one of Good News!

Thank you that the message is for everyone; and it is one of joy.

Please help me to receive and respond positively to that news; and to pass it on to others.

Enable modern society to be more receptive to good news – especially the Good News.

(Include any additional topics for prayer or thanksgiving, arising from this study)

In Jesus' name.

Amen.

'Doers of the word' (aim): To receive the Good News, and pass it on.

Is there anything that you think you might find difficult about achieving the aim?

What the Bible says about **the birth of Jesus (Advent and Christmas)**

A Saviour
16th December

The angel explains exactly who Jesus is.

'To you is born this day in the city of David a Saviour, who is the Messiah, the Lord.'

(Luke 2:11)

'My Journal':

- *'A Saviour', highlights that Jesus' mission is to bring salvation to a world that has been broken as a result of sin and evil – and is reeling from the consequences; which include separation from God. Jesus saves from the consequences of sin. Meditate on this, and make some notes.*

Meditate on the reference to the Messiah. 'The Messiah', highlights that Jesus is the long awaited person, who was to intervene into the course of history, to put right the brokenness in the world. Consider the implications of this.

Risen Jesus.

You are the Messiah, the Saviour of humankind, and my Lord!

Thank you that by your life, death and resurrection, you have paid the penalty for sin; enabled the whole of humankind to be set free from sin's consequences… and provided the way for us to be restored in our relationship with God.

Thank you that you are the answer to brokenness in the world in which we live.

Please strengthen my relationship with you; and set me free from sin's consequences.

Fill me afresh with the Holy Spirit.

And help me to live in obedience to the Father.

(Include any additional topics for prayer or thanksgiving, arising from this study)

In your name.

Amen.

'Doers of the word' (aim): To enter into a personal relationship with Jesus: proclaiming him as Messiah, Saviour and Lord.

Is there anything that you think you might find difficult about achieving the aim?

What the Bible says about **the birth of Jesus (Advent and Christmas)**

The shepherds share the good news

17th December

The shepherds are so overjoyed, after meeting personally with Jesus, that they respond by telling as many people as they can about the Good News.

And all who heard it were amazed at what the shepherds told them.

(Luke 2:18)

'My Journal':

- *Think about the shepherds' eagerness to tell others about meeting personally with Jesus. How did you feel when you met personally with Jesus, and accepted him as your Lord and Saviour? What was your response then? What is your response now?*

Meditate on what you said, or would say to others about your experience of meeting with Jesus?

Lord Jesus.

The shepherds couldn't wait to tell anyone and everyone about meeting with you!

Thank you that we can all meet personally with you today; and get to know you as our Saviour and Lord.

Please help me to know you in this way; and fill me with the same kind of excitement as the shepherds, to tell as many people as I can about that meeting.

(Include any additional topics for prayer or thanksgiving, arising from this study)

In your name.

Amen.

'Doers of the word' (aim): To tell others about meeting with Jesus as our Saviour and Lord.

Is there anything that you think you might find difficult about achieving the aim?

What the Bible says about **the birth of Jesus (Advent and Christmas)**

Mary ponders these things in her heart

18th December

Mary processes everything that has happened; and remembers every last detail – treasuring those memories.

But Mary treasured all these words and pondered them in her heart.

(Luke 2:19)

'My Journal':

- *Consider your own experiences of Jesus – those treasured memories. What was special about them?*

Meditate on this. I am sure that the way the birth of Jesus has worked out so far, is not the birth that Mary expected: the trauma of travelling, not being able to find accommodation, and giving birth in an animal shelter; and the excitement of visitors arriving unexpectedly, as a result of the proclamation of an angel. Consider the fact that our plans are not always the same as God's plans – but God sees the bigger picture, and everything has a purpose.

Almighty God.

Your plans are perfect!

Thank you that you see the bigger picture – that we don't see – so, that way, you know what is best.

Thank you that, even those negative experiences we go through have a positive purpose in your kingdom.

I could ask that you would help me to fully understand why everything happens in my life, in the way that it does; but instead, my prayer is please help me to learn from and accept that which I do not necessarily understand.

(Include any additional topics for prayer or thanksgiving, arising from this study)

In Jesus' name.

Amen.

'Doers of the word' (aim): To treasure and learn from our experiences of Jesus; and to accept God's plans for us – even when they are not according to how we imagine they will be.

Is there anything that you think you might find difficult about achieving the aim?

What the Bible says about **the birth of Jesus (Advent and Christmas)**

Praise God!
19th December

When the shepherds return to the hillside, they don't lie down and sleep after all the happenings of the night, they glorify and praise God.

The shepherds returned, glorifying and praising God for all they had heard and seen, as it had been told them.

(Luke 2:20)

'My Journal':

- *Where, when and how do you praise God?*

Meditate on contrasting ways to praise God, but all of equal value: for example, in a group or on our own; with loud music and singing, or in the peacefulness and beauty of God's creation; with dancing or hands held high, or in stillness on our knees.

Almighty God.

You are worthy of our praise!

Thank you for the beauty and wonder of your creation.

Thank you for your unconditional love.

Thank you that you are the God of salvation.

Thank you for Jesus; and the eternal hope that we have through being in a relationship with him.

Please help me to freely express my praise to you; and not be put off, because I am not doing it in the same way as my neighbour might be.

(Include any additional topics for prayer or thanksgiving, arising from this study)

In Jesus' name.

Amen.

'Doers of the word' (aim): To spend time praising God; and to recognise that there are different, equally as valid, ways to do that.

Is there anything that you think you might find difficult about achieving the aim?

What the Bible says about **the birth of Jesus (Advent and Christmas)**

20th December
Telling the story

In the time of King Herod, after Jesus was born in Bethlehem of Judea, wise men from the East came to Jerusalem, asking. 'Where is the child who has been born King of the Jews? For we observed his star rising, and have come to pay him homage.' When King Herod heard this, he was frightened, and all Jerusalem with him; and calling together all the chief priests and scribes of the people, he enquired of them where the messiah was to be born. They told him, 'In Bethlehem of Judea; for so it has been written by the prophet:

"And you, Bethlehem, in the land of Judah,
are by no means least among the rulers of Judah;
for from you shall come a ruler who is to shepherd my people Israel."'

Then Herod secretly called for the wise men and learned from them the exact time when the star had appeared. Then he sent them to Bethlehem, saying, 'Go and search diligently for the child; and when you have found him, bring me word so that I may also go and pay him homage.' When they had heard the king, they set out; and there, ahead of them, went the star that they had seen at its rising, until it stopped over the place where the child was. When they saw that the star had stopped, they were overwhelmed with joy. On entering the house, they saw the child with Mary his mother; and they knelt down and paid him homage. Then opening their treasure chests, they offer him gifts of gold, frankincense, and myrrh. And having been warned in a dream not to return to Herod, they left for their own country by another road.

(Matthew 2:1-12)

... to be looked at over the next four days.

. . .

Lord God.

Thank you for the truth of scripture, and that it is relevant to every generation.

Thank you for this passage of scripture that speaks about the wise men from the East visiting Jesus.

Please help me to understand what I have just read; and to meditate upon it today.

(Include any additional topics for prayer or thanksgiving, arising from this study)

In Jesus' name.

Amen.

What the Bible says about **the birth of Jesus (Advent and Christmas)**

The wise men seek Jesus

21st December

The wise men seek out Jesus, following a new star in the sky. How important it is that modern society should also recognise the importance of Jesus - and seek him.

'Where is the child who has been born king of the Jews? For we observed his star at its rising, and have come to pay him homage.'

(Matthew 2:2)

'My Journal':

- *Where we can find Jesus in the modern world?*

Meditate on where we can take Jesus in the modern world; as a result of living according to his teaching and example.

Lord Jesus.

In the busyness of daily life, we need to seek you!

Thank you that you are only a prayer away.

Please help me to go on seeking you on a daily basis; finding out more about you and striving to become more like you.

Help me, as I live according to your will and example, to take you into all the places and situations in which I find myself.

(Include any additional topics for prayer or thanksgiving, arising from this study)

In your name.

Amen.

'Doers of the word' (aim): To seek Jesus – meeting with him, and discovering more of him – and then taking him with us, everywhere we go.

Is there anything that you think you might find difficult about achieving the aim?

What the Bible says about **the birth of Jesus (Advent and Christmas)**

Gold
22nd December

The choice of gifts that the wise men bring to Jesus are very relevant to the part he will play in God's plan. Gold is associated with sovereignty: that Jesus would rule as king.

On entering the house, they saw the child with Mary his mother; and they knelt down and paid him homage, Then, opening their treasure-chests, they offered him gifts of gold...

(Matthew 2:11)

'My Journal':

- *Who rules in your life? Make some notes on your conclusions.*

Meditate on the fact that the wise men bring gifts to Jesus. Consider what it means to give ourselves into Jesus' sovereignty – knowing him as our king and ruler. Include things like becoming selfless; learning more about Jesus from the Bible, and wise Christian teachers and friends; allowing the Holy Spirit to work freely in our lives, empowering us to be more Christ like; and putting Jesus first in our lives.

Lord Jesus.

You are the king of kings!

Thank you that you want to be sovereign in our lives.

Please help me to look to you as my king: to learn more about you, to live in obedience to your teaching, and to follow your example.

(Include any additional topics for prayer or thanksgiving, arising from this study)

In your name.

Amen.

'Doers of the word' (aim): To give ourselves into the sovereignty of Jesus, accepting him as our king.

Is there anything that you think you might find difficult about achieving the aim?

What the Bible says about **the birth of Jesus (Advent and Christmas)**

Frankincense

23rd December

The choice of gifts that the wise men bring to Jesus are very relevant to the part he will play in God's plan. Frankincense is associated with deity: Jesus comes to earth as God in human form.

On entering the house, they saw the child with Mary his mother; and they knelt down and paid him homage, Then, opening their treasure-chests, they offered him gifts of ...frankincense ...

(Matthew 2:11)

'My Journal':

- *Consider the deity of Jesus; and its significance. Include things like, Jesus is the great creator God, coming into the world as a human being – reaching out to us, demonstrating the power of God, and revealing to us more about the plans, purposes and nature of God. Make some notes.*

Meditate the significance of God reaching out to humankind in this way, demonstrating God's unconditional love for us, even though we have disobeyed him in many ways; and also highlighting God's desire to be in relationship with us all.

Lord Jesus.

You are both human and divine!

Thank you for entering into the world, in order to reveal to us more about the Triune God and the kingdom.

Please help me to learn from you; and respond positively to you, as God's Son.

(Include any additional topics for prayer or thanksgiving, arising from this study)

In your name.

Amen.

'Doers of the word' (aim): To recognise, and respond to Jesus as God's Son.

Is there anything that you think you might find difficult about achieving the aim?

What the Bible says about **the birth of Jesus (Advent and Christmas)**

Myrrh
24th December

The choice of gifts that the wise men bring to Jesus are very relevant to the part he will play in God's plan. Myrrh is associated with death; and symbolic that Jesus will die on the cross, paying the penalty for sin.

On entering the house, they saw the child with Mary his mother; and they knelt down and paid him homage. Then, opening their treasure-chests, they offered him gifts of ...myrrh.

(Matthew 2:11)

'My Journal':

- *Consider the depth of love that would enable God the Father to send his Son to be born as a baby in the world, knowing what would happen (John 3:16). After all, the death of Jesus was prophesised in the Old Testament (Isaiah 53:7-9). Make some notes.*

Meditate on the sacrificial nature of Jesus' love for us: to be prepared to give his life to pay the penalty for our sin. What is our response to that love? It is Jesus' desire that we should replicate that sacrificial nature as we share God's love with others.

Loving Lord Jesus.

You love us so much; with a sacrificial love!

Thank you for giving your life on the cross; paying the penalty for sin.

Thank you that you paid the penalty for my sin.

Please help me to respond to that sacrificial act by following you; and sharing your love with others, in sacrificial ways.

(Include any additional topics for prayer or thanksgiving, arising from this study)

In your name.

Amen.

'Doers of the word' (aim): To respond to Jesus' love by following him, and loving others sacrificially.

Is there anything that you think you might find difficult about achieving the aim?

What the Bible says about **the birth of Jesus (Advent and Christmas)**

What can we offer to Jesus this Christmas?

25th December

There is a simple answer to the question: What can we offer to Jesus this Christmas? And that answer is: Everything!

He looked up and saw rich people putting their gifts into the treasury; he also saw a poor widow put in two small copper coins. He said, 'Truly I tell you, this poor widow has put in more than all of them; for all of them have contributed out of their abundance, but she out of her poverty has put in all she had to live on.'

(Luke 21:1-4)

'My Journal':

- *Consider the way that this story illustrates the fact that Jesus wants us to give everything to him: all that we have, and all that we are. It is not just a question of 'how much' the people in the story give: it is about how much they give, in relation to how much they possess. The widow gives everything she has. Write down some thoughts.*

Meditate on how you can give all that you have, and all that you are to Jesus.

Lord Jesus.

What can we give to you this Christmas time?

Thank you that Christmas is all about you.

Please help me to give all that I have and all that I am to you this Christmas.

Accept all that I have and all that I am to be used in your service to further your kingdom.

(Include any additional topics for prayer from your journal)

In your name.

Amen.

'Doers of the word' (aim): To offer our all to Jesus, this Christmas.

Is there anything that you think you might find difficult about achieving the aim?

What the Bible says about **the birth of Jesus (Advent and Christmas)**

A humble birth
26th December

The humility of Jesus' birth is a foretaste of what is to come: a ministry that highlights the lifestyle, and sets us the role model of servanthood. God in human form!

But emptied himself,
taking the form of a slave,
and being found in human form.

(Philippians 2:7)

'My Journal':

- Consider the significance of this verse: that God loves us so much (unconditionally) that he is prepared to enter into the world in human form – with no privilege – as a servant. Jot down your thoughts.

Meditate on the fact that Jesus is human and divine. In human form, Jesus understands the things we go through; and in his divinity, he reveals to us more about the nature of God.

Lord Jesus.

You were prepared to enter into the world in human form, because you love us so much – and you want to provide the way to salvation (John 14:6)!

Thank you for your selfless, unconditional love reaching out to us all.

Thank you for your selfless, unconditional love reaching out to me.

Please help me to follow you: to lean on you, in the knowledge that you know and understand what I am going through; to learn more about the nature of God from you; and to strive to follow your example of living a life of servanthood – sharing your love, and witnessing to others.

(Include any additional topics for prayer or thanksgiving, arising from this study)

In your name.

Amen.

'Doers of the word' (aim): To recognise Jesus as being both human and divine; and its significance. And to follow Jesus' example of humility and servanthood.

Is there anything that you think you might find difficult about achieving the aim?

What the Bible says about **the return of Jesus (Advent and Christmas)**

Jesus' return: even he doesn't know when

27th December

Jesus declares that even he doesn't know when his second coming will take place,

'But about that day and hour no one knows, neither the angels of heaven, nor the Son.'

(Matthew 24:36)

'My Journal':

- *If Jesus doesn't need to know the time when he will return, in order to fulfil his calling during his ministry on earth, why do we need to know?*

Meditate on the danger of focusing on trying to work out 'when' Jesus will return - from Bible teaching about the end times - rather than focusing on 'what' we should be doing, and 'how' we should be doing it, as we await that time.

Heavenly Father.

You know when Jesus will return!

Thank you that Jesus is coming again; and that will mark the arrival of your heavenly kingdom in all its fullness.

Please help me to remain focussed on the things to which you have called me to in service – in the meantime – and not to get side-tracked.

(Include any additional topics for prayer or thanksgiving, arising from this study)

In Jesus' name.

Amen.

'Doers of the word' (aim): To focus on 'what' and 'how'; and not 'when'.

Is there anything that you think you might find difficult about achieving the aim?

What the Bible says about **the return of Jesus (Advent and Christmas)**

Jesus' return: the need to be ready

28th December

Jesus instructs us to be ready for his second coming; because we don't know when it could be.

'You also must be ready, for the Son of Man is coming at an unexpected hour.'

(Luke 12:40)

'My Journal':

- *What is the significance of Jesus' return being unexpected: we, none of us, know when that time will be – today, tomorrow, next week, next month, or next year?*

Meditate for a few moments on what it means to be ready for when Jesus comes again. In particular, to be in relationship with the Triune God, through Jesus… and to be busy serving.

Almighty God: Father, Son and Holy Spirit.

We need to be ready for Jesus' second coming!

Thank you for your eternal plan for creation: filled with blessing and promise.

Please help me to be ready: in relationship with you; and busy serving.

(Include any additional topics for prayer or thanksgiving, arising from this study)

In Jesus' name.

Amen.

'Doers of the word' (aim): To be ready for Jesus' return.

Is there anything that you think you might find difficult about achieving the aim?

What the Bible says about **the return of Jesus (Advent and Christmas)**

Jesus' return: it will be unmistakable

29th December

'What if I miss Jesus' return?' could be a question that you are asking. Jesus himself tells us that it will not be an occasion that we will miss.

For as the lightning flashes and lights up the sky from one side to the other, so will the Son of Man be in his day.

(Luke 17:24)

'My Journal':

- *It is an understandable concern that, those of us waiting for Jesus' return, don't want to miss it when it happens. Meditate on Jesus' analogy and be assured that we will all know when he comes again. Make a note of your conclusions.*

Meditate on how you feel about Jesus' second coming. Is it something you are ready for, and to which you are looking forward.

Risen Lord Jesus.

You are coming again – and it will be impossible to miss!

Thank you that you are going to return; in order to fulfil God's plan for creation.

Please help me to recognise, acknowledge and act upon your second coming.

(Include any additional topics for prayer or thanksgiving, arising from this study)

In your name.

Amen.

'Doers of the word' (aim): To recognise, acknowledge and act upon the second coming of Jesus.

Is there anything that you think you might find difficult about achieving the aim?

What the Bible says about **the return of Jesus (Advent and Christmas)**

Jesus' return: found blameless

30th December

Paul speaks about the completeness of the forgiveness that Jesus gives us; when we are in a relationship with him.

So that you are not lacking in any spiritual gift as you wait for the revealing of our Lord Jesus Christ. He will also strengthen you to the end, so that you may be blameless on the day of our Lord Jesus Christ. God is faithful; by him you were called into the fellowship of his Son, Jesus Christ our Lord.

(1 Corinthians 1:7-9)

'My Journal':

- *Consider the concept of being made 'blameless' when Jesus returns. How does that make you feel?*

Meditate on what this verse is saying about being empowered by the indwelling Holy Spirit, during the spiritual battle which we are in: 'To the end.'

Lord Jesus.

Through you, we are made blameless!

Thank you that you offer forgiveness to us all, that is so complete.

Please, let my response to you be a positive one; so that I will know the assurance of being found blameless when you return.

Thank you that, through the indwelling Holy Spirit, you will help me to endure in the spiritual battle, to the end, when your kingdom will reach its ultimate fulfilment.

(Include any additional topics for prayer or thanksgiving, arising from this study)

In your name.

Amen.

'Doers of the word' (aim): To be made blameless through Jesus.

Is there anything that you think you might find difficult about achieving the aim?

What the Bible says about **the return of Jesus (Advent and Christmas)**

Jesus' return: keep busy serving

31st December

Paul warns us not to become complacent as we await the return of Jesus; but to keep on serving.

For you yourselves know how you ought to imitate us; we were not idle when we were with you, and we did not eat anyone's bread without paying for it; but with toil and labour we worked night and day, so that we might not burden any of you.

(2 Thessalonians 3:7-8)

'My Journal':

- *Pick out, and consider any important principles contained within this verse. Make a note of your choices.*

Meditate on the temptation to become complacent as we await the fulfilment of God's amazing heavenly kingdom.

Risen Lord Jesus.

You are going to return!

Thank you that you have entrusted us to continue your work here on earth, as we await that special time.

Please help me not to become complacent, for whatever reason; instead, help me to work hard and conscientiously as I seek to serve you.

(Include any additional topics for prayer or thanksgiving, arising from this study)

In your name.

Amen.

'Doers of the word' (aim): To keep serving Jesus as we wait for the ultimate fulfilment of his heavenly kingdom – when he returns (Acts 1:11).

Is there anything that you think you might find difficult about achieving the aim?